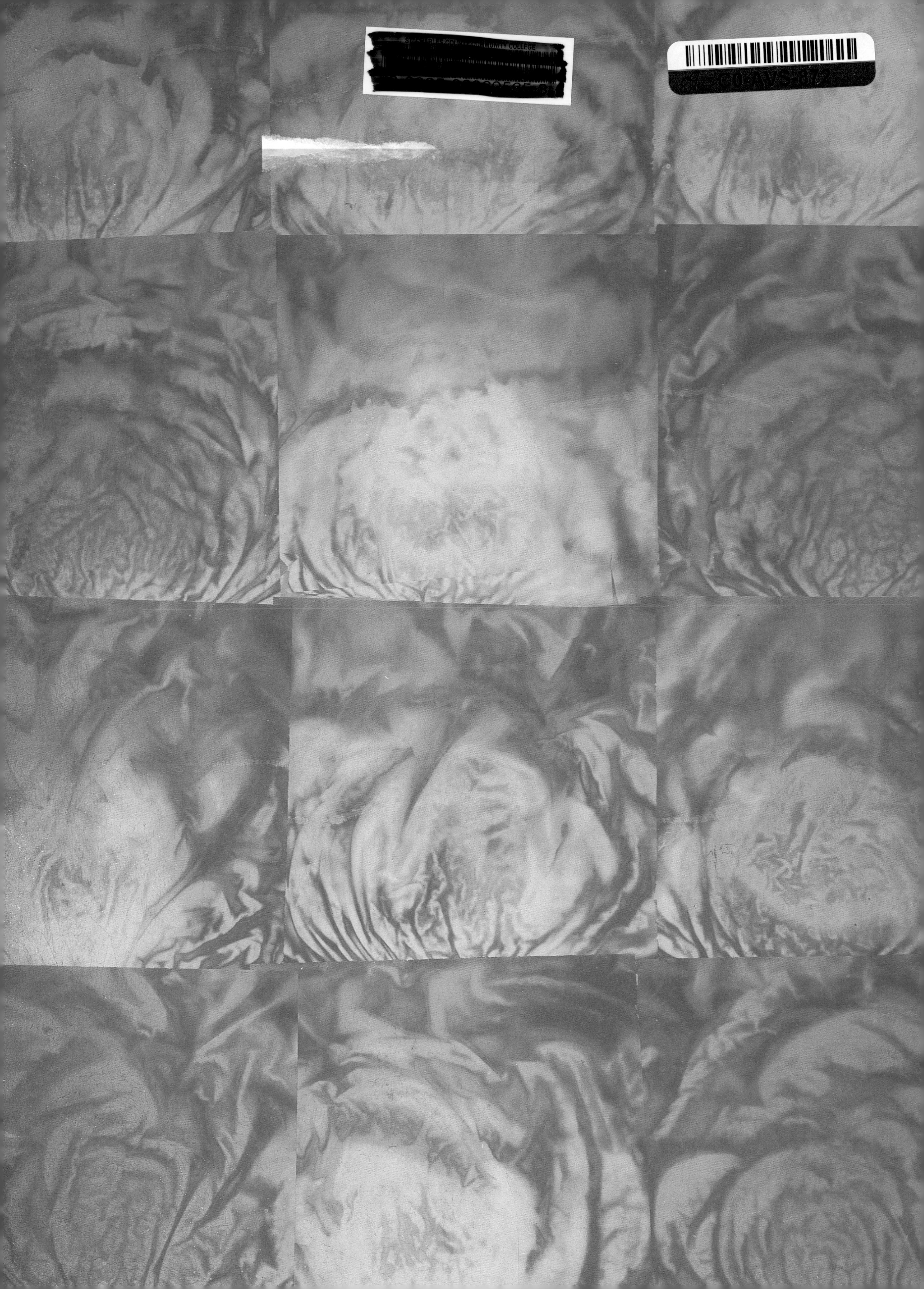

leading
international
designers
select the
best of
their
own work

First Choice

CH
CRAFTSMAN HOUSE

edited by

Ken Cato

First Choice
Edited by Ken Cato
Sub-edited by
Bridgette Newbury

ISBN 976-6410-55-0
Design Cato Design Inc.
Printer Toppan Printing Co.,
(H.K.) Ltd., Hong Kong
Paper stock 157 gsm
Z-Kote Matt
Colour separations Toppan
Printing Co., Singapore

Distributed in Australia by
Craftsman House,
20 Barcoo Street,
Roseville East, NSW 2069
in association with
G&B Arts International:
Australia, Austria, Belgium,
China, France, Germany,
Hong Kong, India, Japan,
Luxembourg, Malaysia,
Netherlands, Russia, Singapore,
Switzerland, United Kingdom,
United States of America

6 4 1 0 - 5 5 - 0

C o n t e n t s

In the past twenty-six years I have been asked many times to choose my best piece of work, my first choice.

It is still a difficult decision to make. The criteria for the decision hasn't changed. Is it the most exciting or the most pleasurable?

The most successful or the greatest artistic breakthough? Each design project presents issues to be overcome.

Finding a way to overcome them is often the most pleasing aspect of a project.

No-one wants to produce work that isn't as good as the last piece but commercial success or the immense scale of a project

can undermine the intrinsic value of the design. When I set out on a new project I believe and hope

that it will be my best work and a new first choice.

After 'First Choice' (First Edition), I realised the difficulty of making a first choice and committing myself to a single piece of work.

I want my first choice to best convey my ongoing commitment to design and demonstrate the scope of my thinking.

I decided to ask over 100 designers to do this again. Rarely are graphic designers given the opportunity to evaluate and display

their first choice in their own words. 'First Choice' (Second Edition) allows designers to define

and redefine their best work, and identify themselves in the world of visual communication.

The result is a definitive collection of the best work of the design profession today

and a record of how the world's best designers evaluate their own work

Ken Cato

Intro duction

CABINET DES ESTAMPES GENEVE

LA BELLA MANIERA

PIECES MAITRESSES DE LA GRAVURE MANIERISTE
1520 – 1640 | COLLECTION DU PEINTRE GEORG BASELITZ

9 JUIN – 11 SEPTEMBRE 1994 | 5, PROMENADE DU PIN | TOUS LES JOURS SAUF LE LUNDI DE 11 A 19 H

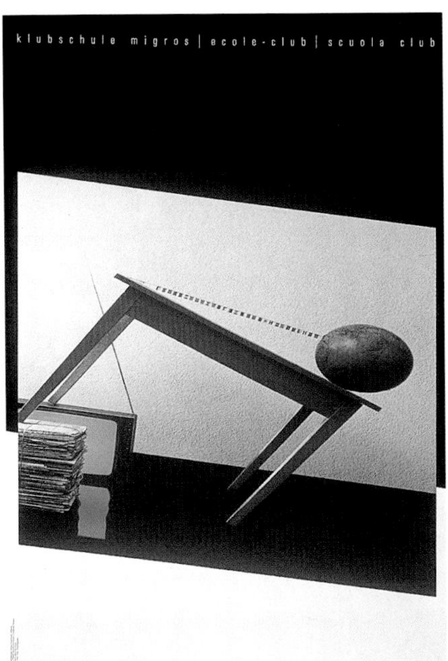

First Choice
Poster for the exhibition at the Cabinet des Estampes Geneva, 'La Bella Maniera'

'The exhibition at the Cabinet Des Center in Geneva presented the 'Druckgraphic des Manierismus' of George Baselitz collection. In order to translate this difficult subject on a poster, I chose the subjects Gods and the God of Love, 'Mars, Venus and l'Amour' by Jean Mignon (between 1537 and 1540), after Luca Penna. In my work I tried to present the subject in a plastic way by choosing the blue crescent of the moon as a night symbol and give at the same time a natural suspension to the sphere'

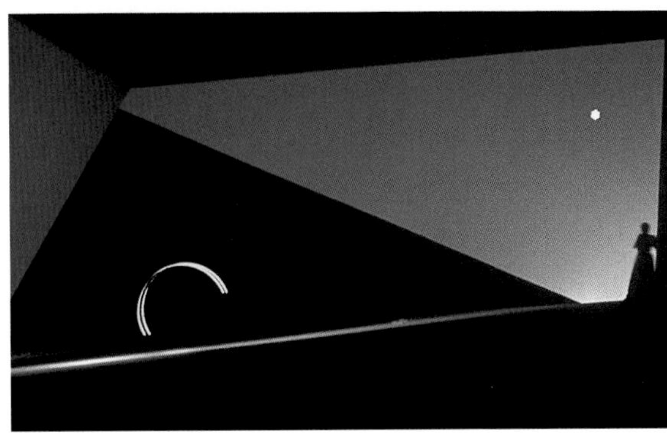

Poster for Klubschule Migros School for development and free time activities

Poster for the Paul Klee collection at the Museum of Fine Arts, Berne, Switzerland

Sets for the opera 'Faust' by Gounod, Opera Montpellier, France

Poster and set for 'Cosi fan tutte', Aalto Theatre, Essen, Germany

NAGANO 1998

THE XVIII OLYMPIC WINTER GAMES

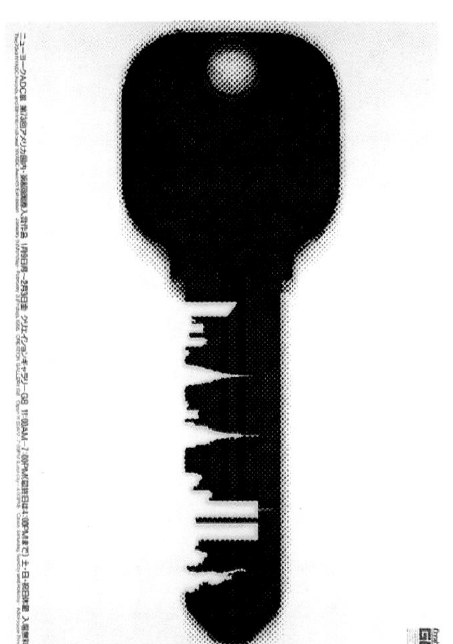

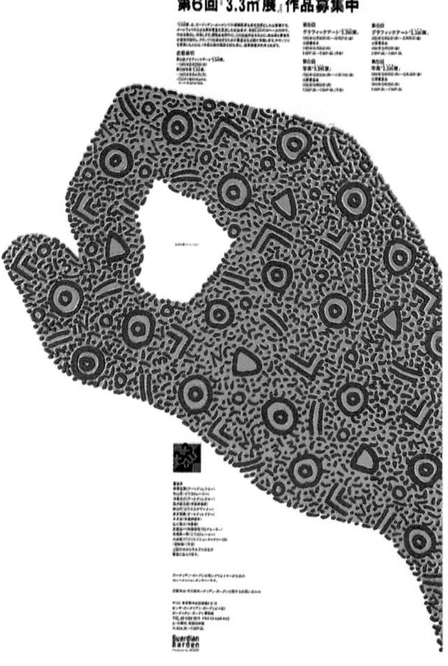

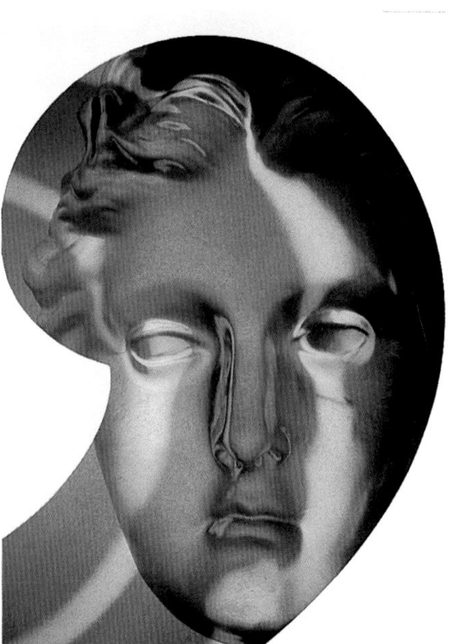

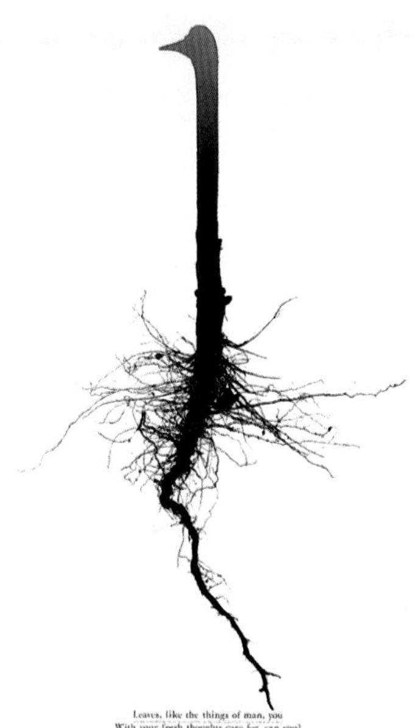

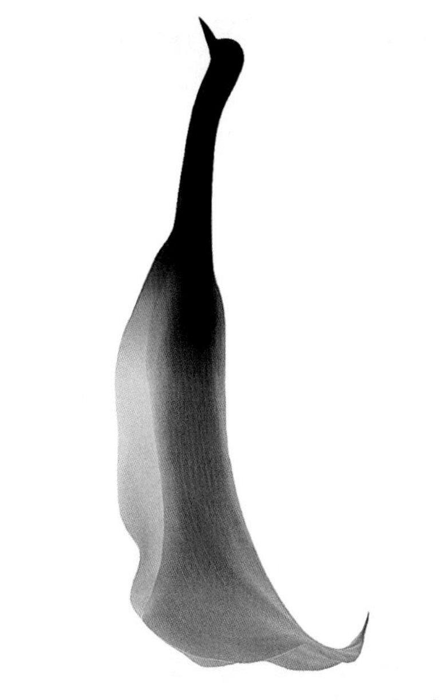

First Choice
Poster for The XVIII Olympic Games, Nagano 1998

'This is the official poster of the 1998 Winter Olympic games which will be held in Nagoya, Japan. Out of the ten designers from inside and outside of Japan who entered the competition, the selection committee chose to use my submission. The theme of this piece is the need for human beings to coexist with our environment. In order to integrate the subject and the Olympics into one picture, I used symbolic images. The silhouette of the thrush, a common migrant bird sits on a ski pole against the beautiful morning glow of the Japanese Alps. In addition to being distributed as a full-size poster, this piece will be reproduced in various media, colours and sizes. With this in mind, I designed the poster so that it would stand out in any medium'

Poster for the Japan Design Committee entitled 'Life'

Poster for the 73rd NYADC Awards and 8th International NYADC Award Exhibition, Japan

Poster for the Guardian Garden Exhibition for the client, Recruit

Poster entitled 'Art Director O∆□ (Circle, Triangle and Square) Exhibition II'

Environmental posters for A & A

MONTREUX 28TH **JAZZ FESTIVAL**

JULY 1-16

1994

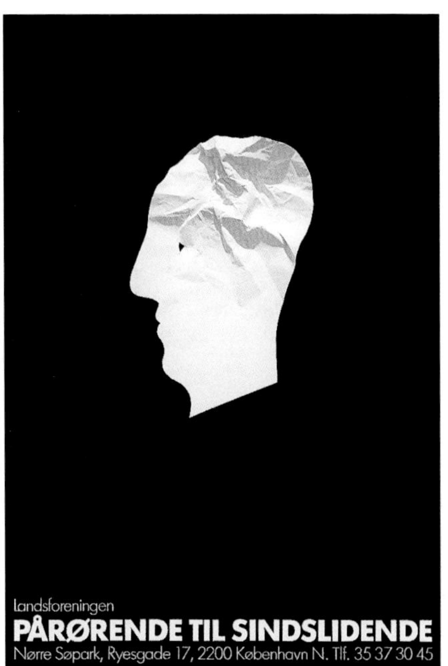

First Choice
Poster for Montreux Jazz Festival

'The case story is very simple. Each year on the shore of Lac Leman, the jazz festival takes place. My first question: What is unique about the place? The lake. Second question: What is the purpose of the festival? Art and tourism...and the parallel with another lakeside seasonal 'monster' came to my mind...Loch Ness. Good old nessie, who's as steady as a Swiss clock, pops up her lovely head and makes a strange sound, same thing here...only the monster is the ultimate jazz cliche, the sax, and the sound is pure delight, so here it is. Lake jazz and little old Jazzie stomping around'

Poster promoting Communication

Poster for relatives of the mentally ill

Poster for Save the Alps

Poster for Chicago Lyric Opera 40th season

Poster for the 50th Anniversary of Denmark's resistance to the Nazi occupation

Poster for 'Odense'

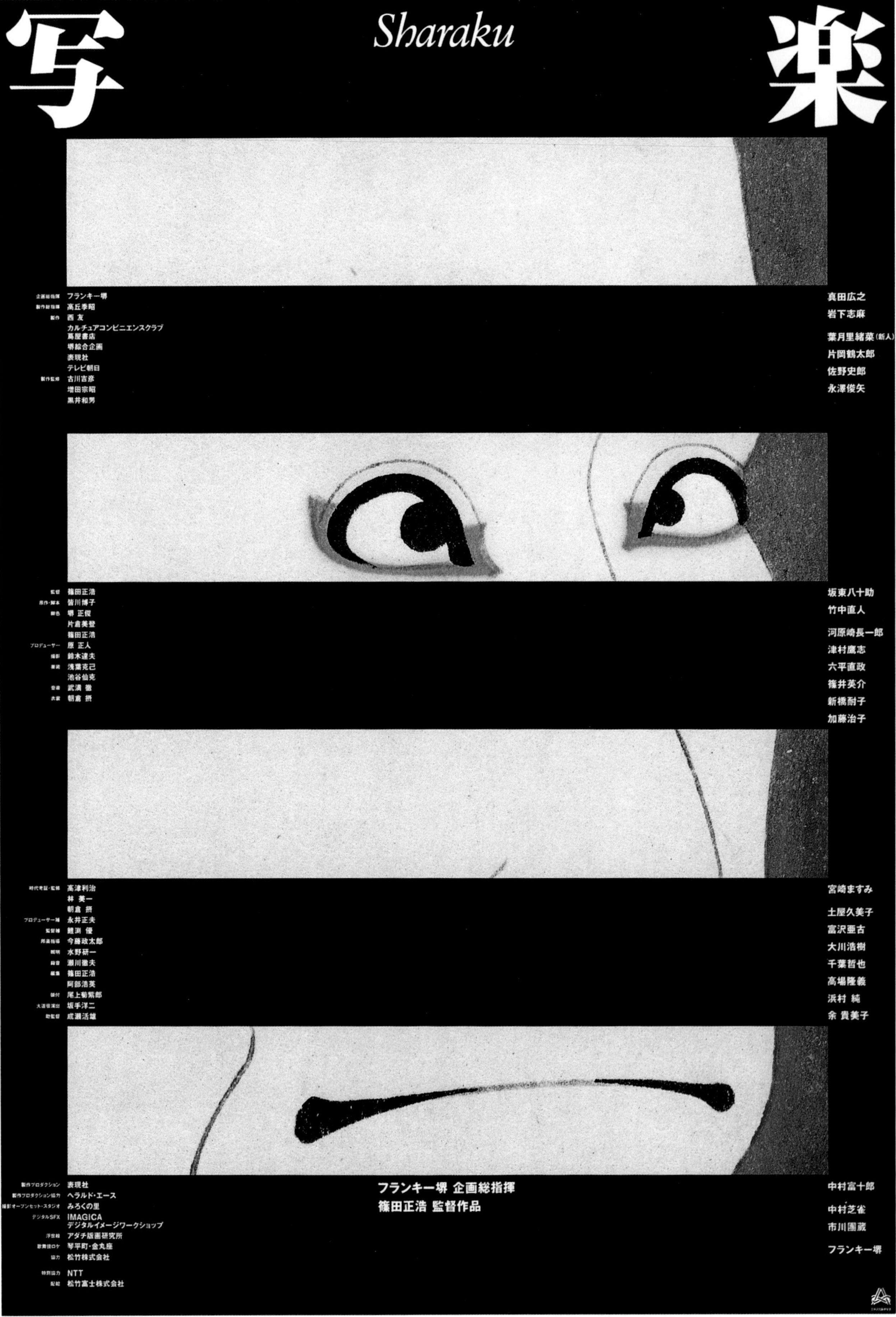
写
Sharaku
楽
企画総指揮 フランキー堺
製作総指揮 高丘季昭
製作 西 友
カルチュアコンビニエンスクラブ
蔦屋書店
堺綜合企画
表現社
テレビ朝日
製作監修 古川吉彦
増田宗昭
黒井和男
真田広之
岩下志麻
葉月里緒菜(新人)
片岡鶴太郎
佐野史郎
永澤俊矢
監督 篠田正浩
原作・脚本 皆川博子
脚色 堺 正俊
片倉美登
篠田正浩
プロデューサー 原 正人
撮影 鈴木達夫
美術 浅葉克己
池谷仙克
音楽 武満 徹
衣裳 朝倉 摂
坂東八十助
竹中直人
河原崎長一郎
津村鷹志
六平直政
篠井英介
新橋耐子
加藤治子
時代考証・監修 高津利治
林 美一
朝倉 摂
プロデューサー補 永井正夫
監督補 鯉渕 優
邦楽指導 今藤政太郎
照明 水野研一
録音 瀬川徹夫
編集 篠田正浩
阿部浩英
振付 尾上菊紫郎
大道具演出 坂手洋二
助監督 成瀬活雄
宮崎ますみ
土屋久美子
富沢亜古
大川浩樹
千葉哲也
高場隆義
浜村 純
余 貴美子
製作プロダクション 表現社
製作プロダクション協力 ヘラルド・エース
撮影オープンセット・スタジオ みろくの里
デジタルSFX IMAGICA
デジタルイメージワークショップ
浮世絵 アダチ版画研究所
歌舞伎ロケ 琴平町・金丸座
協力 松竹株式会社
特別協力 NTT
配給 松竹富士株式会社
フランキー堺 企画総指揮
篠田正浩 監督作品
中村富十郎
中村芝雀
市川團蔵
フランキー堺

アジア太平洋博覧会—福岡'89
1989年3月17日→1989年9月3日
ASIAN-PACIFIC EXPOSITION: FUKUOKA '89 FUKUOKA, JAPAN. MAR. 17→SEP. 3. 1989

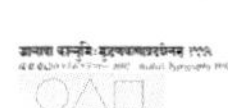

World Cup Japan 2002 Bidding Committee

See you in 2002.

Typography in Asia; A View from Tokyo

日本文化デザイン会議 '93山形
Japan Inter-Design Forum '93 Yamagata
1993年10月21日(木)・22日(金)・23日(土)・24日(日)

First Choice
Poster for the film, 'Sharaku'

'This is the first time that I worked as the art director on a film. Frankie Sakai led the production of the 1995 project, directed by Masuharu Shinoda. The film was about a mysterious Ukiyo-e artist named 'Sharaku', who, during the Edo period about 200 years ago, produced 140 works on Kabuki actors and was never heard of again. Films begin firstly from a script, and I was asked to design the script format. Upon reading the script, it seems that the actors intuitively knew that the film would be different from anything they had done previously. This poster was produced prior to the completion of the film, and many posters were put up around each filming location'

Poster for 'Asian Pacific Exposition: Fukuoka'

Asaba's Typography 1992

Poster for 2002 World Cup Japan (Soccer) 'See you in 2002'

Poster for 'Typography in Asia; A View from Tokyo'

Japan Inter-Design forum '93 Yamagata

'Father is the man' Billboard version

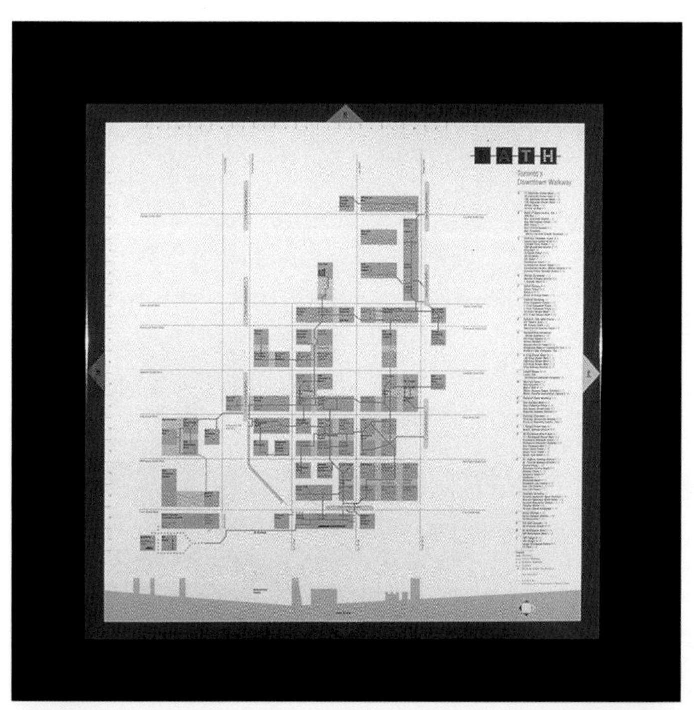

P
A
T
H

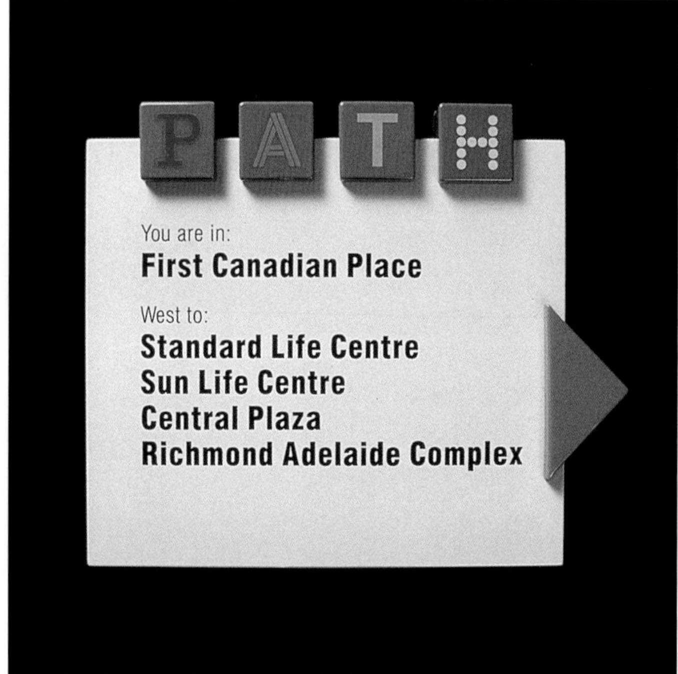
PATH
You are in:
First Canadian Place
West to:
Standard Life Centre
Sun Life Centre
Central Plaza
Richmond Adelaide Complex

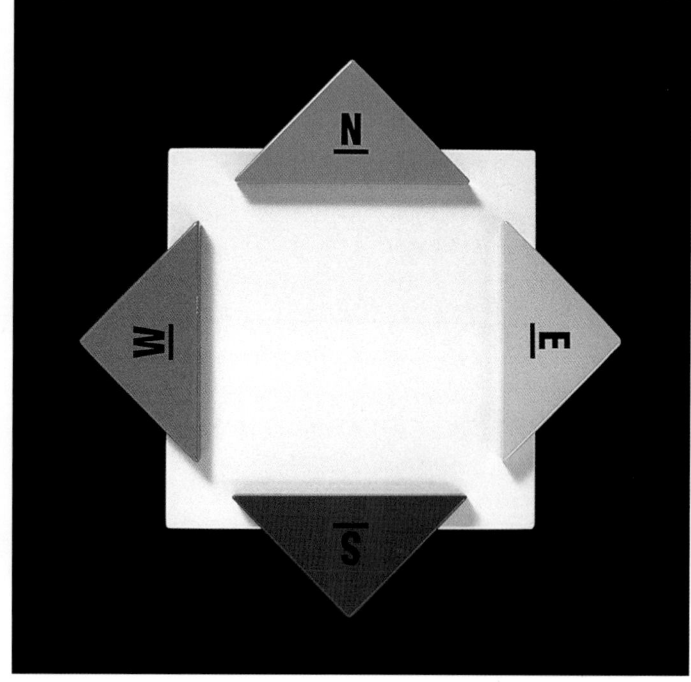
N
W
E
S

First Choice
Design for PATH Underground Wayfinding Program

'The 8.5 km Toronto underground pedestrian walkway (PATH) is an information system that functions to simplify the downtown pedestrian core passageways.
By using a simple but effective system of maps and signs, G & A was able to provide a comprehensive, coherent communication and wayfinding system'

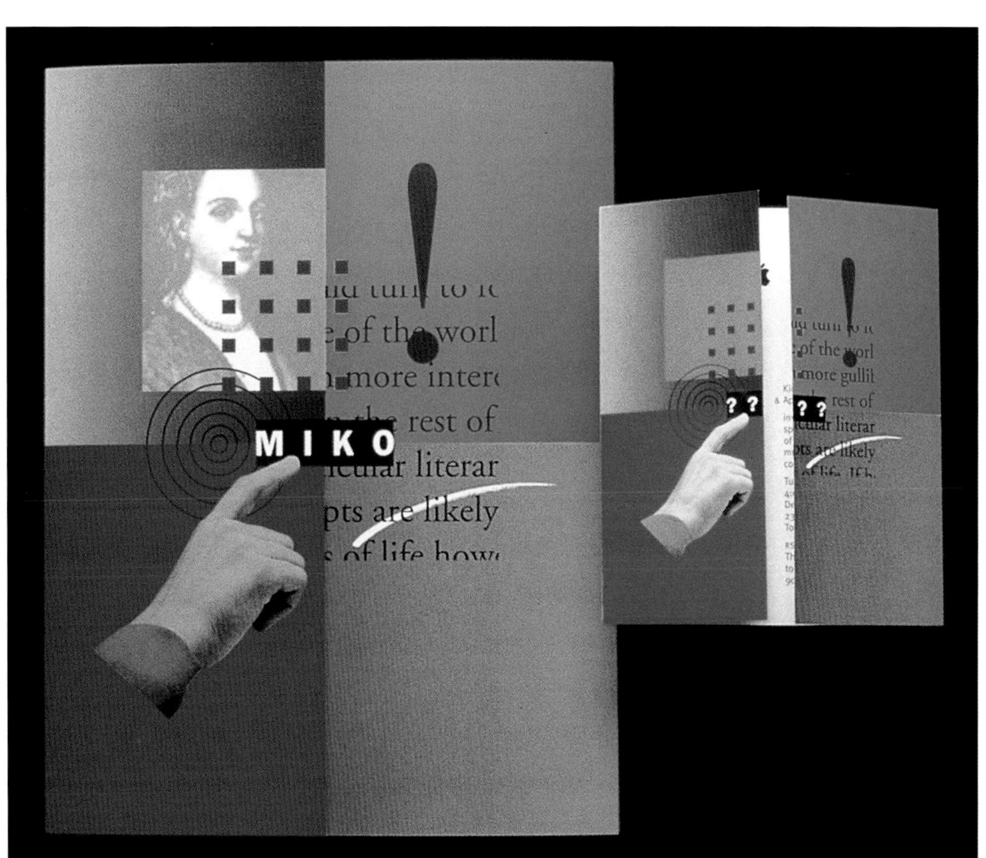

Image program for MIKO, interactive multimedia kiosks

Corporate Identity program for CAE Inc

Corporate Identity program for Canada Trust

Stamp design for International Civil Aviation

Celebrating the Establishment of the Foundation for Human Rights in Asia,
the Concert for Human Rights in
Asia
Neither dominating nor dominated, all people are equal and the same.
ザ・コンサート
［アジアの人権］
東京交響楽団
1991年7月2日火
東京芸術劇場大ホール

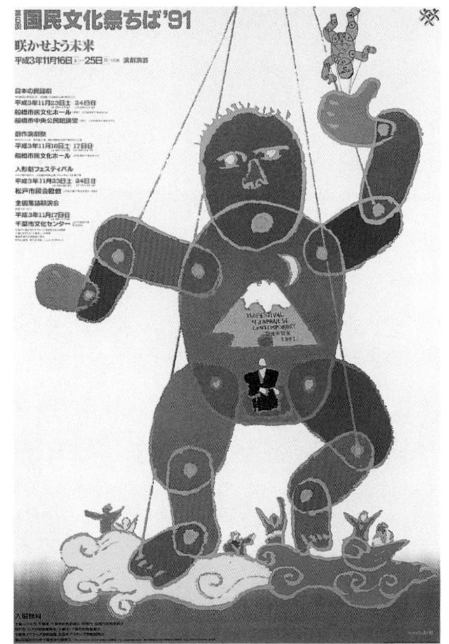
国民文化祭ちば'91
咲かせよう未来

The 14th Exhibition Of Contemporary Japanese Sculpture '91
第14回・野外彫刻30周年記念
現代日本彫刻展

SAVE THE SEA
21世紀に残そう!美しい海
Credo of the Seas
海を救おうキャンペーン

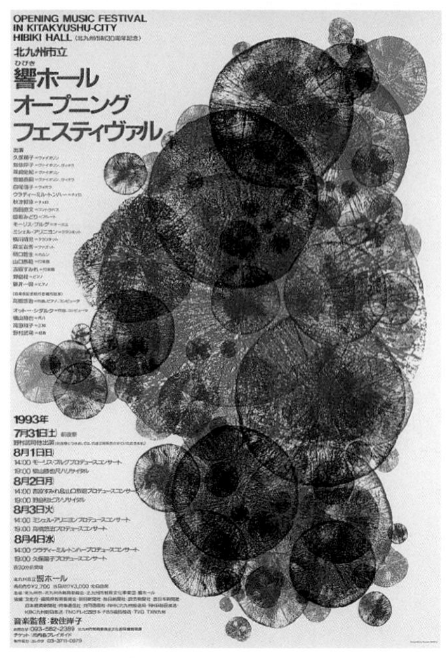
OPENING MUSIC FESTIVAL
IN KITAKYUSHU-CITY
HIBIKI HALL
北九州市立
響ホール
オープニング
フェスティヴァル
1993年

First Choice
Poster for an exhibition of Japanese Style Artists, the Awazu Design Room

'The original drawing for the poster is oil on canvas (1620mm x 1300mm). It took me about 60 days to finish it. That's why I feel a strong attachment to this work'

Public poster for peace

Poster for the Concert for Human Rights in Asia,1992

Poster for The Festival of Japanese Contemporary Theatre

Poster for the 14th Contemporary Japanese Sculpture exhibition

Public poster for Save The Sea

Poster for the Opening Music Festival in Kitakyushu City, Hibiki Hall

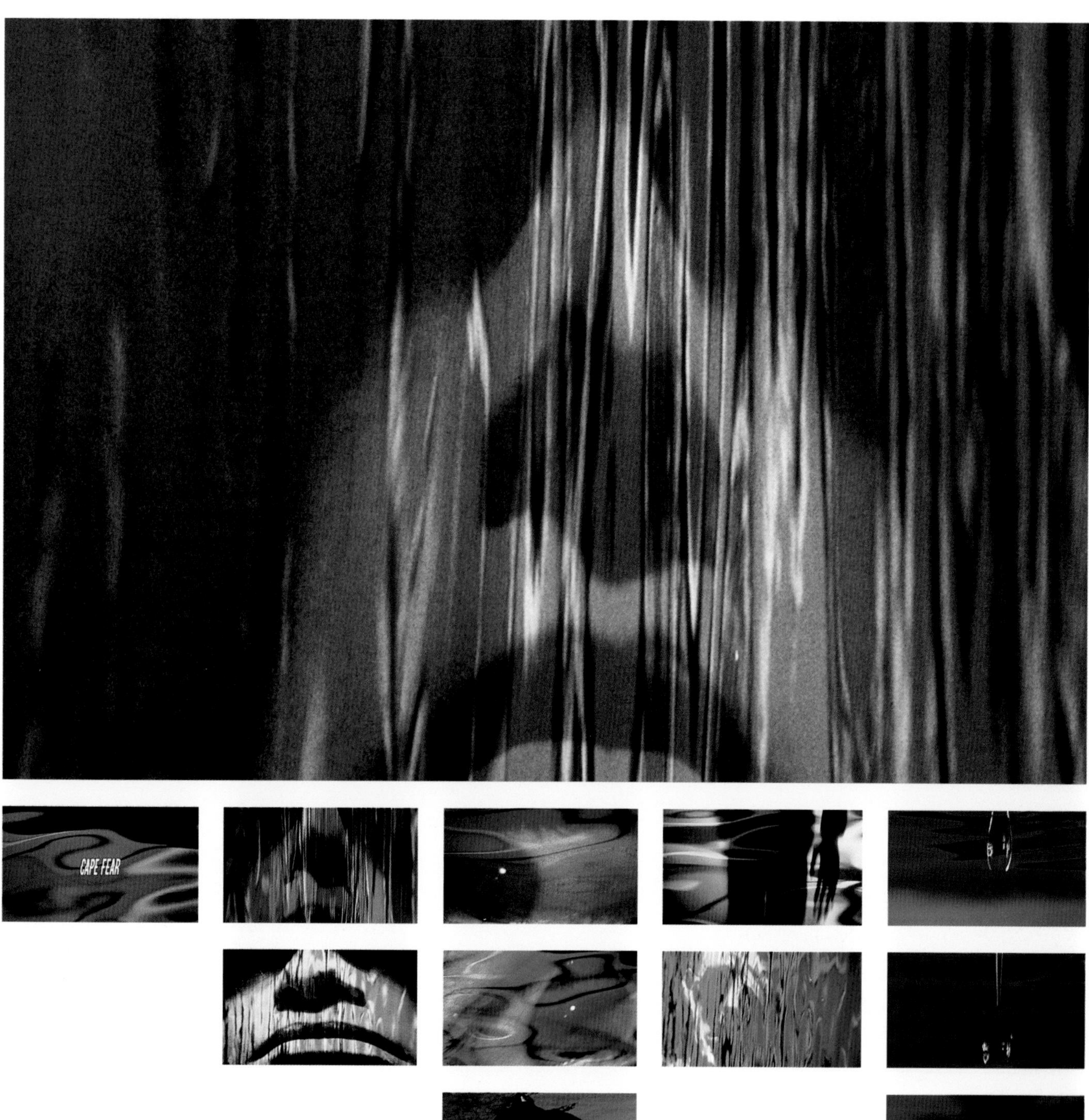
CAPE FEAR

First Choice
Opening title for the film 'Cape Fear'

'I selected this piece of film for several reasons. Because it marks a satisfying return to film titles after a long hiatus from my early work in this genre. Because it's part of an ongoing, rich and joyous film collaboration with my wife Elaine Bass. And because it's part of a rewarding relationship with a great director Martin Scorese (having also created the openings for his films 'Good Fellas', 'Age of Innocence', and now working on his new film 'Casino')'

Poster commemorating the Bicentennial of the French Revolution

Poster for 'Schindler's List'

Two posters for a book on Psychology

Poster for the Academy Awards broadcast

Poster and course catalogue cover for UCLA

abbaye
du Bec Hellouin

First Choice
Panel designs from the Highway Paris-Normandie

'It is difficult to decide what is the preferred project, because very often our realisations can't be summed up in one image. My first choice is a wonderful collaboration with a photographer, Fabien, conceiving forty-two visuals that represent important places along the highway. Each image is on a support of nearly 20 metres square, even a motorist driving at a speed of more than 100 km/h, is able to read them. Our project spans the highway like a space in time, in which the visuals appear like a play with forty-two acts. Also, the client has been ready to fight with us against the local authorities who try to level down, or even prevent the realisation of this project'

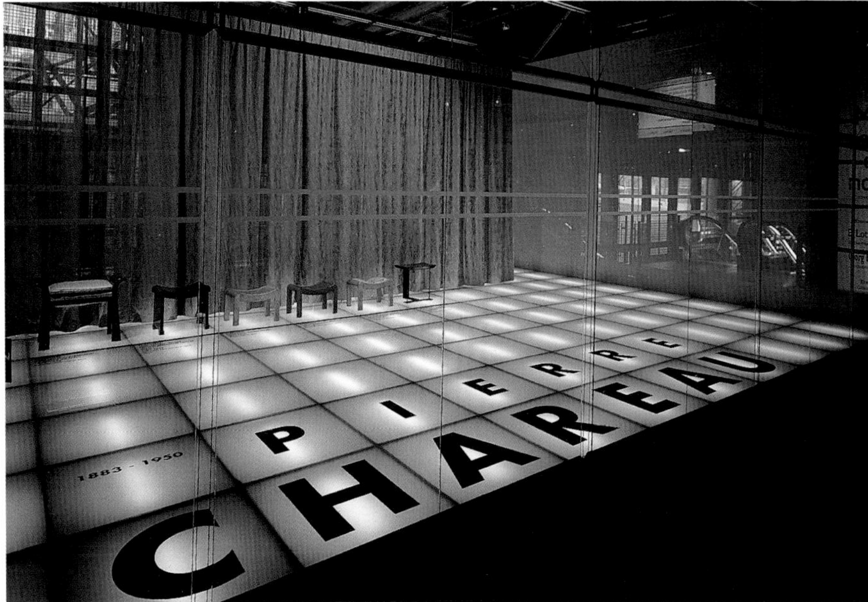

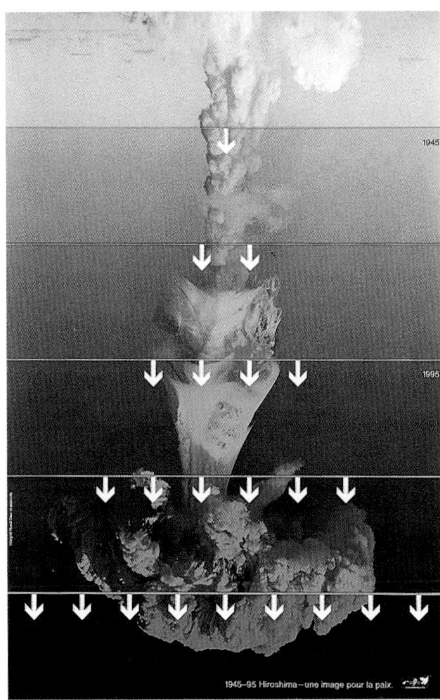

ville de Nancy.

la cité
internationale

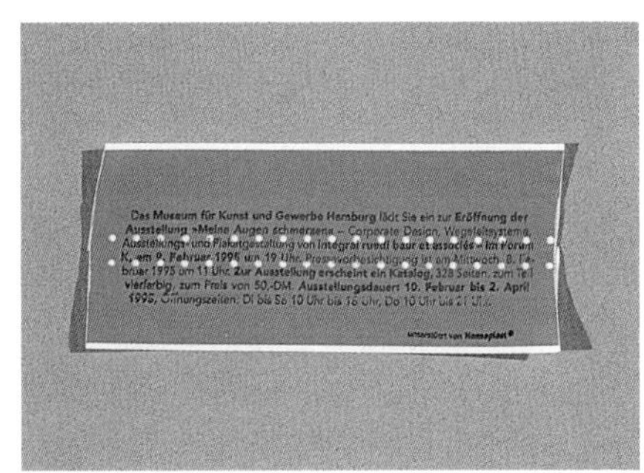

Design for the Pierre Chareau exhibition at the Georges Pompidou Centre, Paris

Poster for the 50th Anniversary of the bombing of Hiroshima for the Movement for Peace

Visual identity for the Museum of Modern and Contemporary Art, Geneva, Switzerland

Visual identity for the town of Nancy, France

Visual identity and signage for the Cité Internationale, Lyon, France

Invitation cards for an exhibition of personal works entitled Meine Augen Schmerzen (My eyes hurt)

AIDS
THE KILLING
BITE OF
LOVE

First Choice
Poster entitled 'Aids, the Killing Bite of Love'

'Although every poster can be interpreted as a reflection upon life in present society, the poster 'Aids' carries a contemporary message of utmost significance for the general public. The statement it makes is more direct than that of other posters in the cultural sector'

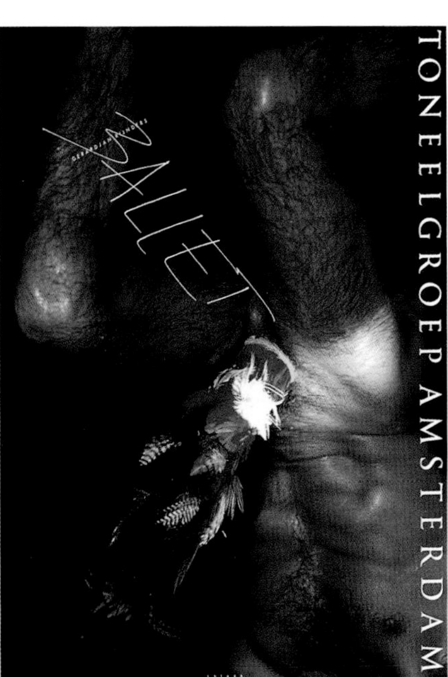

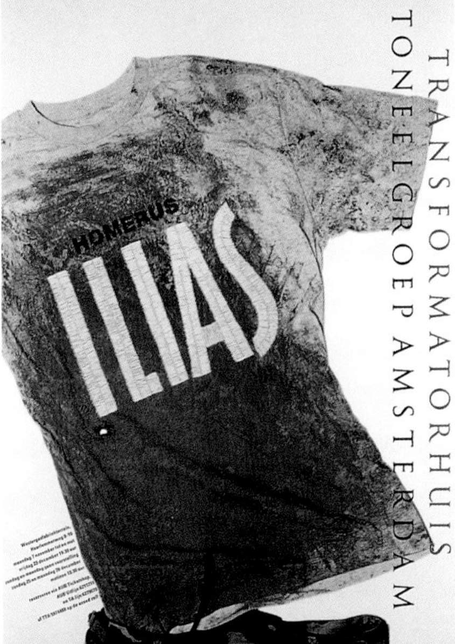

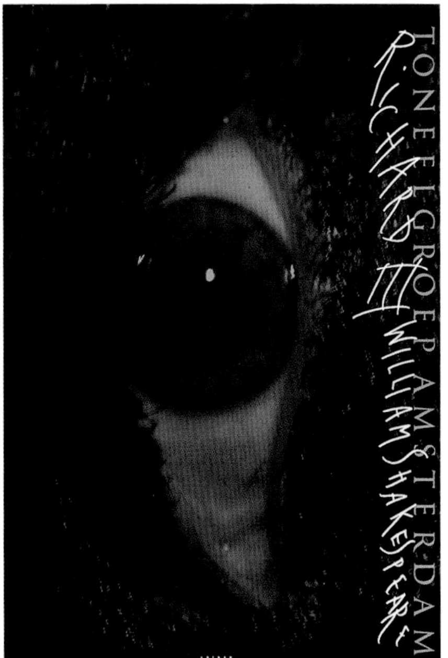

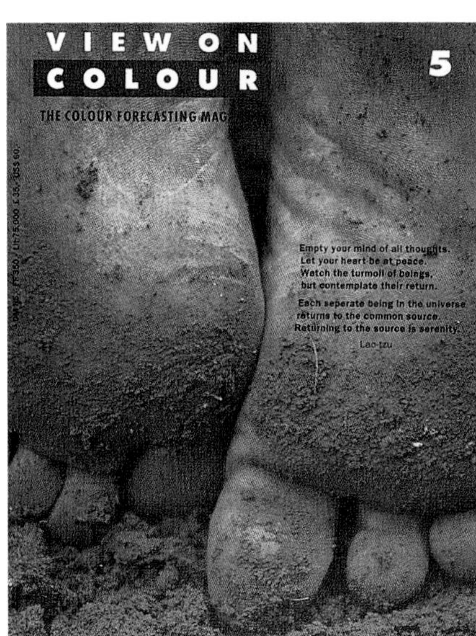

Poster promoting the Amsterdam ballet

Poster promoting the production 'Klaagliederen'

Poster promoting the production 'Ilias'

Poster promoting the production 'Richard III'

Cover for View on Colour No.5

Cover for Interior View No.5

En ambos supuestos aparentemente antagónicos: la cámara que nos lleva al inframundo o la cámara que nos conduce penosamente por la vía de la redención profunda, los actos fotográficos de Oweena Fogarty se nos revelan como verdaderas conmociones rituales: estremecimientos radicales que nos hacen ir con certeza más allá de nosotros mismos. De ahí que la expresión que utilicé al principio de estas líneas: la **fuerza tremenda**, adquiera un sentido radical y casi primigenio: la palabra **tremenda** se usaba antiguamente en su vínculo con rituales religiosos, queriendo decir que algo es **tremendo** cuando es digno de hacer temblar a quien lo observa. Como se supone que son ciertas divinidades, incluyendo las prehispánicas y la católica. En ésta se sigue considerando como una de las virtudes teologales "el temor de Dios", la posibilidad de estremecerse ante su presencia **tremenda**. Y los rituales cristianos tienen muchas veces la finalidad de transmitirnos, de incluirnos en el espectáculo de esa **fuerza tremenda** de la divinidad. En muchos de los rituales prehispánicos la dimensión del horror es esencial a su existencia, por el mismo motivo de conmoción profunda y trascendente de la vida religiosa. De ahí que, como lo hace notar una y otra vez el historiador del arte Paul Westheim, la cualidad primordial del arte prehispánico no sea la belleza sino el horror, factor que no nos deja olvidar que lo que llamamos arte prehispánico es primordialmente un conjunto de objetos religiosos, casi imposibles de entender fuera de sus contextos religiosos, muchas veces plenamente rituales.

La obra de Oweena Fogarty nos recuerda plenamente esa dimensión del arte que consiste sobre todo en romper el tiempo lineal para instaurarnos en un tiempo profundo donde realidades desconcertantes, trascendentes, agudas, acuciantes, se mezclan y ejercen sobre nosotros su poder de conmoción. El tiempo unívoco se vuelve polivalente en esta obra. Una línea es de pronto una estrella. Un instante fijo es súbitamente un punto de fuga infinito en el alma, como un hueco sin límites. El tiempo continuo da de golpe vueltas sobre sí mismo y nos hace regresar a lo primigenio de nuestras

31

sensaciones más elementales. Estas tienen que ver con diferentes dimensiones de nuestra existencia: por una parte, con el origen de nuestra percepción, y por ahí con lo más elemental de nuestra percepción de la fotografía.

El ritual de Oweena Fogarty nos hace volver también a lo que fueron nuestras primeras sensaciones fotográficas. Ritual de la percepción que se enrosca sobre sí mismo sin proponérselo, como una manera más de penetrar realidades, de crear espacios profundos. De nuevo, **fuerza tremenda** puesta en obra. Así, de pronto tengo fresca en mi memoria la primera sensación que tuve al ver con detenimiento una fotografía. La sensación fuerte de que los familiares ahí retratados eran otros, de que yo mismo era otro. Tenía la percepción de la imagen fotografiada como la llave para entrar en una otredad. En otra dimensión de la vida que no era la de mi conciencia de las cosas y de las personas. La obra de Oweena Fogarty es sin duda una llave de entrada más radical a una realidad que podemos llamar otra, a una otredad fundamental. Pero es una otredad que está en la base de nosotros mismos. Es nuestra otredad profunda que estas fotografías de pronto nos muestran. Su obra es ritual de la otredad de nuestro tiempo, ritual de tiempos otros, cruzados, convergentes, anudados. Tiempos enroscados ante nuestra mirada.

Oweena Fogarty pertenece de lleno a la nueva sensibilidad artística que se va perfilando hacia el final de este siglo en México. Sensibilidad que van conformando varios artistas, y sobre todo artistas plásticos, para quienes la dimensión ritual del arte es, consciente o inconscientemente, clave y sentido de sus obras. La búsqueda del arte está cada vez menos en plasmar una versión de la historia o del progreso de la humanidad, como en la época de los muralistas, o en estar a la vanguardia del arte contemporáneo universal, como en los sesenta. La búsqueda de los nuevos artistas va a los fundamentos de la naturaleza artística en cuanto a los materiales que emplea, y a los fundamentos de las realidades espirituales que llevamos dentro. Es una búsqueda rayada de misticismo, de

16

First Choice
Cover for an invitation for an exhibition of the TDC works

'For some time now, I've been the International Liason for the Type Directors Club of New York in Mexico where I've been presenting the annual exhibition of the awarded works. In order to promote the last exhibition I made up an invitation. On the cover a texture of the letters 'T' in positive and negative using the colours of the flag of the USA in order to thus evoke many of the characteristics of the competition. The invitation was printed in silk screen with brilliant inks over opaque paper and the results were quite attractive. At least such were the comments of the public'

Spreads from a book for a photographer

Cover of a brochure for a textile manufacturer

Christmas card for a computer manufacturer

Illustration for a brochure for a box manufacturer

Trademark for a film festival for the Red Cross

Cover of an invitation for an exhibition of Belgian graphic designers

O Z O N O

O Z O N O
MUS ICA
PRESENTACION AL PUBLICO DE SU PRIMERA PRODUCCION. OTOÑO • 1993

First Choice
Visual Identity for the jazz rock group Ozono

'My favourite work is the logo for a jazz rock group called Ozono (Ozone) made in 1993. This is an exotic bird and you can see it in two positions. This makes the symbol more interesting. In the first position you see a falling bird dying, and in the second position you see the bird flying. Death or life is our choice. The hole inside the bird represents the results of pollution in the atmosphere. This group's music has an environmental message for young people'

Poster to promote the Mexican pavilion at the International Fair in Genova, Italy

Logotype for the Trama Visual Graphic Designers Association

Corporate Identity for Metropolis, a company which conducts night tours in Mexico City

Poster for the 4th Latin American Theatre Encounter

Corporate Identity for Mexican activities in Spain

Typographic design for a 'Merry Christmas' postcard

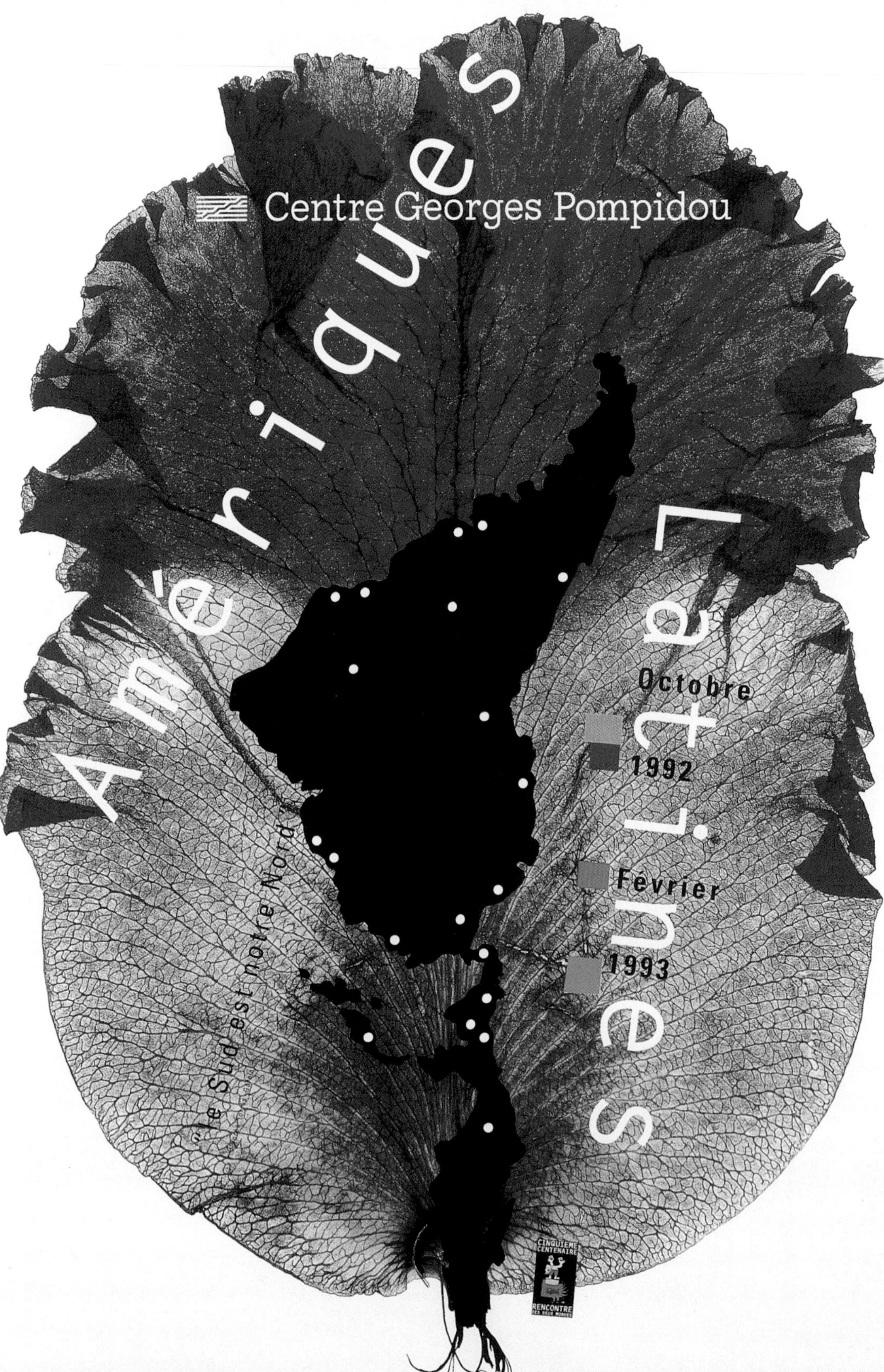
Centre Georges Pompidou
Amériques Latines
"le Sud est notre Nord"
Octobre 1992
Fevrier 1993
CINQUIEME CENTENAIRE
RENCONTRE
Atelier de Création Graphique '92 - Grapus

First Choice
Poster announcing an exhibition of South American Art at the Georges Pompidou Centre

'It is based on a quotation from Torres Garcia (a painter) who once said: 'South is our north'. I like the idea that a poster is as fragile as a petal, and that flowers are as beautiful and significant as a poster can be...sometimes'

Poster for the National Parks of France

Poster for an ICOGRADA event in Glasgow

Poster announcing a theatre event for children designed with my daughter, Héloïse

Corporate Identity for the Louvre Museum, Paris

Poster announcing an exhibition of our Atelier du Creation Graphique entitled 'Tomorrow is the result of today'

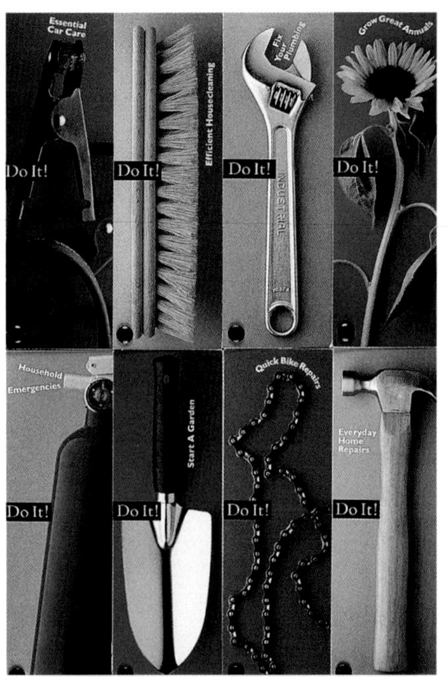
Essential Car Care
Do It!
Efficient Housecleaning
Do It!
Do It!
Grow Great Annuals
Do It!
Household Emergencies
Do It!
Start A Garden
Do It!
Quick Bike Repairs
Do It!
Everyday Home Repairs
Do It!

7th Annual
New York Book Fair
to Help the Homeless
A joint project of Goddard Riverside Community Center and the New York Publishing Community
Saturday and Sunday November 20 and 21, 1993 at
Goddard Riverside Community Center
10a.m. to 6p.m.
593 Columbus Avenue at 88th Street
Admission $3.00 adults
$1.00 children

THE GOOD DINER
42ND ST & 11TH AVE

E.G.SMITH
E-MAGINATION

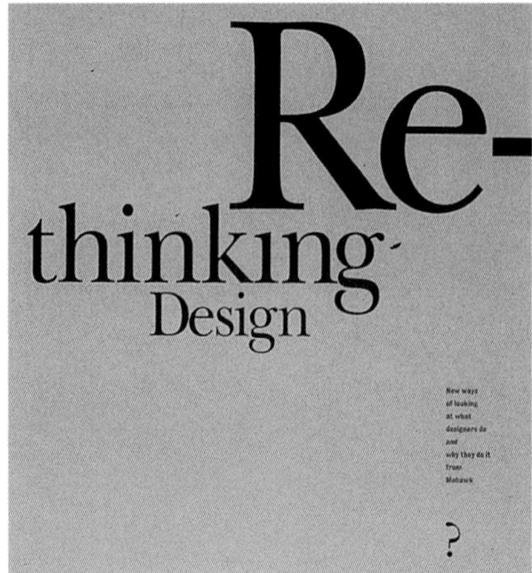
Re-
thinking
Design
?

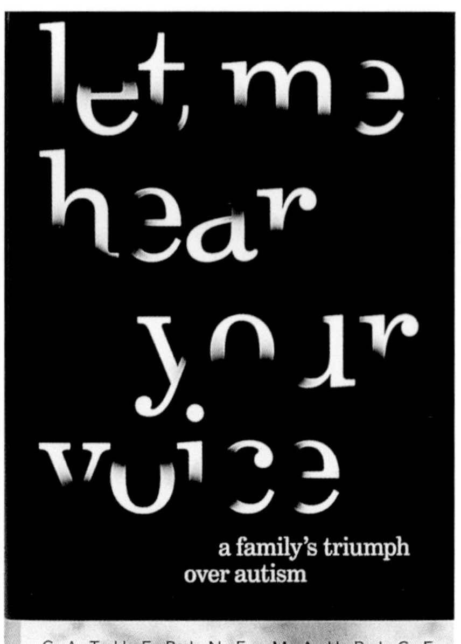
let me
hear
your
voice
a family's triumph
over autism
CATHERINE MAURICE

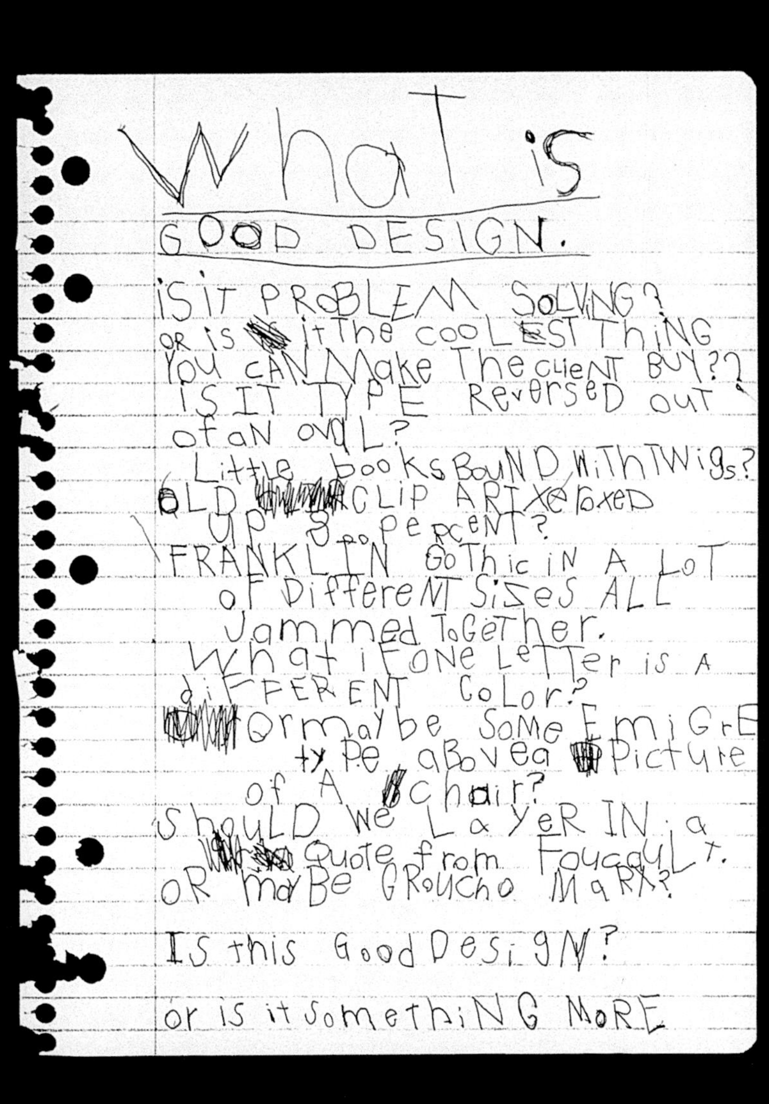

Call for Entries
The Fifteenth Annual American Center for Design
One Hundred Show

Alexander Isley, Jilly Simons, Erik Spiekermann, Judges
Michael Bierut, Chair

Entry Deadline: May 1, 1992

Design: Michael Bierut / Pentagram
Lettering: Elizabeth Ann Kresz Bierut / Transfiguration School

First Choice
Poster promoting Call for Entries for the annual competition of the American Centre for Design

'Being asked to serve as chairman for one of my country's most controversial design competitions forced my personal ambivalence about the current state of design out into the open. I was completely at a loss as how to design a call for entries announcement that could at once express a point of view and yet step outside the boundaries of style and influence, until this solution occurred to me. Dictating a statement letter by letter to my barely literate four-year-old daughter produced an effect that I find peculiarly moving every time I see it. And Elizabeth got it exactly right in one try'

Cover for 'Do it!' guides for Redefinition Books

Poster for an annual book fair to benefit New York's homeless

Corporate Identity for The Good Diner, New York

Identity and packaging for Hanes Hosiery for the client EG Smith

Cover for 'Rethinking Design' a publication for Mowhawk Paper Mills

Cover for 'Let me Hear Your Voice', a non-fiction account of raising an autistic child

Blechman

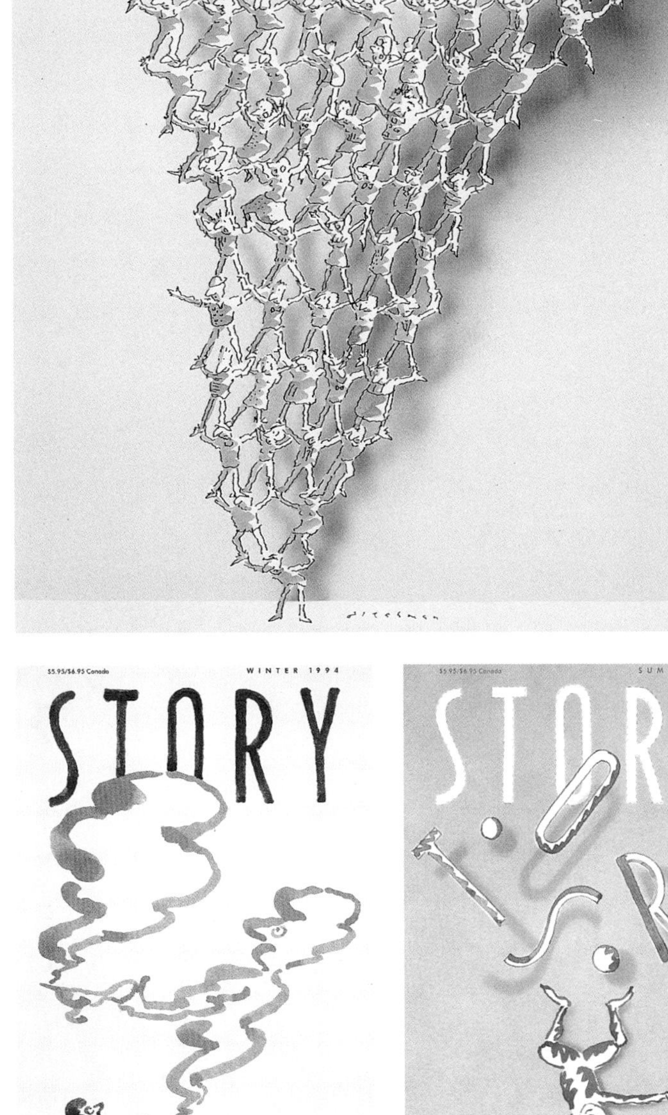

First Choice
Cover for 'The New Yorker' entitled, 'Halloween Cat'

'I always like it when I try something new and succeed. My Halloween Cat was an experiment in painting and collage, neither of which I had done much of before. So I was thrilled when it worked out so well. I was not so thrilled when it was bought by 'The New Yorker' as a cover and ran as a spot (without the photo collage!) but that's another story'

Cover illustration for a lead article on the population explosion for 'The Atlantic' magazine

Cover for 'Story' magazine, Winter Edition

Cover for 'Story' magazine, Summer Edition

Advertisement for 'Adweek' magazine

'Labour Day' unpublished drawing

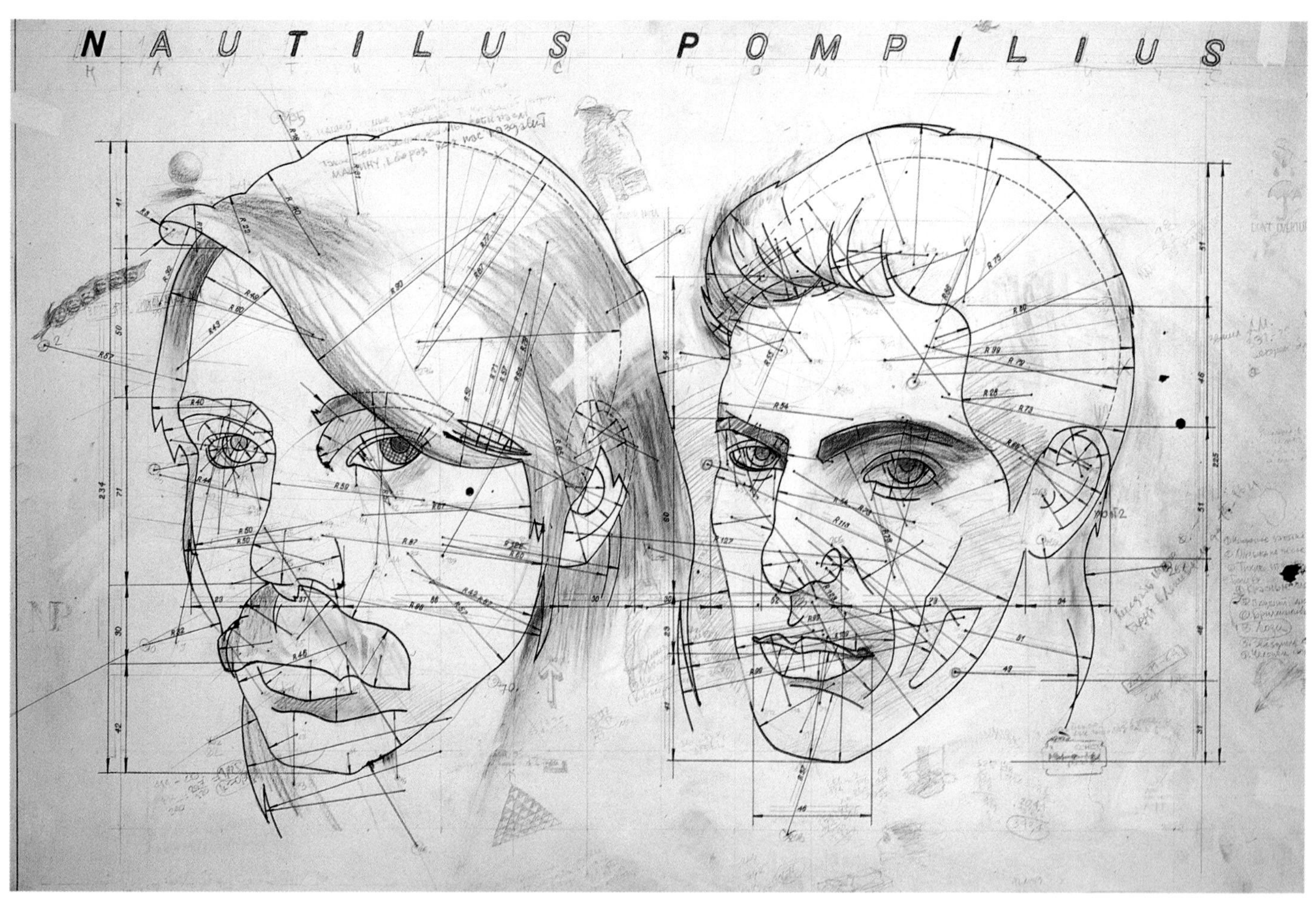
NAUTILUS POMPILIUS

First Choice
Design for rock group Nautilus Pompilius

'I love these people and their music. I spent two or three weeks making these stupid technical drawings of people, writing up on the sheet real telephone numbers and questions, doing small sketches on it, so it is a kind of two week diary. The print was very cheap in a small size and of course it did not have even a shadow of commercial success'

Poster for the film 'Stalin's Funeral'

Poster advertising Benedictine

Poster advertising Premier SV

Self promotion entitled 'A Political Map of the World'

Self promotion entitled 'The Most Human Man'

Self promotion, 'The Calendar' 1989

RICHARD STRAVSS: HIS LIFE AND WORK

Richard Strauss (1864 - 1949), one of the most prolific composers of his day, enjoyed a career spanning some seven decades, which represent some of the most turbulent and productive periods in Germany's cultural history. Duke University will host the first musicological conference on Strauss in the United States (April 5th - 8th, 1990). The international roster of participants represents musicology, theory, music criticism, arts administration, and German literature. Strauss was not only a successful composer, but a major conductor and organizer for the rights of composers. The Duke symposium intends to provide a clearer picture of the artist, his time, and his work.

An International Symposium
Duke University: 5 - 8 April 1990

Sessions

Strauss: The Musical and Historical Context

Strauss and his Contemporaries

The Instrumental Works

The Operatic Works

Strauss Research: Past, Present, and Future (Plenary Session)

Graduate-Student Session: Works in Progress

Participants

V. Kofi Agawu
(Cornell University)
Robert Bailey
(New York University)
George Buelow
(Indiana University)
Günther Brosche
(Austrian National Library, Vienna)
Kate Covington
(University of Kentucky)
Bryan Gilliam
(Duke University)
Stephen Hefling
(Case Western Reserve)
James A. Hepokoski
(University of Minnesota)
Michael Kennedy
(London Daily Telegraph)
Stephan Kohler
(Richard Strauss Institute, Munich)
Rey Longyear
(University of Kentucky)
Lewis Lockwood
(Harvard University)
Barbara Petersen
(Broadcast Music Incorporated)
Pamela Potter
(Yale University)
Reinhold Schlötterer
(University of Munich)
R. Larry Todd
(Duke University)
Ulrich Weisstein
(Indiana University)

Concerts
Nelson Music Room, East Duke Building

An Evening of Strauss Lieder
Steven Kimbrough, baritone
Dalton Baldwin, piano
Friday, April 6th, 8:00pm

The Early Piano Works of Strauss
Tibor Szász, piano
Saturday, April 7th, 8:30

Conference Advisory Committee:
Bryan Gilliam (director),
Alexander Silbiger,
R. Larry Todd

Conference Administrator:
Susan Ashley Wilson

With special thanks to: Anne Parks, Olivia Moore, and Marcia Doerr

For more information contact:
Bryan Gilliam
Conference Director
Box 6695 College Station
Department of Music
Duke University
Durham, NC 27708

Design: Bonnell Design Associates
Printing: W.E. Andrews of Connecticut

This conference is funded by a grant from the National Endowment for the Humanities, an independent federal agency; the Duke Center for International Studies; the Mary Duke Biddle Foundation; and The Josiah Charles Trent Memorial Foundation.

First Choice
Poster for a concert of Strauss compositions

'The Strauss poster is my favourite for two reasons. I love the music of Richard Strauss, and the client, Duke University, gave me complete freedom. A continuing debate revolves around Strauss staying in Germany during the war and lending his prestige to the Nazis. That's where the red and black came in juxtaposed against the early and late photos of Strauss; his composing career spanned 80 years. The remaining detail is all musical quotations from his major works'

Exhibition design for a temporary three day installation for a sales meeting in Grand Rapids entitled 'So What's New'

Construction sign for the Swiss Bank Tower for the developer, The Galbreath Company

CD ROM interface, graphics packaging and guidebook design for John Wiley and Company entitled 'Calculus Connections'

Format promotional brochure design for Lightolier Inc

Format book design for Continuum Publishing Company used for over fifty books a year

Ongoing communications development for new architectural systems product entitled 'Pathways', project book for the client Steelcase

REVOLT

First Choice
Invitation card for Amsterdam Stedelijk

'Before my creative directorship at Total Design (1963-1991) I worked with Ahrend, a leading company in office equipment and furniture. Frisco Kramer designed their Revolt chair (1954) which was really a new concept and the first of a broad revolutionary series. I was thrilled when Ahrend offered Frisco the opportunity to redesign this famous design classic. I was asked to design the graphics for the reintroduction in 1993. I made a poster and an invitation card for the presentation in Amsterdam's Stedelijk Museum. The front of that card is my favourite design. Frisco did not like the concept of showing a vague photographic image, distorted by the use of a xerox copy. But his real thing was a kind of copy in itself...'

Series of stamps for Dutch Post Fepapost Stamp exhibition, The Hague

Cover for Kieler Woche, The Winning Event design programme

Poster to celebrate twenty years of Randstad Intérim, Brussels

Cover for brochure for Mehes office furniture, Ahrend

Poster to commemorate Hiroshima's bombing for the Movement for Peace

Logotype for ECT, Europe Combined Terminals

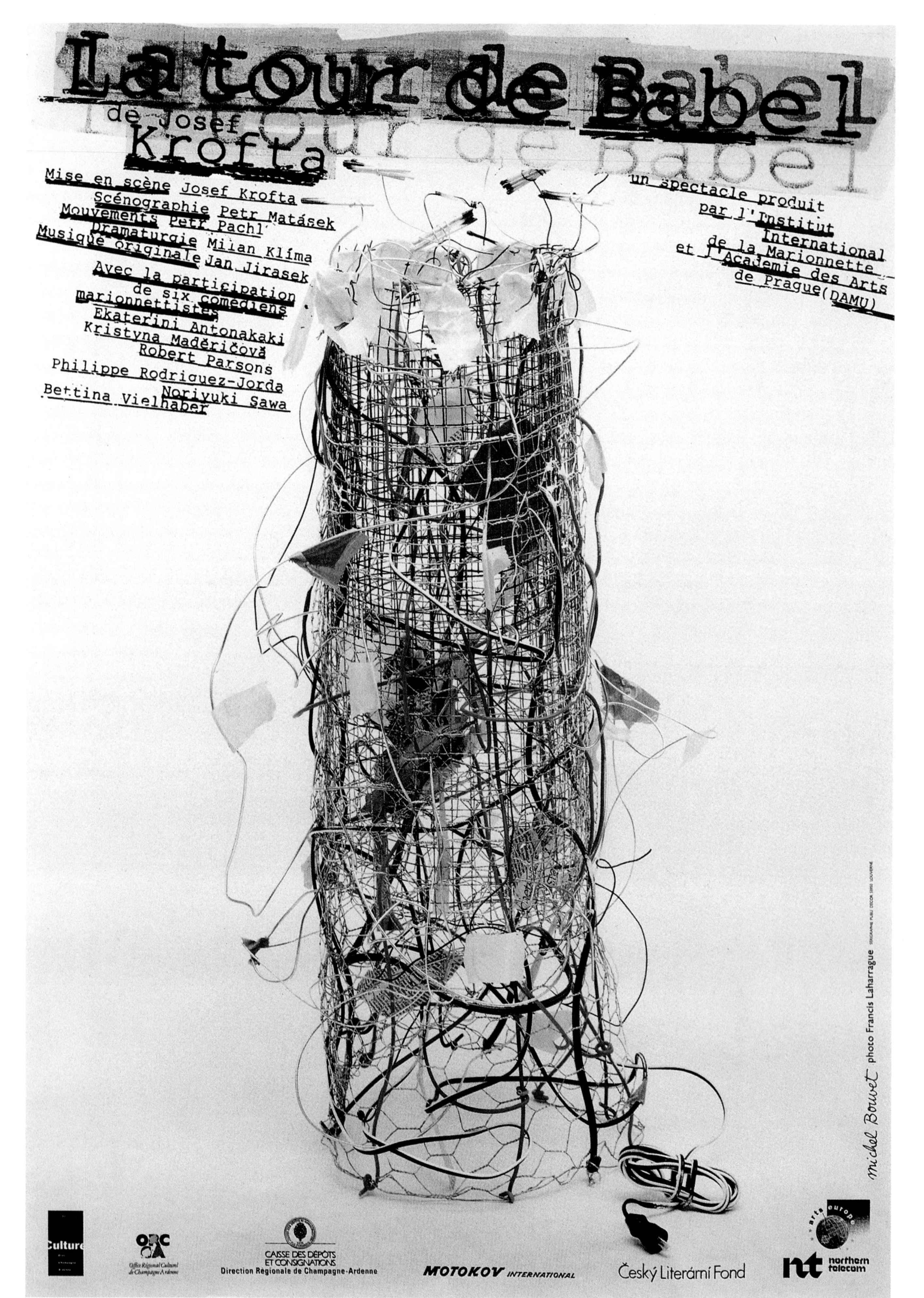
La tour de Babel
de Josef
Krofta
Mise en scène Josef Krofta
Scénographie Petr Matásek
Mouvements Petr Pachl
Dramaturgie Milan Klíma
Musique originale Jan Jirasek
Avec la participation
de six comediens
marionnettistes
Ekaterini Antonakaki
Kristyna Maděričová
Robert Parsons
Philippe Rodriguez-Jorda
Noriyuki Sawa
Bettina Vielhaber
un spectacle produit
par l'Institut
International
de la Marionnette
et l'Académie des Arts
de Prague (DAMU)
michel Bouvet photo Francis Laharrague
Culture
ORCCA
Office Régional Culturel de Champagne Ardenne
CAISSE DES DÉPÔTS ET CONSIGNATIONS
Direction Regionale de Champagne-Ardenne
MOTOKOV INTERNATIONAL
Český Literární Fond
arts europe
nt northern telecom

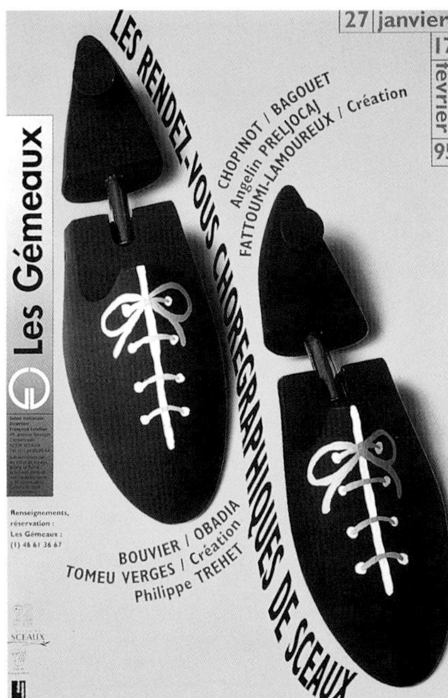

First Choice
Poster entitled 'The Tower of Babel'

'This poster has a special meaning for me. It represents a stage in my work as a poster artist, establishing a link between my interest in contemporary art (I studied at the School of Fine Arts in Paris) and my love of typography. This three dimensional work, this 'sculpture' was my way of expressing the derision and absurdity of our world, 'The Tower of Babel' terminating in burned out matchsticks. The poster was produced by the International Puppet Institute in Charleville-Mezieres, France, and the Academy of Arts in Prague, Czech Republic'

Poster for a stage play 'Français, encore un effort'

Poster for Mozart's 'Marriage of Figaro'

Poster for a stage play, 'Marie Tudor'

Poster for a stage play, 'Les Paravents'

Poster for the ballet, 'Les Rendez-vous chorégraphiques de Sceaux'

Poster promoting the 1990 'In the City' festival

Banca d'Italia

Pagabili a vista
del Portatore
Il Governatore

Il Cassiere

400

LireQuattrocento

48765876548765

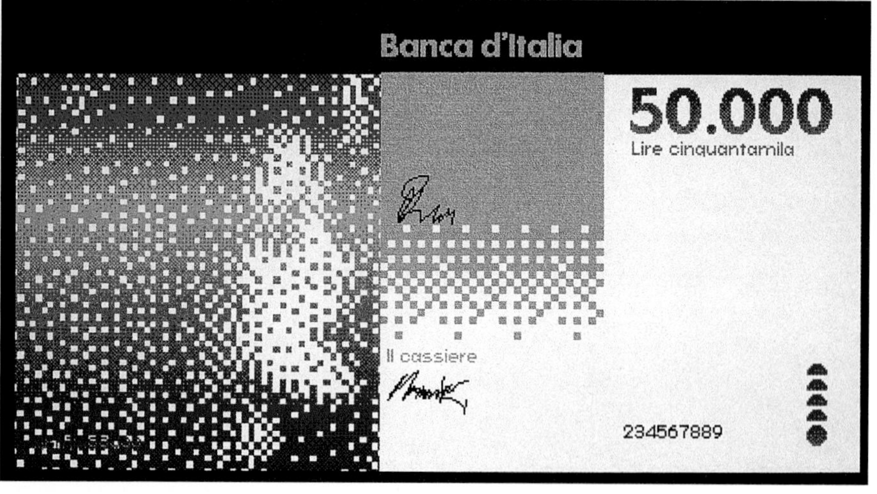

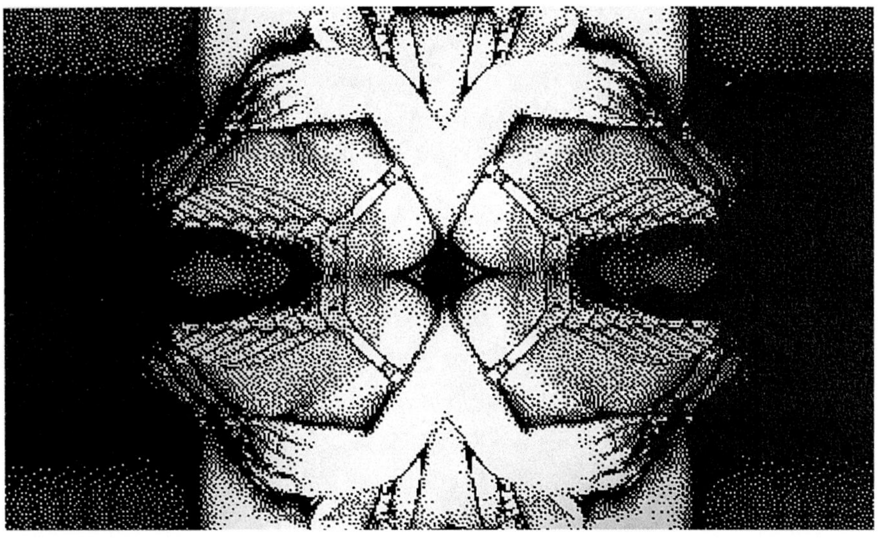

First Choice
Personal work modelled on a banknote

'I absolutely prefer this, the entertaining banknote form which we all want in our pockets, outside of the pomp and rhetoric of the money currently in use'

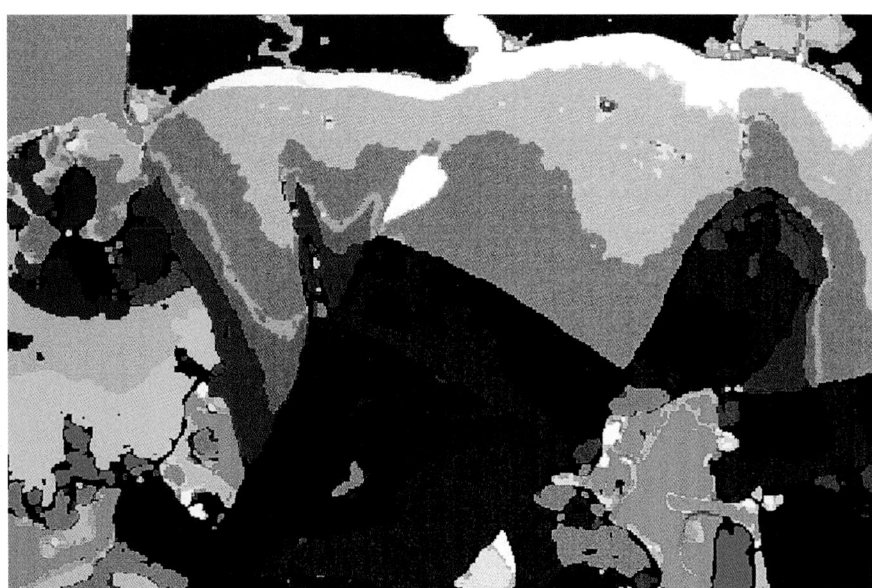

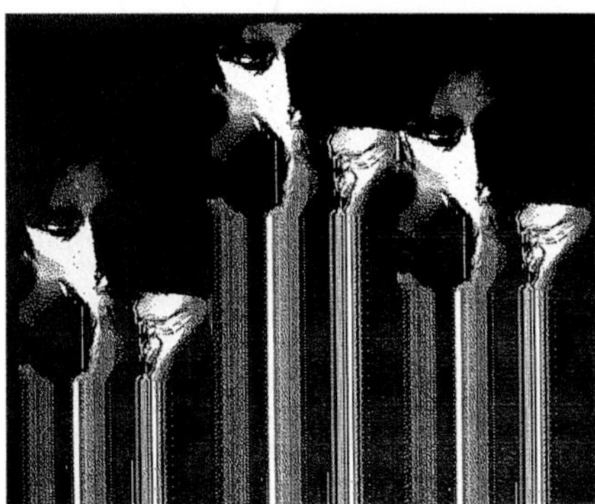

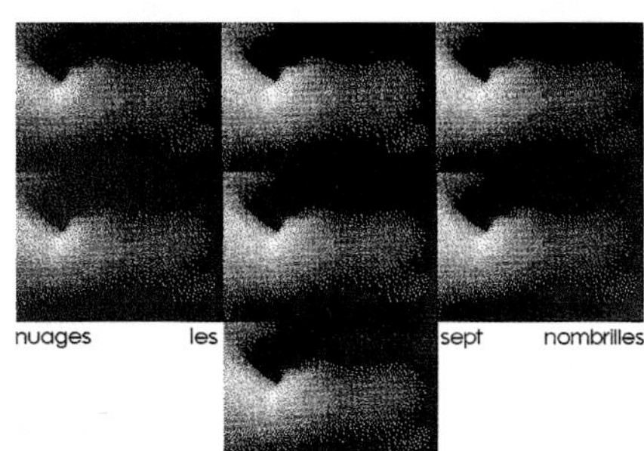

Nouveau motif for a buckle in silver

A personal piece, colourisation of a black and white original

Illustration for a volume of poetry

Personal work entitled 'Clouds, the Seven Navels'

T'GALLIANT
HOLY
STONE
1994

First Choice
Label design for
T'Gallant Holystone

'Working with a client and breaking a few traditional rules to produce a result that creates a unique position for a product and a company are factors strongly influencing my selection. Not only has this package design had a profound effect on sales but it has also won its share of design awards and critical acclaim.
I believe our profession is about a number of things, amongst them is having a major influence on the performance of business'

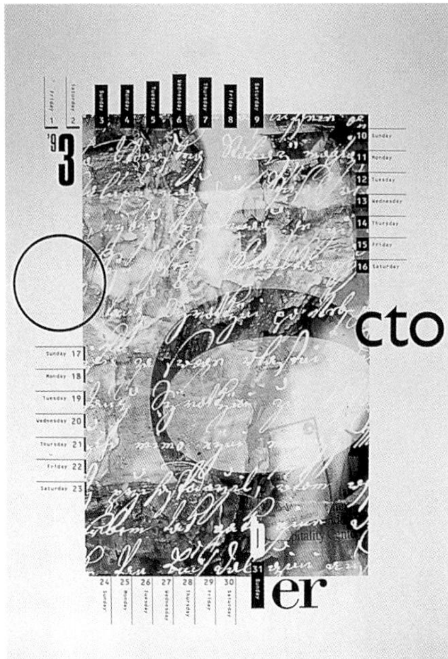

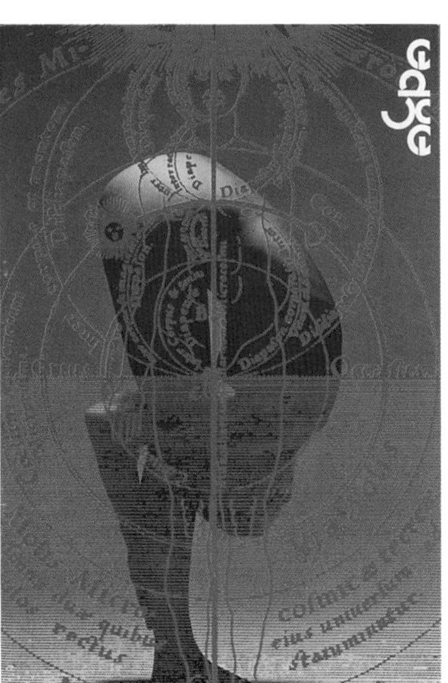

Environmental sculptures for Melbourne Olympic Bid city decorations

Label design for T'Gallant Demi-vache

Promotional calendar design for Eurasia Press, Singapore

Cover design for 'Edge' magazine

Corporate Identity design for Poppy King Industries

Symbol and logotype design for Melbourne Olympic Bid

MELBOURNE
1996

EXPOSIÇÃO
CASSIANO
BRANCO E
O EDEN
LISBOA · 91
PELOURO
CULTURA
EDEN
TEATRO

CIÊNCIA E COMUNICAÇÃO
COOPERATIVA CULTURAL, C.R.L.
RUA PASCOAL DE MELO, 84-1º 1000 LISBOA
tel: (01) 315.15.71

mário ruivo
director

First Choice
Poster for the exhibition of the Eden Cinema Theatre in Lisbon

'This poster was designed to advertise the exhibition of Portugal's most controversial modernist architect, Cassiano Branco. His most important and polemic work, the Eden cinema theatre in Lisbon, sought inspiration in the designs of the 1930s. The exhibition logo in the top left hand corner was based on the lettering found on the facade of another Cassiano Branco work. The search for a suitable design led me to rework typefaces derived from a number of sources from that period, in particular a typography manual published in Argentina in the 1930s. The facade of the building was photographed with different lighting to highlight the wealth of sculpture found beneath the stone and neon lettering, atop the main body of the building'

6 de Dezembro de 1993 100$00 Culturgest

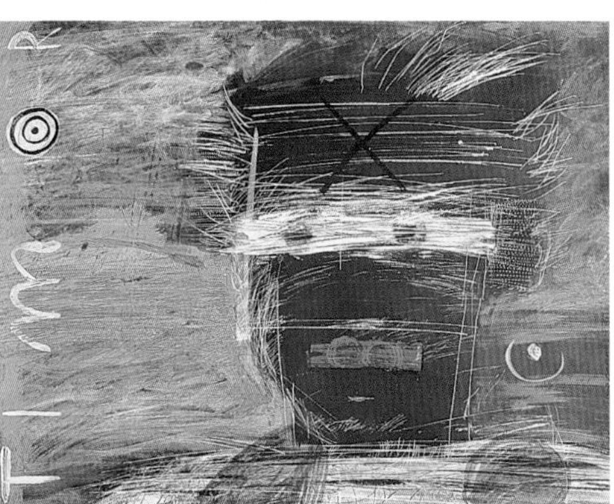

PUBLICO

Corporate Identity design for Ciência e Comunicacão

Cover of a catalogue for an architecture exhibition

Cover for exhibition newspaper

Illustration, a personal piece

Painting, a personal piece

Logotype for the Público daily newspaper

S

First Choice Symbol for Credito Sardo Bank design competition

'I chose a small piece of work, a trademark for a competition (that I did not win) because this work reflects, better than many others, the process I follow. Credito Sardo is a developing bank, based in Sardinia, one of the most beautiful Italian islands. The design of the trade mark represents a recumbent 'S' (for Sardinia). The curves forming this unusual figure also represent a lower case 'c' and a lower case 's' the initials of the bank. I believe a message can be conveyed through tiny shafts of meaning, capable of provoking a light and naive amazement'

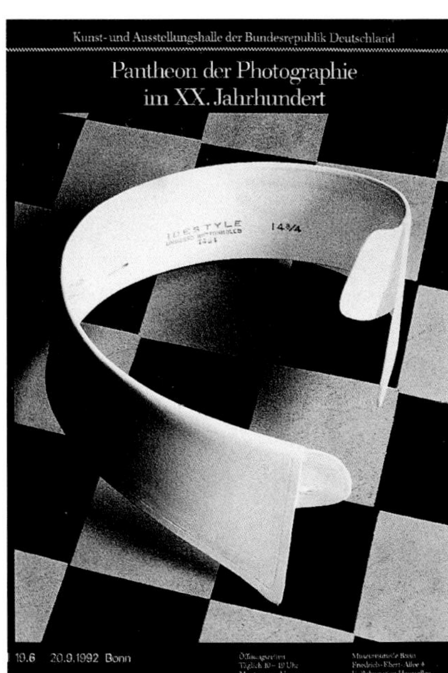

Logotype for the Saroil oil company

Poster for a Mario Merz exhibition, at the Peggy Guggenheim Collection, Venice

Poster for Unifor office furniture system

Poster for a photographic exhibition at the Kunst Halle, Bonn

Logotype for a series of interactive publications 'Encyclomedia'

Logotype for a music foundation

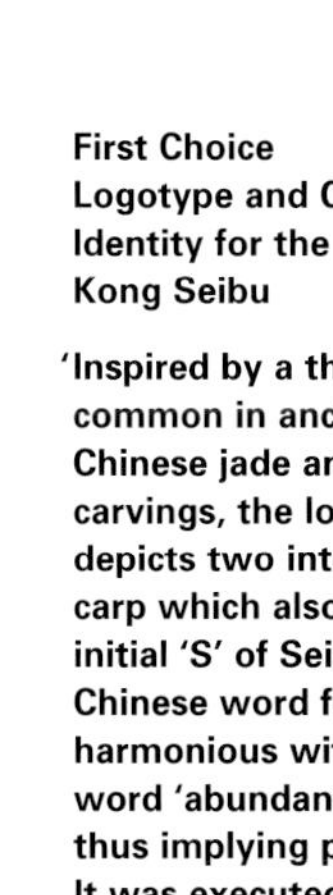

First Choice
Logotype and Corporate Identity for the Hong Kong Seibu

'Inspired by a theme common in ancient Chinese jade and wood carvings, the logo mark depicts two intertwining carp which also form the initial 'S' of Seibu. The Chinese word for 'fish' is harmonious with the word 'abundance', thus implying prosperity. It was executed in a contemporary style without losing its cultural context.
The logo runs continuously, flowing like an eternal cycle and symbolising the non-stop energy of the fishes, representing the growth of Seibu's business. The wrapping paper similarly repeats the carp image, this time in an all over design which was inspired by Furoshiki, the traditional Japanese gift wrapping fabric'

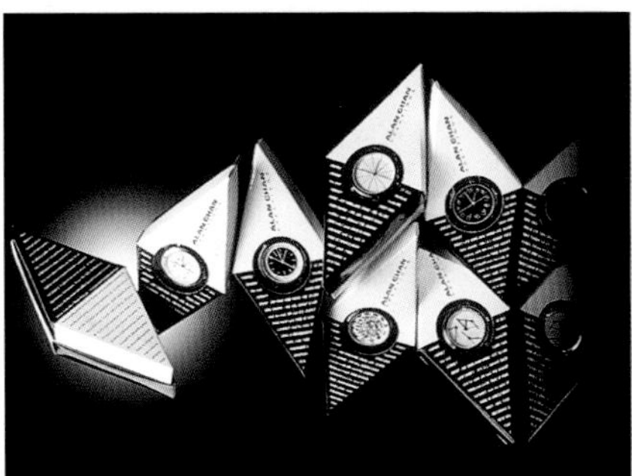

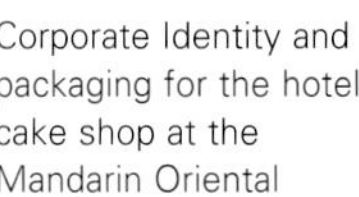

Corporate Identity and packaging for the hotel cake shop at the Mandarin Oriental

Mooncake packaging for a homemade bakery for Chung King Szechwan Restaurant

Corporate Identity and packaging for the Swank Shop

Packaging range for Mr Chan Fine Teas

Product and packaging design for Alan Chan Creations Watches, six limited edition timepieces

A series of spectacle cases for the Optical Shop, manufactured in mock tortoiseshell, marble and plain colour

carefully to first
ticisms of your work.
just what it is that
critics don't like, the
tivate it. That's the
t of your work that's
keeping.
an Cocteau
VISITA
INFERIORA
TERRAE
RECTIFICANDO
INVENIES
OCCULTUM
LAPIDEM
VITRIOL

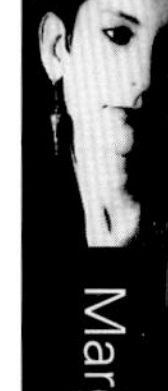

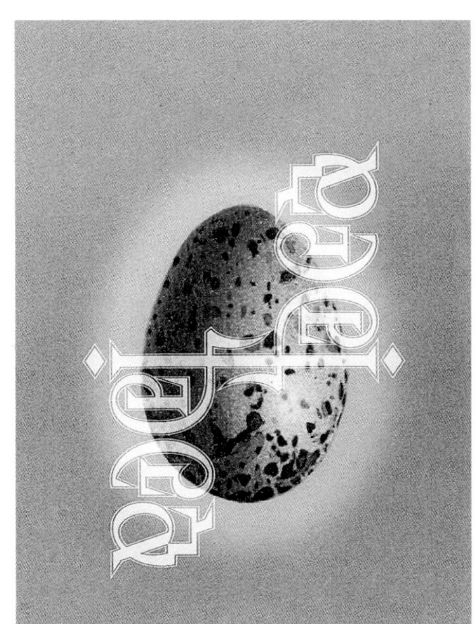

First Choice
Vitriol, the acid test

'Historically, vitriol was a symbolic formula of the alchemists, often used to describe the transformation of base metals into precious metals, especially gold. The word VITRIOL is an acronym of the Latin phrase Visita Inferiora Terrae Rectificando Invenies Occultum Lapidern ('Seek out the lower realms of the earth, perfect them, and you will find the hidden stone', ie the Philosophers Stone) Vitriol has now come to be synonymous with sulfuric acid and other caustic substances, or an adjective (vitriolic) to mean caustic, biting and painful. As designers and artists, exposing our work to public view and comment is the acid test by which we are judged'

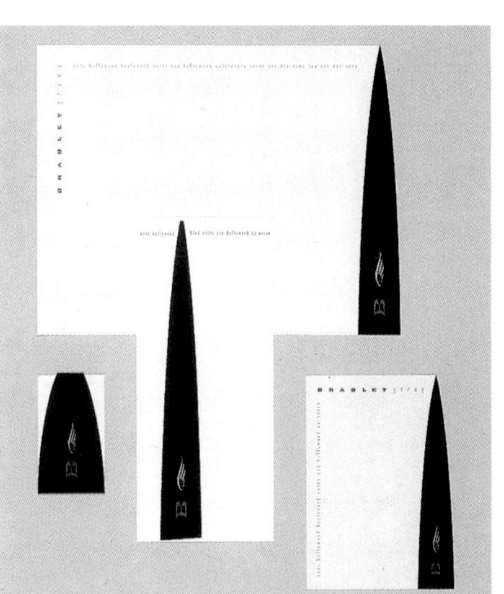

Poster for 'Germs', Margo Chase Design Lecture for Dallas Society of Visual Communication

Cover design for 'IDEA' magazine, issue 245, 1994

Logotype and packaging for Bone Dry Beer

Stationery for the Bradley Group, computer consultants

CD cover for Ten Inch Men entitled 'Pretty Vultures'

CD cover for Loreena McKennitt entitled 'Mask and Mirror'

The Master Series: Ivan Chermayeff Graphic Design: Art & Process
Eighth in the series, Exhibition: October 2nd to October 20th 1995
Lecture: Thursday, October 5th, 7 pm. Museum hours:
Monday–Thursday 9 am–8pm, Friday 9 am–5pm
Visual Arts Museum at the School of Visual Arts
209 East 23rd street, New York, New York 10010

First Choice
Self promotional poster

'I love garbage, accidents and odd, new connections. The glove is found; the rainbow pencil, a tool awaiting an opportunity. This poster for myself makes a new connection'

Poster for the 1994 IDCA 'Design and Human Bodies' conference

Figure for 'Jacob's Pillow' dance company'

Catalogue cover for the UCLA, 1992

Cover for the Corcoran School of Art

Collage entitled 'Russian side table'

Catalogue cover for the Corcoran School of Art

DE STIJL
DESIGN & STYLES

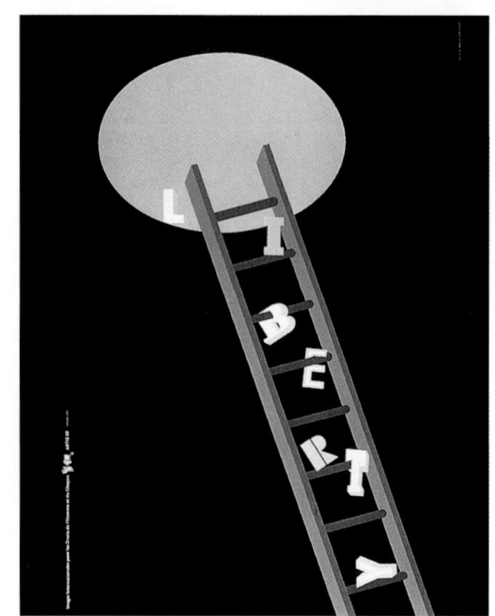
LIBERTY

GROWING BY DESIGN
THE 40th INTERNATIONAL DESIGN CONFERENCE IN ASPEN
JUNE 17-22, 1990

EARTH DAY
NEW YORK
APRIL 22, 1990
REDUCE
REUSE
RECYCLE

SEYMOUR CHWAST IN AMBROSIANA

First Choice
Poster promoting a series of lectures by designers for the Cooper Union School of Art in New York

'It is a solution I rarely use, that is, to have the letter forms express the message. I decided not to use an illustrated image. It would be too personal, since I was only one designer among eight to give a talk. I think it succeeds because, while conveying no particular style, it has concise immediacy in a way that does not take itself too seriously'

Promotional brochure entitled 'Design and Style No.7 Bauhaus' from a series of seven created to profile Mohawk Papers and celebrate different genres of graphic design

Promotional brochure entitled 'Design and Style No.5 De Stijl' from a series of seven created to profile Mohawk Papers and celebrate different genres of graphic design

Poster to commemorate the celebration of the 200th Anniversary of the French Revolution entitled 'Liberty'

Poster for the 40th International Design Conference in Aspen entitled 'Growing by Design'

Poster for Earth Day, 1990

Poster created to promote Design Biennale in the Czech Republic entitled 'Seymour Chwast in Ambrosiana'

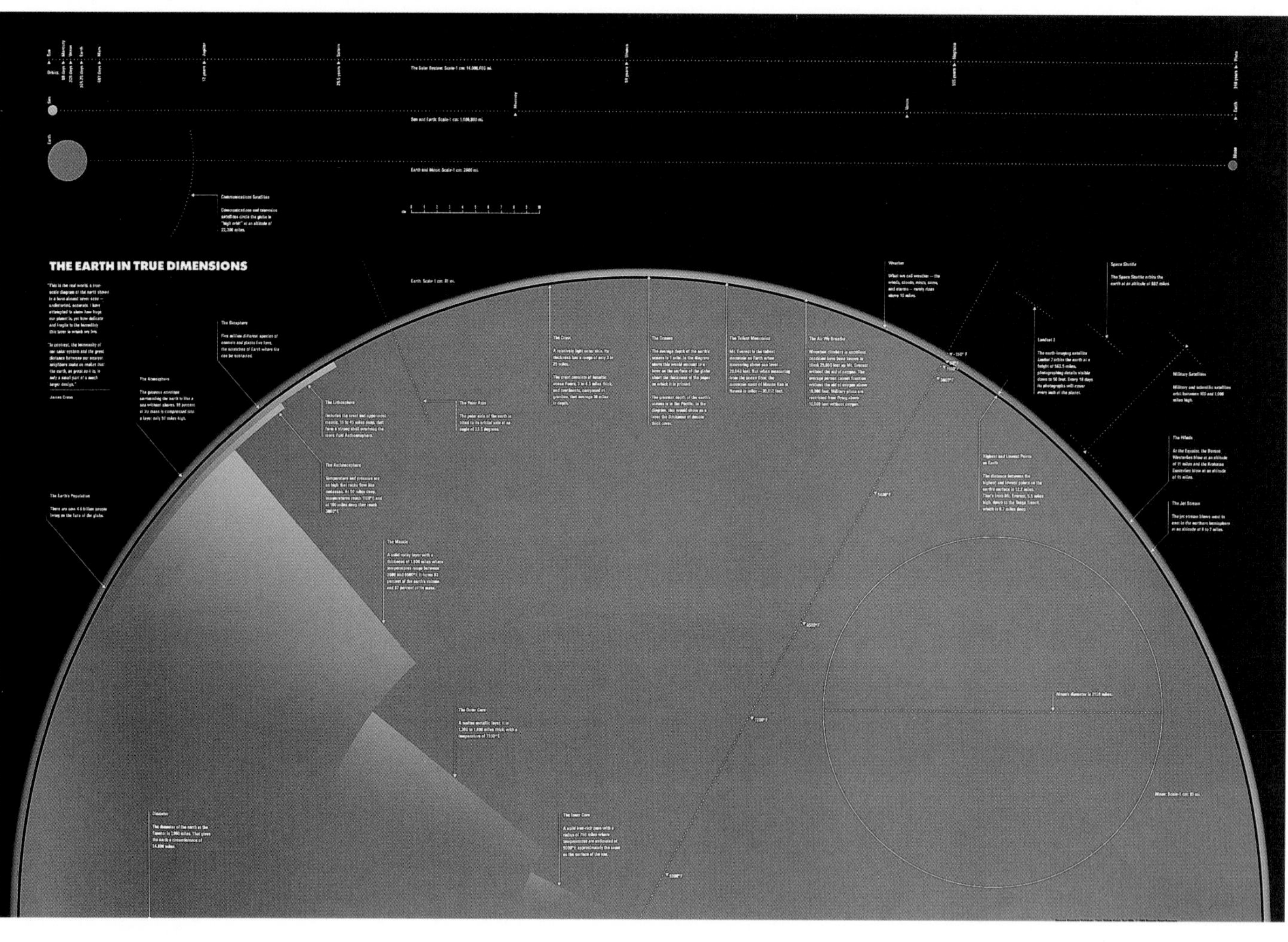
THE EARTH IN TRUE DIMENSIONS

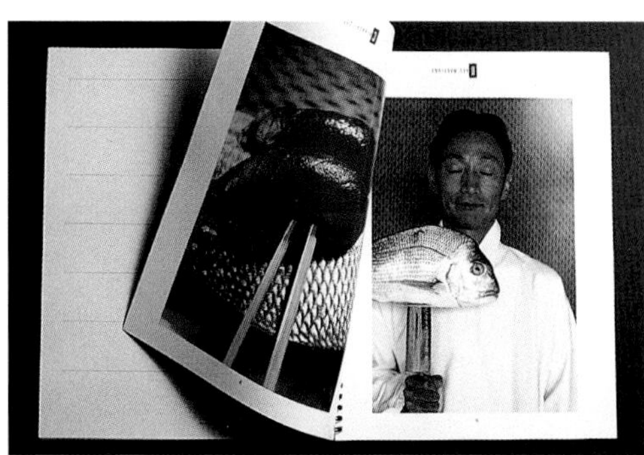

First Choice
Poster depicting a diagram of geological and astronomical features of the earth in true scale

'I have always been concerned that man's perception of the physical dimensions of the earth's structure, its surface, interior and surrounding atmosphere, is a very distorted one. This is the result of depictions of the planet and space in popular magazines, some atlases and other non-scientific media. If we see the dimensions of these features in true scale, we begin to understand the fragile nature of our world and become more aware of the delicate balance of the environment in which we inhabit'

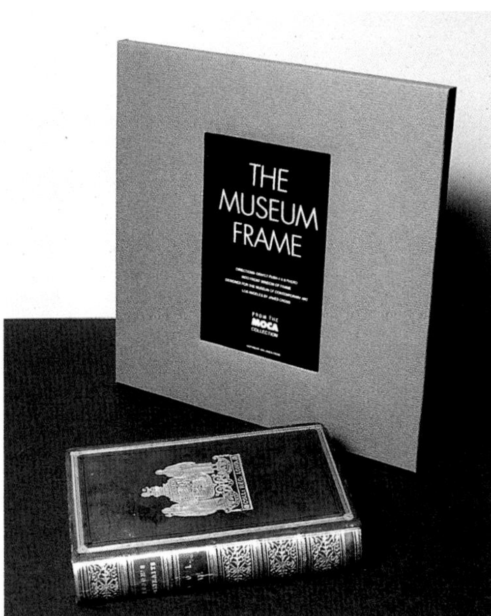

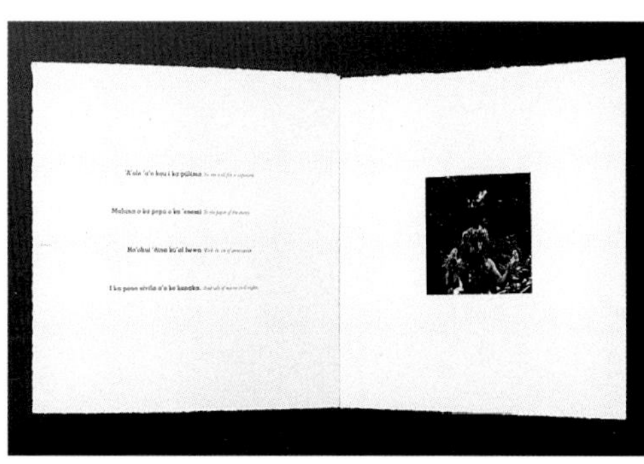

1993 desk calendar for Alan Lithograph Company featuring fifteen award winning chefs and their favourite recipes

1994 desk calendar for Alan Lithograph Company featuring fifteen award winning chefs and their favourite recipes

Artist book entitled 'Hiilawe', handprinted letterpress featuring original James Cross intaglio prints

Artist book entitled 'Hilo Hanakahi', handprinted letterpress featuring original James Cross wood cuts

Picture frame made of recycled paper, manufactured in eight colours and sold as part of James Cross paper products

Artist book entitled 'Kaulana Na Pua', printed letterpress featuring original James Cross photographs

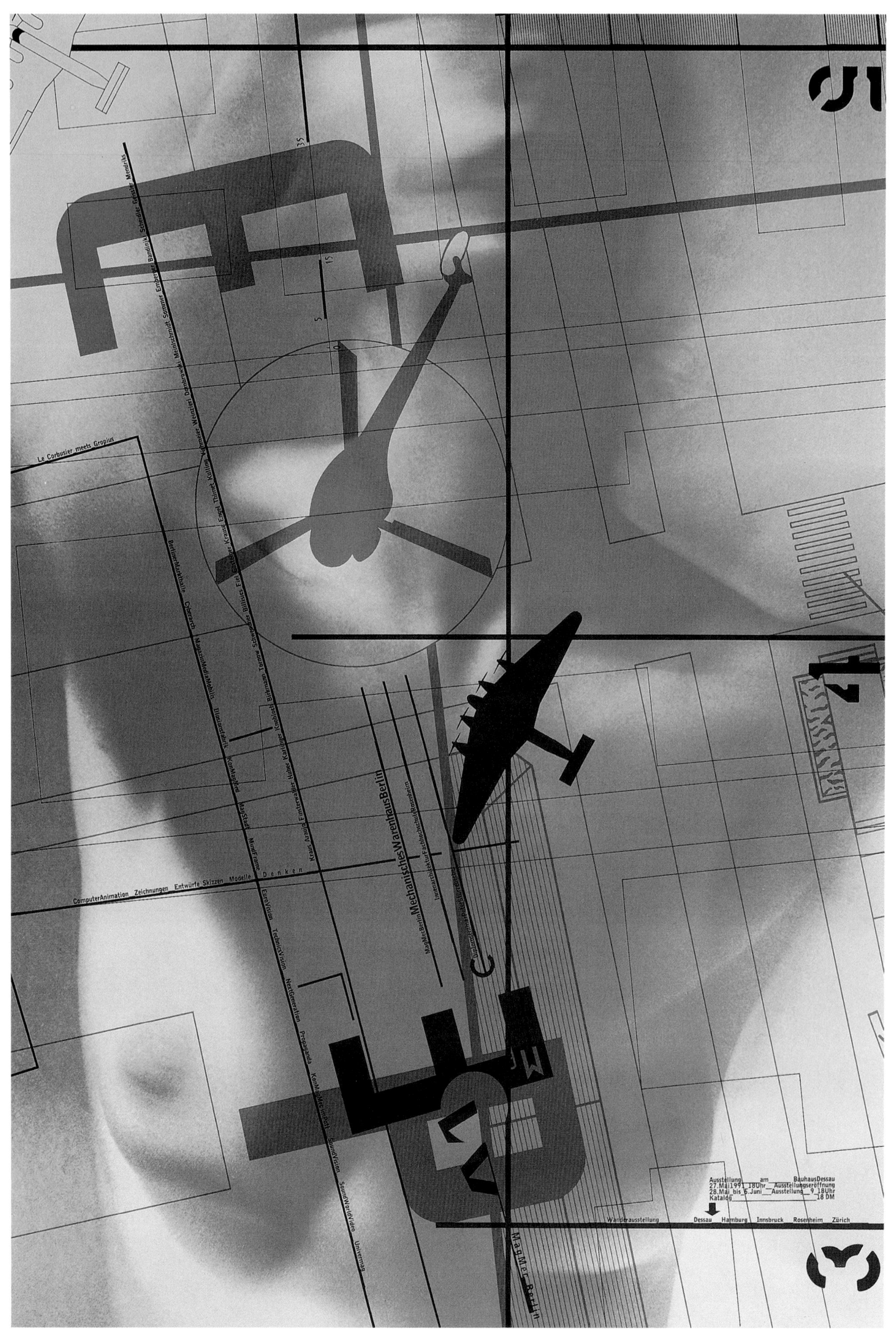

Le Corbusier meets Gropius
ComputerAnimation Zeichnungen Entwürfe Skizzen Modelle Denken
MechanischesWarenhausBerlin
Ausstellung am BauhausDessau
27.Mai1991 18Uhr Ausstellungseröffnung
28.Mai bis 6.Juni Ausstellung 9 18Uhr
Katalog 18 DM
Wanderausstellung Dessau Hamburg Innsbruck Rosenheim Zürich

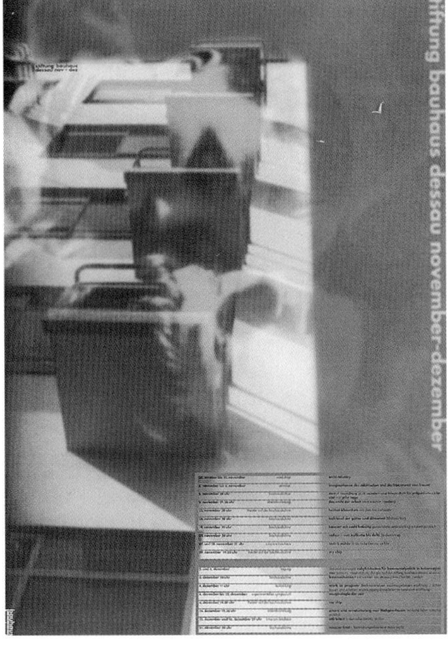

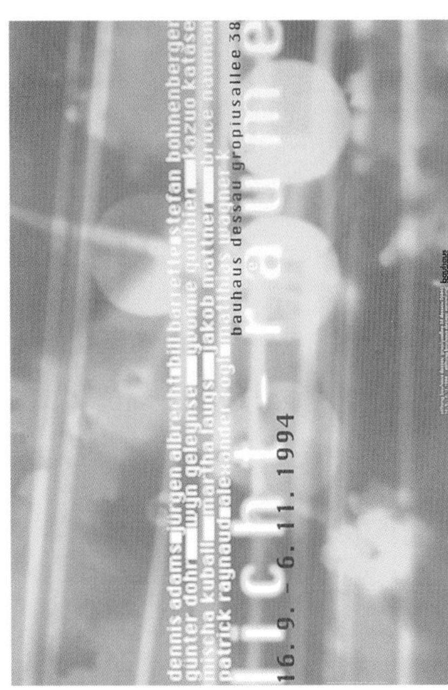

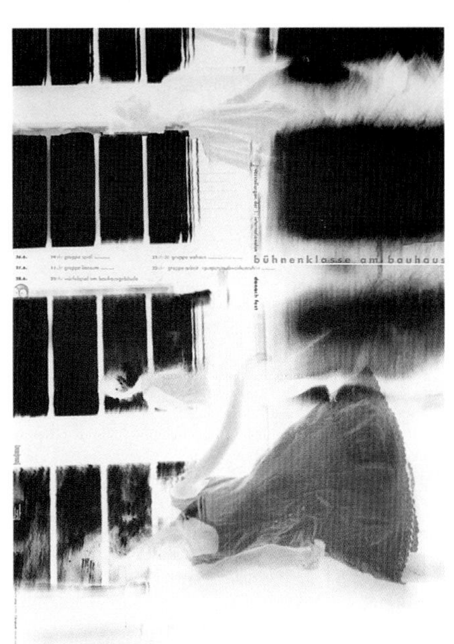

First Choice
Poster for Mag Mec Berlin

'Our fascination with the aesthetic potential of computers was at first restrained by our allegiance with the traditions of the early 20th century avant-garde (the Bauhaus etc). These seven 2-colour posters resulting from three years of cooperation with the Bauhaus Dessau are important to us because in the course of time an aesthetic evolution (concerning both the cooperation between the client and us, and the technical development) became not only possible but also evident. This led to a close approach to our idea of poster design. Our work may not conform to the conventional claims of functional communication, and much less still are they meant to trivialise'

Two poster programmes for Bauhaus Dessau

Exhibition poster for Lichträume for the Bauhaus Dessau

Poster for a concert in the Bauhaus

Two posters for the theatre class at Bauhaus

F. I. T.
50
YEARS

First Choice
Clothing range for F.I.T.

'This year is the 50th Anniversary of the Fashion Institute of Technology. Coincidently, it marks my 25th anniversary as graphic design consultant to this unique college. It's unusual to be associated with a client over such a long period of time, and I'm delighted to be part of this spirited milestone in the life of F.I.T.'

F.I.T. recruiting book sent to high school students

Retail items created for Barnes & Noble College Shop

T-shirts featuring TSMSS anniversary symbol and logotype

F.I.T. Continuing Education brochures

100th Anniversary materials for the Third Street Music School Settlement

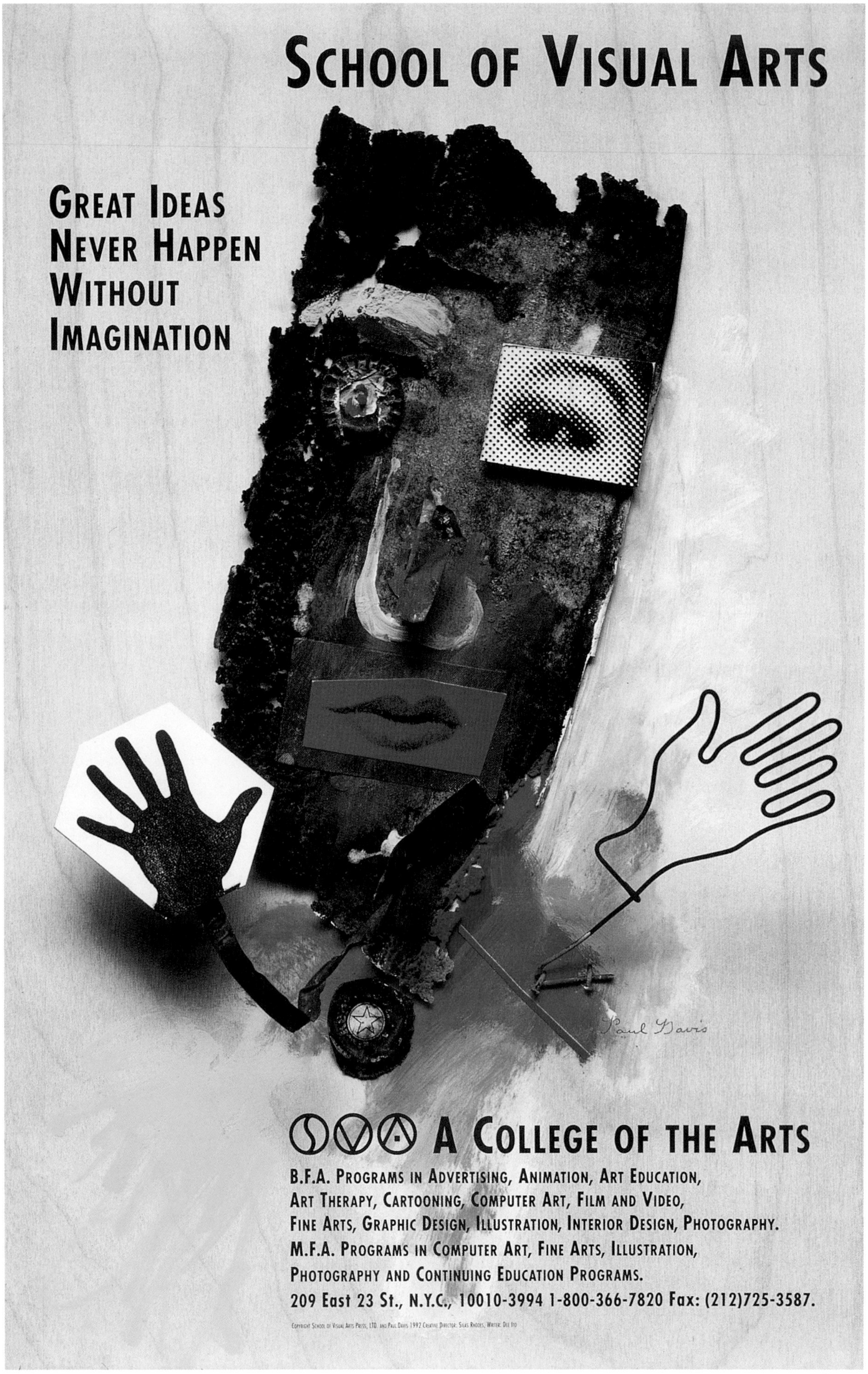

GREAT IDEAS
NEVER HAPPEN
WITHOUT
IMAGINATION

Paul Davis

SVA A COLLEGE OF THE ARTS

B.F.A. PROGRAMS IN ADVERTISING, ANIMATION, ART EDUCATION,
ART THERAPY, CARTOONING, COMPUTER ART, FILM AND VIDEO,
FINE ARTS, GRAPHIC DESIGN, ILLUSTRATION, INTERIOR DESIGN, PHOTOGRAPHY.
M.F.A. PROGRAMS IN COMPUTER ART, FINE ARTS, ILLUSTRATION,
PHOTOGRAPHY AND CONTINUING EDUCATION PROGRAMS.
209 East 23 St., N.Y.C., 10010-3994 1-800-366-7820 Fax: (212)725-3587.

First Choice
Collage illustration for SVA, Great Ideas

'I have always made collages and drawings outside of my commercial work. Some elements of these experiments tend to spill over into my design projects. In this case I wanted to make something special for the School of Visual Arts that was fresh and striking, and I like the sense of playfulness and spontaneity that this assemblage brought to the poster'

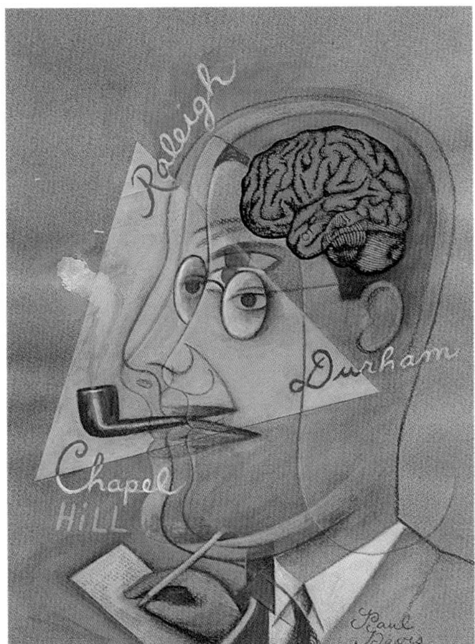

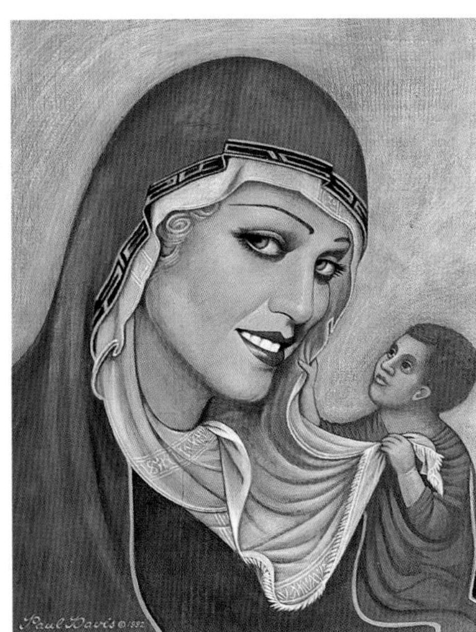

Illustration for greeting card for Spazio, Japan, entitled 'Janus'

Collage for the Manhattan Community College

Illustration entitled 'Sales Man', for 'Selling' magazine

Illustration entitled 'Hearing About the Bomb, August 1945, Kansas'

Illustration of Madonna for Rolling Stone

Illustration of Denzel Washington as Richard III, New York Shakespeare Festival

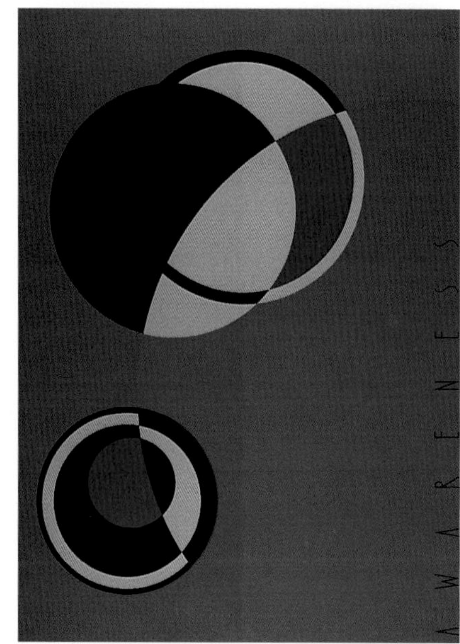
AWARENESS

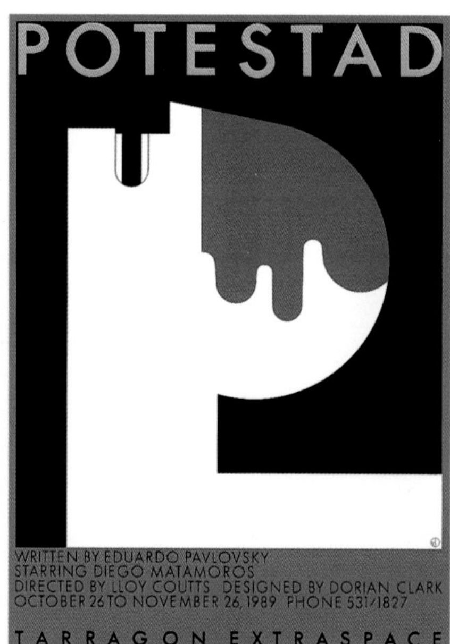
POTESTAD
WRITTEN BY EDUARDO PAVLOVSKY
STARRING DIEGO MATAMOROS
DIRECTED BY LLOY COUTTS DESIGNED BY DORIAN CLARK
OCTOBER 26 TO NOVEMBER 26, 1989 PHONE 531-1827
TARRAGON EXTRASPACE

THE FATHER
BY AUGUST STRINDBERG
ADAPTED BY JOHN OSBORNE DIRECTED BY DEREK GOLDBY
STARRING JOYCE CAMPION PAUL HADDAD MICHAEL POLLEY
LEON POWNALL LISA ROBERTSON DAVID SCHURMANN KATE TROTTER
SET & COSTUMES BY ARNDT VON HOLTZENDORFF
LIGHTING BY ROBERT THOMSON
FEBRUARY 20 TO MARCH 25 PREVIEWS FEBRUARY 13 TO 18 PHONE 531-1827
TARRAGON MAINSPACE

1492
1992

First Choice
Concept for column design for my one man show at the Royal Ontario Museum

'Because of my Greek heritage I based the symbol for the show on the classic Greek style. It was kind of nice to know that a couple of floors above my show, The Real Thing created by my ancestors was being exhibited'

Brochure cover for the Ontario College of Art, Toronto

Poster for Gitanes

Poster for Aids awareness

Poster for Tarragon Theatre, Toronto

Poster for Tarragon Theatre, Toronto

Design for Kiosk - 2nd International Litfass Art Biennale

WOMAN SUFFRAGE!
CONSTITUTIONAL AMENDMENT.
THE RIGH
OF CITIZENS
SHALL N
BE
DENIED
or abridged
United States
ny State
State
CELEBRATE THE 75TH ANNIVERSARY OF THE 19TH AMENDMENT

ON

February 14, 1989, the religious leader of one country issued a death edict against a citizen of another country. Five years later Salman Rushdie is still a man with no fixed address.

The novel that provoked the death sentence, *The Satanic Verses*, continues to be available in bookstores and libraries throughout the United States and many other countries. But Rushdie is in hiding, still writing nearly every day, making public appearances on occasion— but effectively under threat, marked as with an incandescent X on his chest and back.

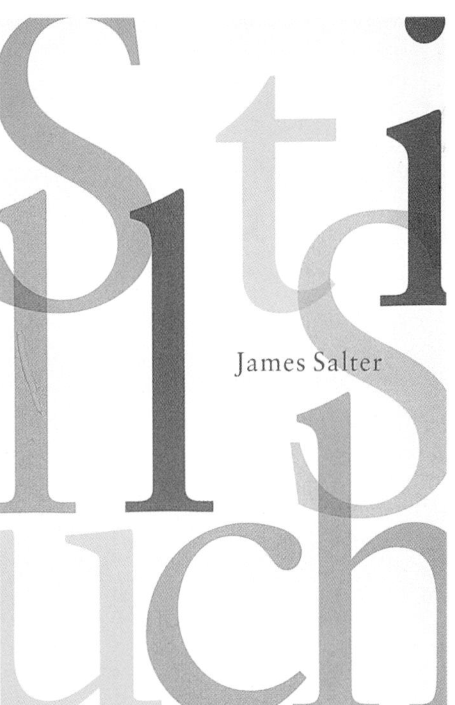

First Choice
Installation to celebrate the 75th anniversary of the granting of American women's Right to Vote

'Our favourite project is always the most recent because it reverberates with freshness. Our 19th Amendment installation to celebrate the 75th anniversary of American Women's Right to Vote is full of energy, so much so that it literally filled one of our grandest spaces in New York City, the main waiting room of Grand Central Terminal. Its impact is its simplicity. These twenty-eight words affected the course of American history, so they seemed worth repeating and in a scale one cannot forget'

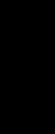

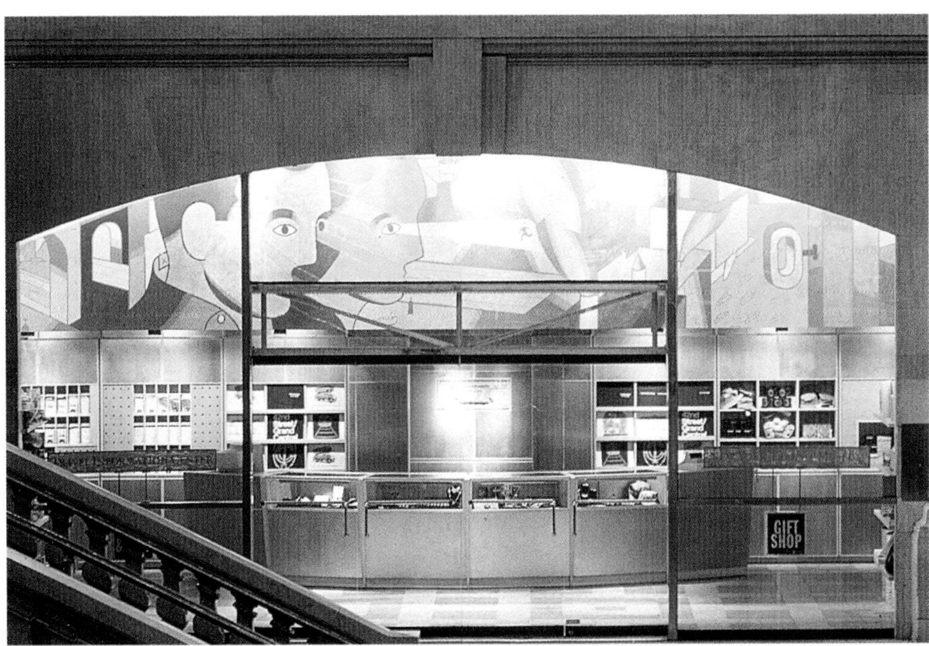

Design for a flyer which was distributed in 450,000 bookstores on the Fifth Anniversary of the fatwa against author Salman Rushdie

Book design for the publication 'Still Such' written by James Salter, designed by Stephen Doyle and published by William Drenttel, New York

Exterior and interior design for the Transit Museum Gift Shop, located in the main concourse of the Grand Central Terminal

Catalogue design for the Dislocations installation at the MoMA

Hand lettered design for the first issue of Champion International's 'Subjective Reasoning' Series, based on Vaclav Havel's speech about the end of communism

TRAIL MARK
MARK
MARK

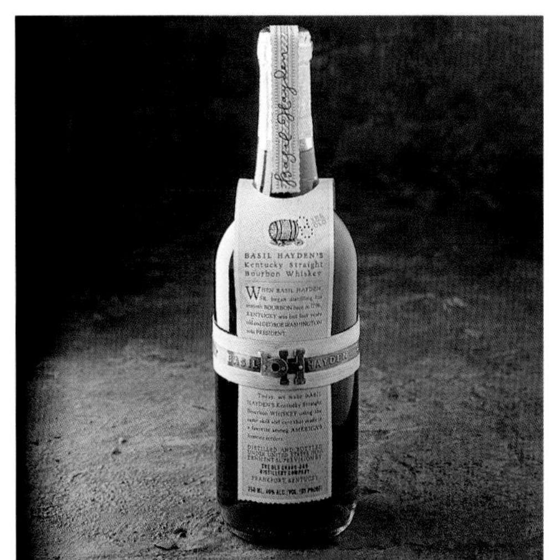

First Choice
Corporate Identity for Trailmark stores

'Why?'

'The best client I've ever worked for. Someone who understood the need for consistency of message in building a brand personality. Someone who allowed us to attend to every last detail from name and store design, to sales staff name tags, with the same amount of care and concern'

'The Client?'

'Me, of course'

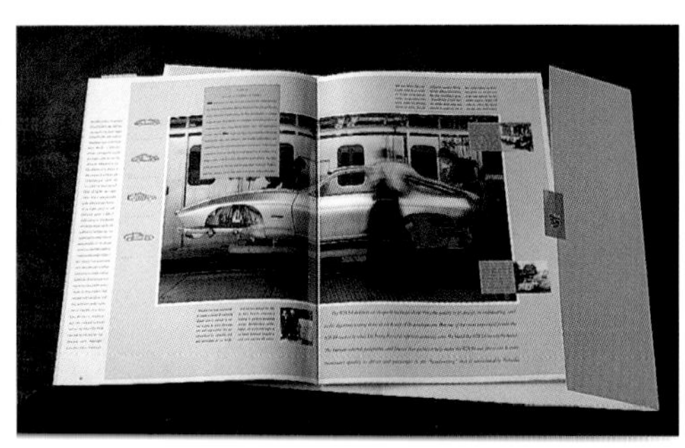

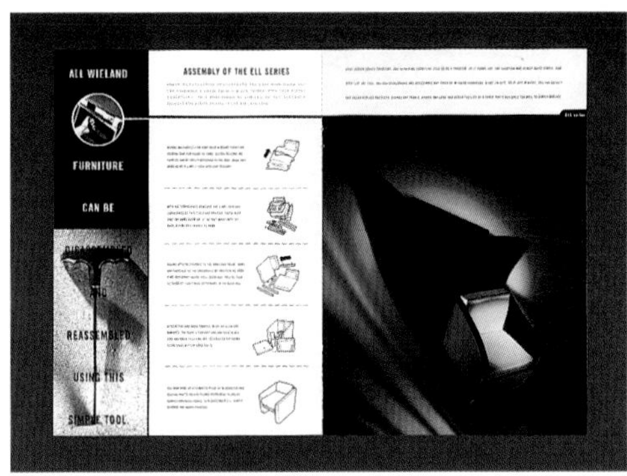

Packaging design for the Stroh Brewery Company, Barrel #12

Packaging design for Jim Beam brands, Basil Hayden's

Brand identity for Fruitopia

Brand identity for a purified ice company, Paradise

Brochure design for Porsche

Brochure design for Porsche

Identity campaign for Wieland Furniture

Identity campaign for Wieland Furniture

POLITIE

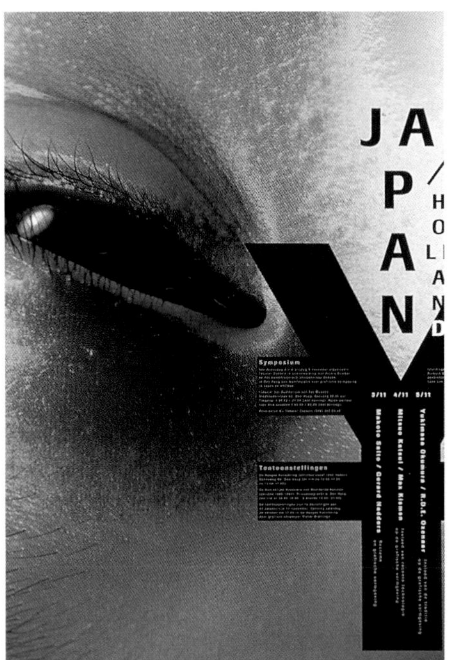

First Choice Corporate Identity program for the Dutch Police

'The main reason for this choice is that it is the first time in history that the Dutch Police (an organisation for the public sector) has chosen one integrated visual identity program. The Corporate Identity was developed after a fusion between the state police and the municipal police forces. The new logo integrates the two symbols of the former separated forces. Apart from the logo, Studio Dumbar developed systems for printed matter and for striping on cars. The striping system has been developed in such a way that it can be applied on 14 different car models. This resulted in a reduction of the production and implementation costs. The application of the striping does not require any spray paint and can therefore be restored very easily'

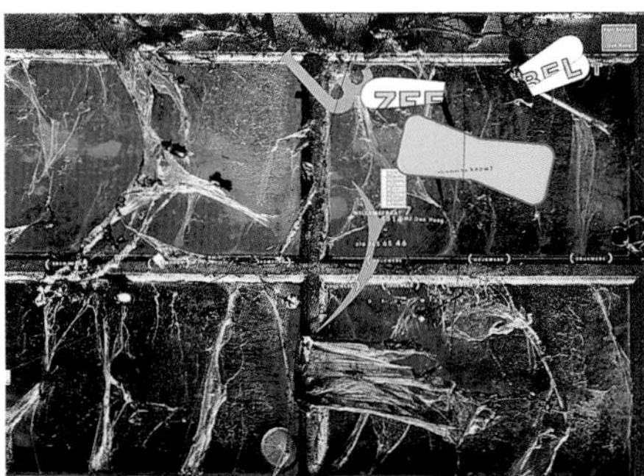

Poster for Nike

Poster for Symposium entitled 'Japan/Holland about graphic design'

Variations of logo for Het Nationale Toneel

Poster for exhibition, Rijksmuseum, Amsterdam

Program for Zeebelt Theatre

Corporate Identity for the Dutch Police (striping on Porsche)

First Choice
create-face-mask-works

'During my travels to many museums in different countries, I saw art works from past to present. When I saw Maleric's 'Black Square' at Georges Pompidou Centre in Paris, I felt that this picture was the most modern and abstract picture that I ever saw before. For me it was a high point of contemporary art. And I saw many contemporary artists going this way, like 'Black Square' in other situations. And these famous artists are 'big names' in contemporary art. I decided to create work with a black square. I used it for a poster 'Art and Business'. And it was published by a Polish art magazine for advertising in 1992'

Poster for International Puppet Festival in Bielsko Biala, Poland

Poster for Kloun

Poster entitled 'Stairs'

Poster entitled 'Holiday'

Poster entitled 'Hommage a Leo Castelli' (a New York Art dealer)

Poster entitled 'For Mother'

CONFERENCIA

INTERNACIONAL DE DISEÑO GRAFICO IXTAPA 93

First Choice
Poster announcing the Conferencia International De Diseno Grafico Ixtapa in Mexico

'I have selected this poster because it expresses some of the characteristics often associated with Australians. The image is hybrid, simple, direct, a cliché and slightly irreverent'

Corporate Identity for new colour printing enterprise Spectro

Poster invitation to Designers' Saturday event, promoting an exhibition of Australian bush furniture for Carmen

Advertisement for Carmen, a manufacturer of commercial systems furniture

New identity for Gollings Photography

Commemorative plaque for the Governor Phillip Tower

Magazine about avant-garde Australian architecture for Haig Beck and Jackie Cooper

Tokyo Art Directors Club 40th Anniversary Exhibition : FROM TOKYO
EARTH CRISIS

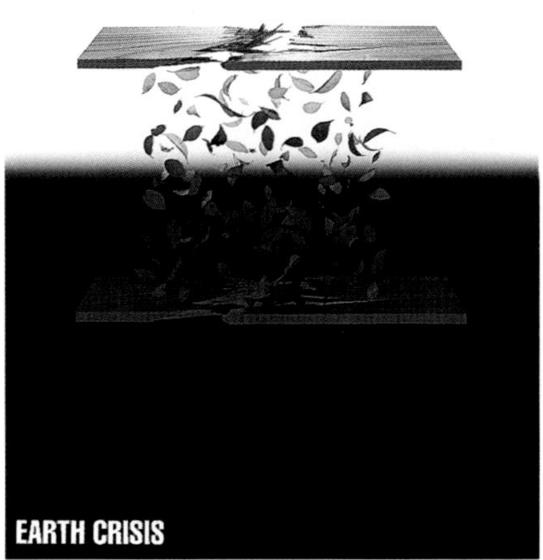

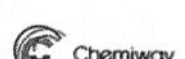

First Choice
Poster for Tokyo Art Directors Club Exhibition entitled 'Earth Crisis/Wood II'

'In the past few years, the open spaces scattered around my house have either featured the sign 'land for sale' or become deserted parking spaces. The house opposite mine was only ten years old, and yet because of the fall in the stock market, the owner had to part with it, leaving it vacant. One day a bulldozer came and tore it down. The electric bulb swinging in the stylish room being ruthlessly torn away and the ragged edges of the broken pillars still remain as vivid and distressing images in my mind'

Poster for Tokyo Art Directors Club entitled 'Earth Crisis/Can & Sea'

Poster for Tokyo Art Directors Club entitled 'Earth Crisis/Wood I'

Two pages from a promotional calendar for Maruzen Petrochemical Company Limited

Poster for an exhibition for the Japan Design Committee, entitled 'Life/I'

Poster for an exhibition for the Japan Design Committee, entitled 'Life/II'

levis
Style Center
levis

levis

levis

levis

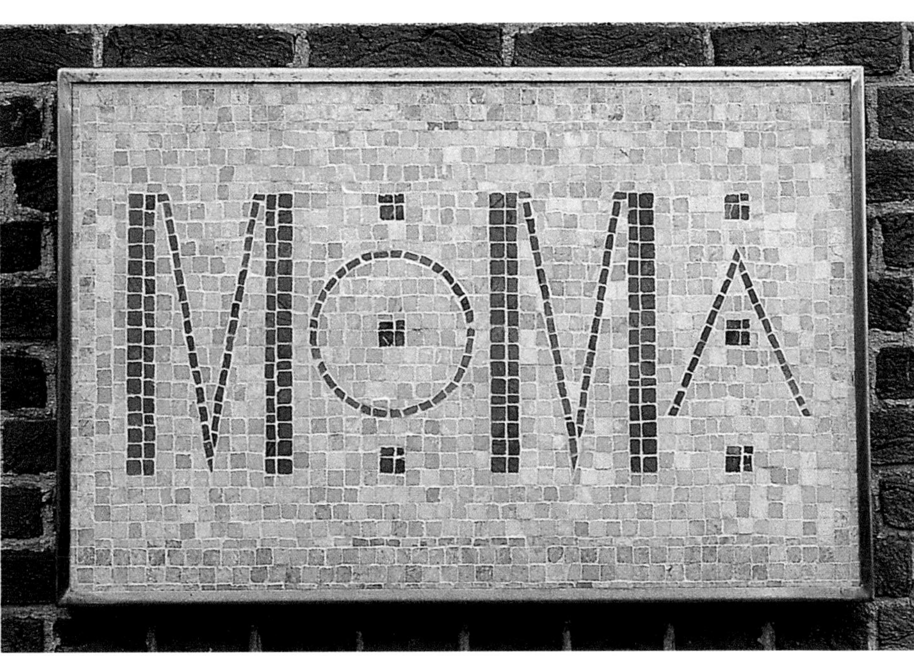

First Choice
Identification system for the paint brand Levis, a leader in the Belgian market

'My first choice is motivated by the problem I had to resolve and also by the results obtained in terms of notoriety of the brand. First I had to redefine the graphic identity of the brand, and then to imagine an identification system for the points of sale. I chose the symbol of the hand, an obviously human tool, as the identifying and directional element that integrates the logo of the brand. The same signals are also used for points of sale inside signage, on flags, vehicles, and other visual material'

Logotype for the MOMA marble mosaic company

Logotype for the National Theatre of Belgium

Naming and logotype from a Corporate Identity for an insurance company

Logotype for the Loan Servicing Center (mortage company)

Logotype for French Speaking Community Institution in Belgium

Naming and logotype for a new game for the Belgian National Lottery

DOWN WITH DOGMA

Design Renaissance/Glasgow/September 1993 Alan Fletcher Printed by CTD Printers Ltd

First Choice
Poster for Chartered Society of Designers/Pentagram

'The British Chartered Society of Designers, in association with Pentagram, commissioned five designers to produce a poster on any subject related to design. The posters were exhibited at Design Renaissance, an International Design Congress held in Glasgow in 1993. The event was organised by the three major international design associations: ICOGRADA; ICSID; and IFI. This poster utilises a standard commercial label to make an ironical comment'

Cover for 'Domus' magazine, entitled 'The hazards of town planning'

Cover for 'Domus' magazine, 1994, entitled 'De gustibus non est disputandum'

Cover for 'Domus' magazine, 1994

Cover for 'Domus' magazine, 1994

Cover for 'Domus' magazine, 1994, entitled 'Concepts have Wings'

Cover for 'Domus' magazine, 1994

QUIMPER CENTRE D'ART CONTEMPORAIN
FUKUDA C'EST FOU
15 NOVEMBRE 1991
Le Quartier
28 FEVRIER 1992

DESIGN
RENAISSANCE

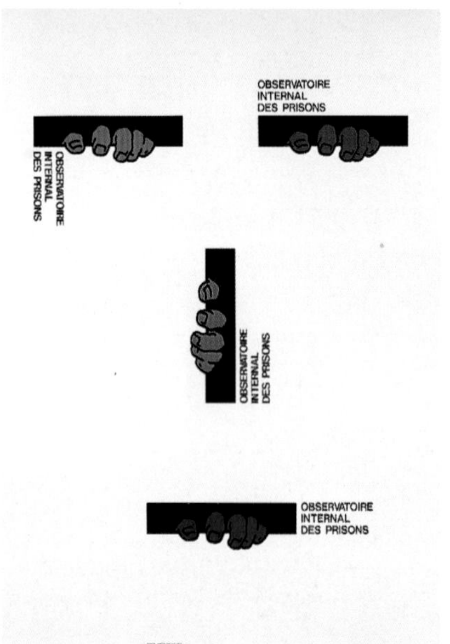
OBSERVATOIRE
INTERNAL
DES PRISONS
OBSERVATOIRE
INTERNAL
DES PRISONS
OBSERVATOIRE
INTERNAL
DES PRISONS
OBSERVATOIRE
INTERNAL
DES PRISONS

LES ACTEURS A L'ÉCRAN
LES ACTEURS A L'ÉCRAN

miroir du siècle
DESIGN
GRAND PALAIS
du 19 mai au 25 juillet 1993
ELLE

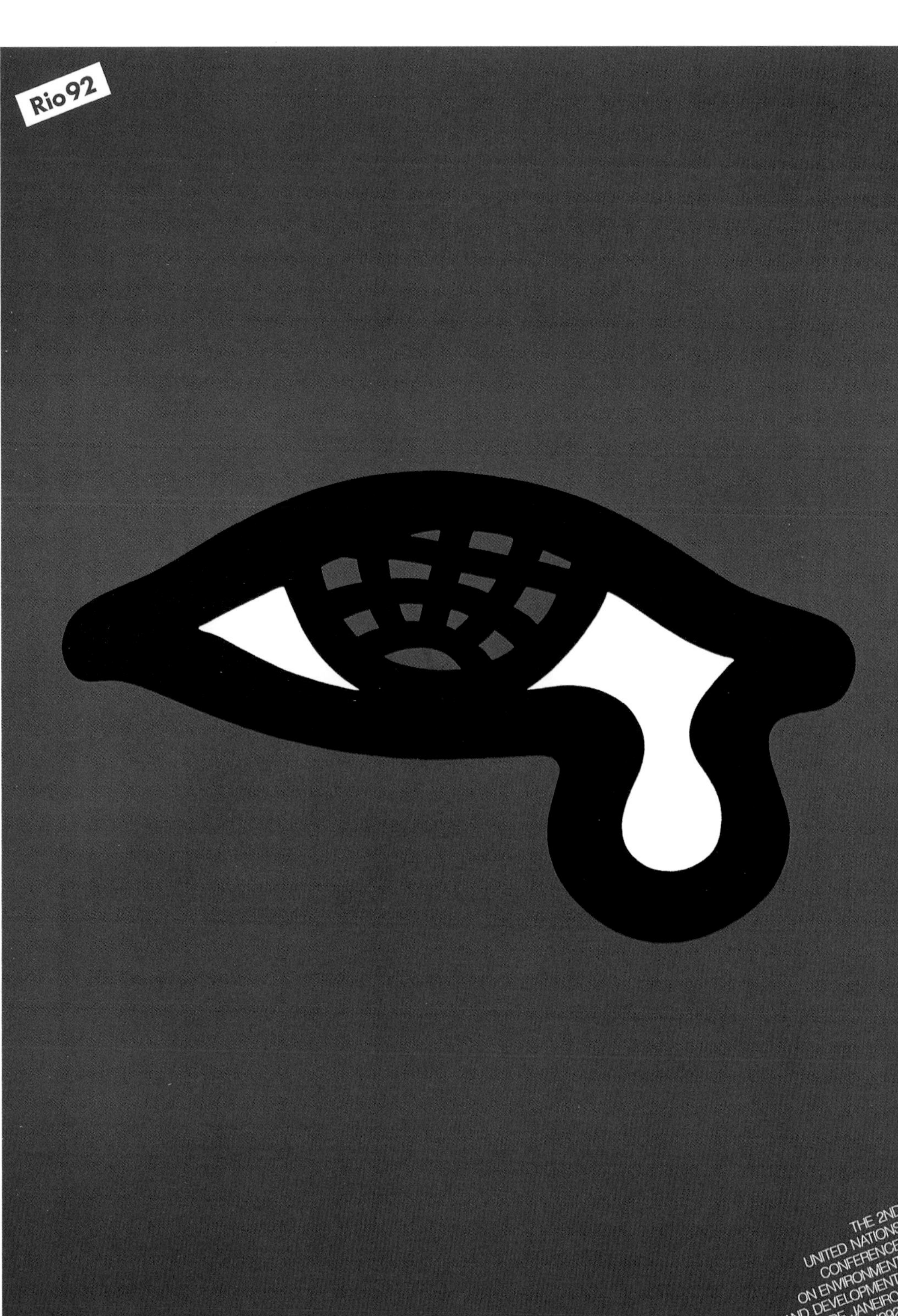

First Choice
Poster for 2nd United National Conference on Environment and Development

'Even if we know that our computers present us with incomplete images from birth, we remain unable to escape the charm of these illusions. Trying to produce designs not just to be looked at, but grappling with the creation of designs that deceive. Believing in miracles that can make a black and white surface come alive like a colourful three-dimensional object. Awed by the phenomenon of non-existent forms that emerge from gray shadow...Never using an electric pencil sharpener...Never calling for help from others... Secretly slipping into my studio when an appealing idea comes to mind... Sometimes giving myself flattering encouragement saying. 'Hang in there a little longer. This could be a masterpiece''

Poster for Quimper Centre D'Art Contemporain entitled 'Fukuda C'Est Fou', France

Poster for Design Renaissance Conference, Glasgow

Poster for One Man Exhibition Fukuda Prism, Nagoya

Poster for Exhibition Observatoire International des Prisons, France

Poster for Saint-Denis Les Acteurs A L'écran, Paris

Poster entitled Mirror du Siécle for Gran Palais design, Paris

First Choice
Sculpture for The Museum of Immigration

'This large 'flag' acts as a symbol in the new Museum of Immigration at Ellis Island. It is actually made of large triangular prisms, so that from one direction the visitor sees the US flag, but passing by the image changes to 1000 portraits of American citizens of all races and ages'

Poster to promote Aids research entitled 'For the love of life'

Poster 'F' taken from a series featuring the 26 letters of the alphabet

Corporate Identity for Knoll, an international furniture company

Announcement for an AGI Annual Meeting

Design for stone seating for Gemini Consulting

Corporate Identity for Univision (US Spanish language television network)

...5th Anniversary
Bunkamura
Shibuya · Tokyo

First Choice
Poster for 5th Anniversary
Bunkamura, Tokyo

'It seems difficult for a designer to choose his best work. Each one has its own story, which made it difficult to get you on the right track. Sometimes you succeed more, sometimes less. Bunkamura's Fifth Anniversary is one of my favourites from my latest works. It was a challenge for me to create a poster for another culture (Japan) (And I love 'Norma', the opera, very much)'

5 posters for the Opera House, Zurich

Poster for Art Museum, Zurich

NEW YORK IS
DANCE
New York City Department of Cultural Affairs
Edward I. Koch, Mayor
Mary Schmidt Campbell, Commissioner
For information call: (212) 956 ARTS
PHILIP MORRIS
Provided as a public service by
Philip Morris Companies Inc.
New York and the Arts: A Cultural Affair Martha Graham Dance Company Joffrey Ballet Lar Lubovitch P.S. 122 Merce Cunningham BCBC El
Vagoner Rod Rodgers Dinizulu and his African Dancers David Gordon/Pickup Performance Company Paul Taylor Dance Company Dancewave/Diane
cers Trisha Brown New York City Ballet Bill T. Jones/Arnie Zane Jubilation! Laura Dean Asian American Dance Theatre Joyce Theater Eiko and
Gonzalez Limon Dance Company Nikolais Dance Company Alvin Ailey American Dance Theater Lucinda Childs Dance Company Meredith Monk/T
mon Ballet Hispanico Erick Hawkins Murray Louis Dance Company Feld Ballet American Ballet Theatre Saeko Ichinohe and Company Bronx Dar
river and Harry Dance Theater Workshop Eleo Pomare Chen & Dancers City Center Theater Dance Theatre of Harlem and much, much more...

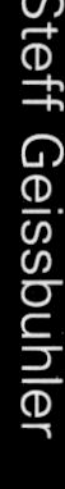

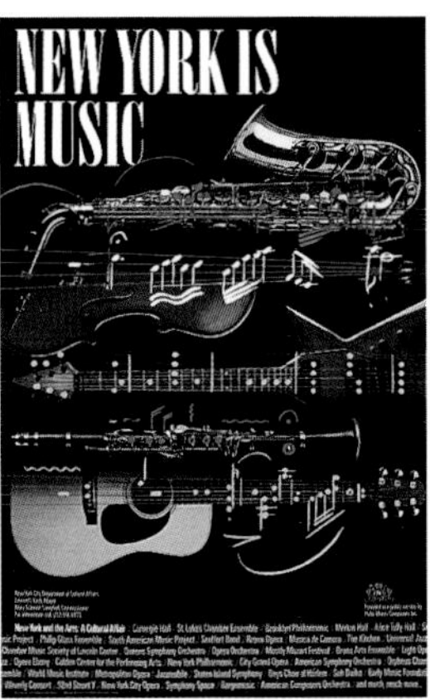

First Choice
Poster for New York and the Arts entitled 'New York is Dance'

'Four of nine posters designed for the New York City Department of Cultural Affairs. Each poster promotes, illustrates and lists the multitude of institutions available to visitors of the city within one of these cultural categories: Dance; Music; Theatre; Gardens and Zoos; Children; Heritage; Museums; and Art. The posters were and in some cases still are, displayed at all major ports of entry to the city including airports, and bus and train terminals. To me, 'New York is Dance' was one of the most successful posters in communicating the vitality, excitement and variety of ballet, classic, jazz and modern dance organisations in our city'

Poster for New York and the Arts entitled 'New York is Music'

Poster for New York and the Arts entitled 'New York is Theatre'

Poster for New York and the Arts entitled 'New York is Garden and Zoos'

Construction Barricade for Madison Square Building

Symbol and entrance sign for Time Warner (media and entertainment)

Animated on-air signature for Telemundo (US Hispanic language television network)

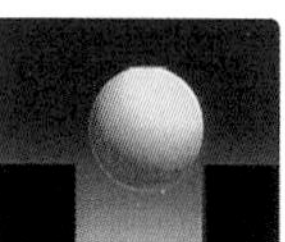

Words

In words as fashions the same rule will hold,
Alike fantastic if too new or old.
Be not the first by whom the new are tried,
Nor yet the last to lay the old aside.

Alexander Pope

Image

Thoughts

This poem is impossible. Silas usually has a better touch with his choice of quotations. This one generates no imagery at all. Maybe the words can make the image without anything else happening. What's the heart of this poem? Don't be trendy if you want to be serious. (Isn't doing the poster this way trendy in itself?) I guess one could reduce the idea further by suggesting that the new emerges behind and through the old, like this.

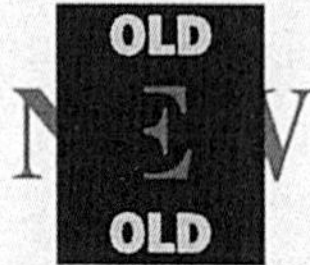

Not bad, but more didactic than visual. Maybe what wants to be said is that the old and the new are locked in a dialectical embrace–a kind of dance where each defines the other.

Am I being simple-minded? Is it the kind of simple that looks obvious or the kind that looks profound? There is a significant difference. This could be embarrassing. Actually, I realize fear of embarrassment drives me as much as any other ambition.

Do you think this sort of thing could really attract a student to the school?

Milton Glaser

First Choice
Poster for School of Visual Arts entitled 'Old/New'

'I think this poster represents a set of somewhat more complex situations than occurs in my usual work. It attempts to address the viewer in an unexpected way, that is, by subverting the usual confidence that a poster must suggest and instead dealing with questions of self doubt. The small text under the heading of 'Thought' investigates the process of marking the poster and admits to confusion and uncertainty. At the same time, it engages the reader in a more interesting conversation than normally occurring in this medium'

Illustration entitled 'Fire Eater' for a book of Baudelaire's poems

Book jacket design for the Pulitzer Prize winning play 'Angels in America'

Poster entitled 'La Guardia Flowers'

Poster for Olivetti's new minicomputers, Quaderno

Illustration entitled 'Monet Seated' as part of a series for a show called 'The Imaginary Life of Claude Monet'

Vereinsbank

First Choice
Corporate Identity for Germany's third largest bank, Vereinsbank

'The logotype was specifically developed to fuse the past and the future, hence the serifs to evoke tradition and the logical choice of sans-serif type to represent the future. The switch adds movement and therefore is the element that transforms the word into a high-recognition mark'

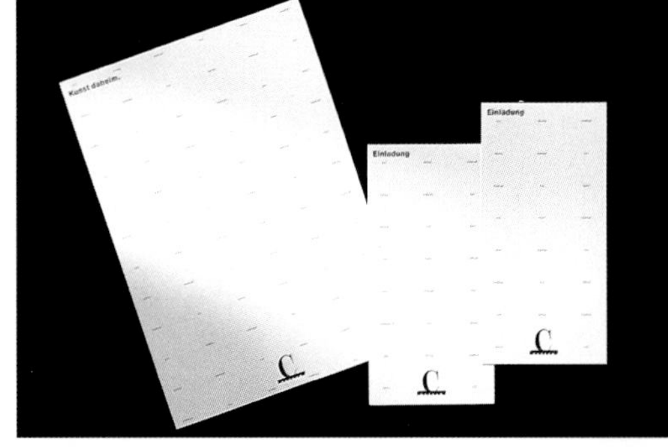

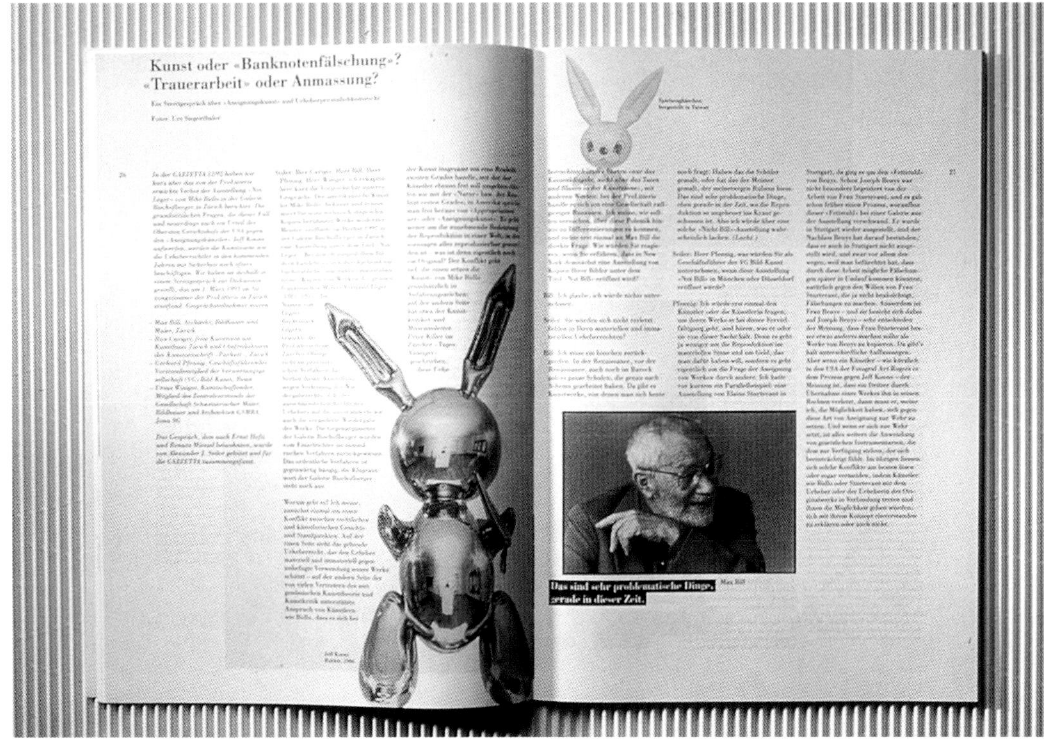

Supergraphic story for ZKB Training Centre, Zurich

Give away package as part of the Corporate Identity design for Vereinsbank

Brochure design as part of a series entitled 'Spektrum' for a Vereinsbank subsidiary, The Bethmann Vermögensbetreuung

Cover of 'ProLitteris GAZZETTA', magazine of the Swiss Copyright Society for Literature and the Visual Arts

Corporate Identity for Coninx Museum, Zurich

Double page spread from 'ProLitteris Gazzetta'

Kitchens and Bathrooms
Furniture, Accessories, Tiles, Mirrors, Appliances, Architectural Hardware, Surfacing Materials, Planning Services and Fittings
idi
You'll find it all at IDI 93
The Interiors Show
Earls Court, London
6-10 June 1993
Interior Design International
IDI 11 Manchester Square London W1M 5AB Tel 071 486 1951
Designs by Pentagram

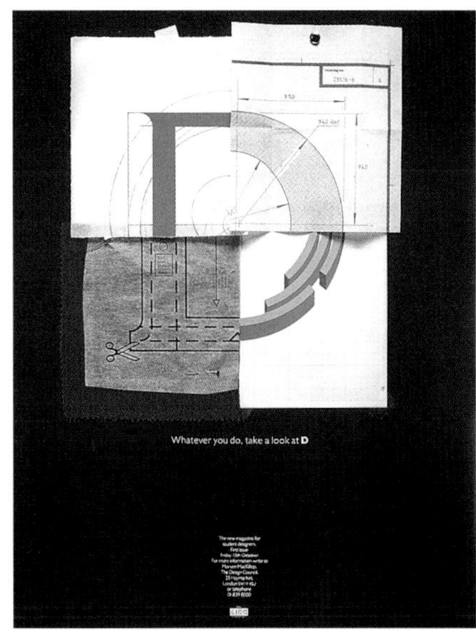

First Choice
Identity and poster series for Interior Design International

'The commission to design an identity for the Interior Design International, organisers of a major interiors show at London's Earls Court, had two significant advantages. A client with a sense of adventure, and a subject with 1001 elements. A designer's dream. The combination resulted in seeming contradiction, a consistent mark with infinite variety. While the basic letters 'idi' remain constant, the bowl of the 'd' transforms from a bath plug to a tiffany lamp, to every other household item imaginable. Each application is treated as a variation on a theme'

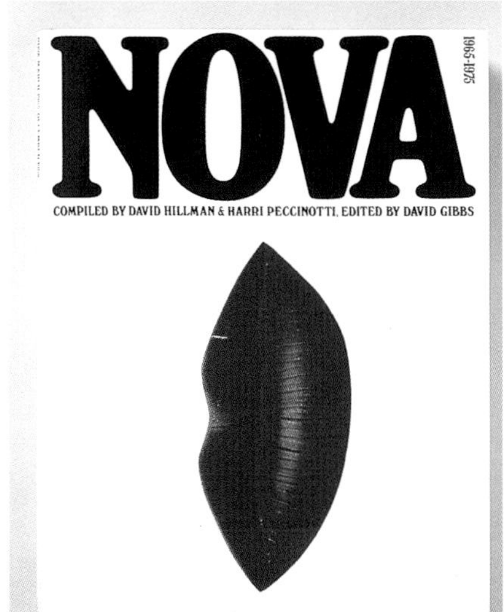

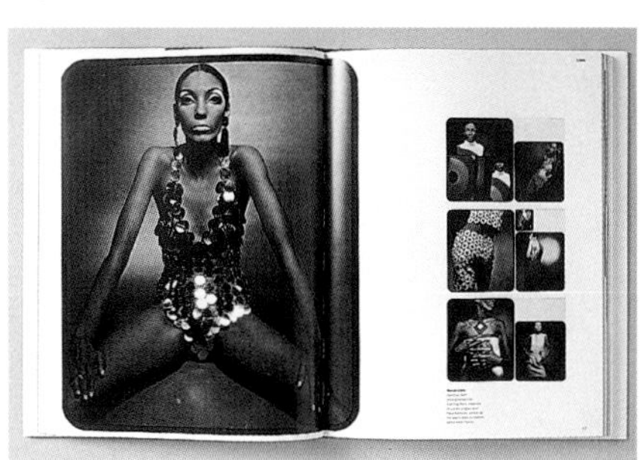

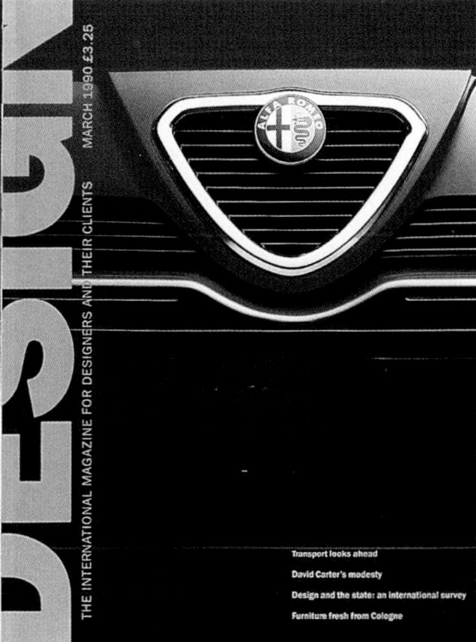

Book design and exhibition graphics for 'The Sixties' art scene book

Design for 'D' magazine launch poster/launch booklet

Cover and spread design for book which highlighted the best of the Nova years

Poster for the Third Annual Pentagram Lecture

Magazine design for The Design Council, a publication promoting British design to industry

Identity and Branding Programme for Phaidon Press

First Choice
One of a series illustrating ghost stories in the magazine 'High Quality'

'I choose this illustration because I think its idea works with a minimum of effort to achieve its effect: just leaving a drawing unfinished, in this case a second person I had intended to place behind the man on the beach is not there. Another of my reasons is that the image reminds me of nightmares in which I escape from one danger only to run into another'

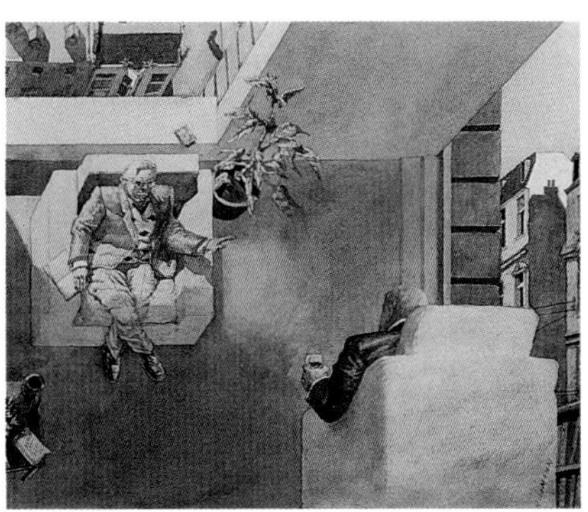

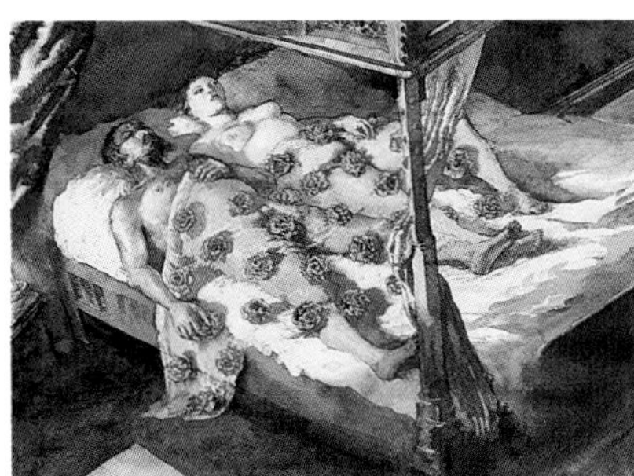

Illustration for the magazine 'Natur'

Illustration for the magazine 'High Quality' entitled 'Spriggans'

Illustration for an essay on triviality

Illustration for a short story by Raymond Chandler 'No crime in the mountains'

Illustration from a series of love stories of famous people

Illustration for an article entitled 'The detective story as a religious category'

OLD & NEW GLORY

CALIFORNIA CRAFTS MUSEUM

JULY 2 - SEPTEMBER 7, 1992

GHIRARDELLI SQUARE 11A.M.- 6P.M. DAILY

SAN FRANCISCO

First Choice
Poster design promoting an exhibition of old and new flag memorabilia

'Seeing the countless ways that the stars and stripes have been interpreted serves as a continual reminder that there is always another solution to a design problem and that I am limited only by my own imagination in finding a new direction'

Poster design for lecture series in Australia

Cover design for 'Hemispheres' magazine

Book design for the publication 'Typewise'

Layout design for 'Hemispheres' magazine

Poster design for the anniversary of the restaurant, Square One

Design for paper promotions brochures for Simpson entitled 'Evergreen'

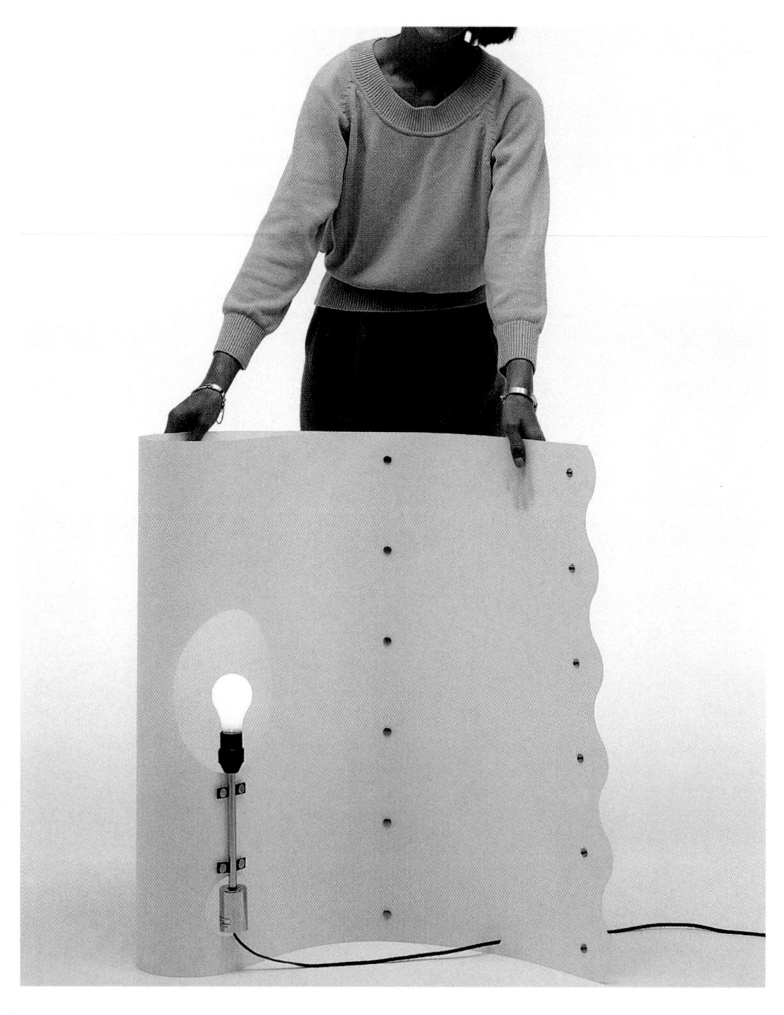

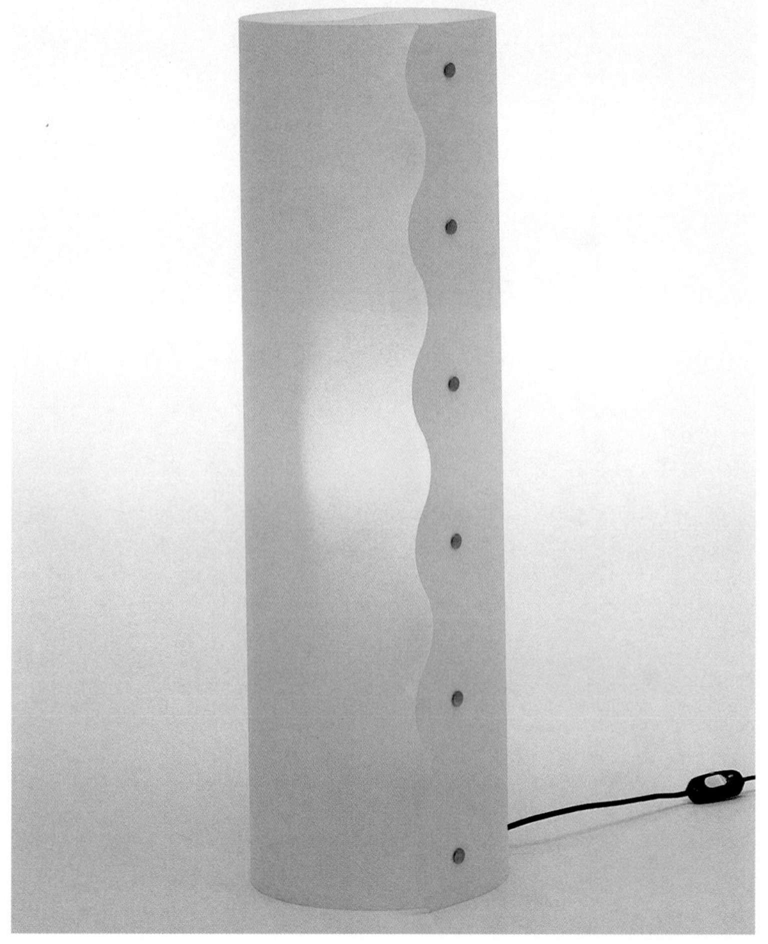

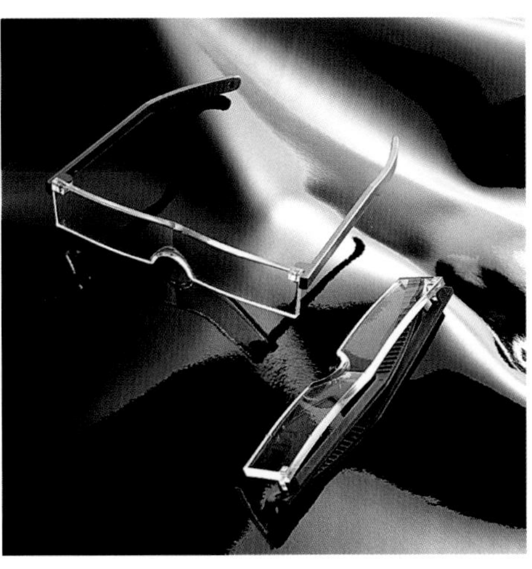

First Choice
Design for AndOn NAMI Lighting Fixture

'There is something appealing about turning a flat surface into a functional, three-dimensional object. A good interface like this is what is expected in the design of the future. When I set out to design a foldable lamp from a single plastic sheet, I bore this in mind. Both the S-shaped cylinder into which the sheet is folded, and the socket connected to the sheet are fastened together by snaps. There are only two possible combinations for the snaps, so it is very easy to figure out how to construct it. In other words, it's as easy to assemble as buttoning up a shirt'

Product design for reading glasses 'eyemeganetta'

Product design for the YMD original cutlery collection

Corporate Identity for AIM Limited

Poster design for Igarashi's one-man exhibition at Deutsches Plakat Museum, Germany

Design for MoMA Playing Cards

Shopping Bag for MoMA

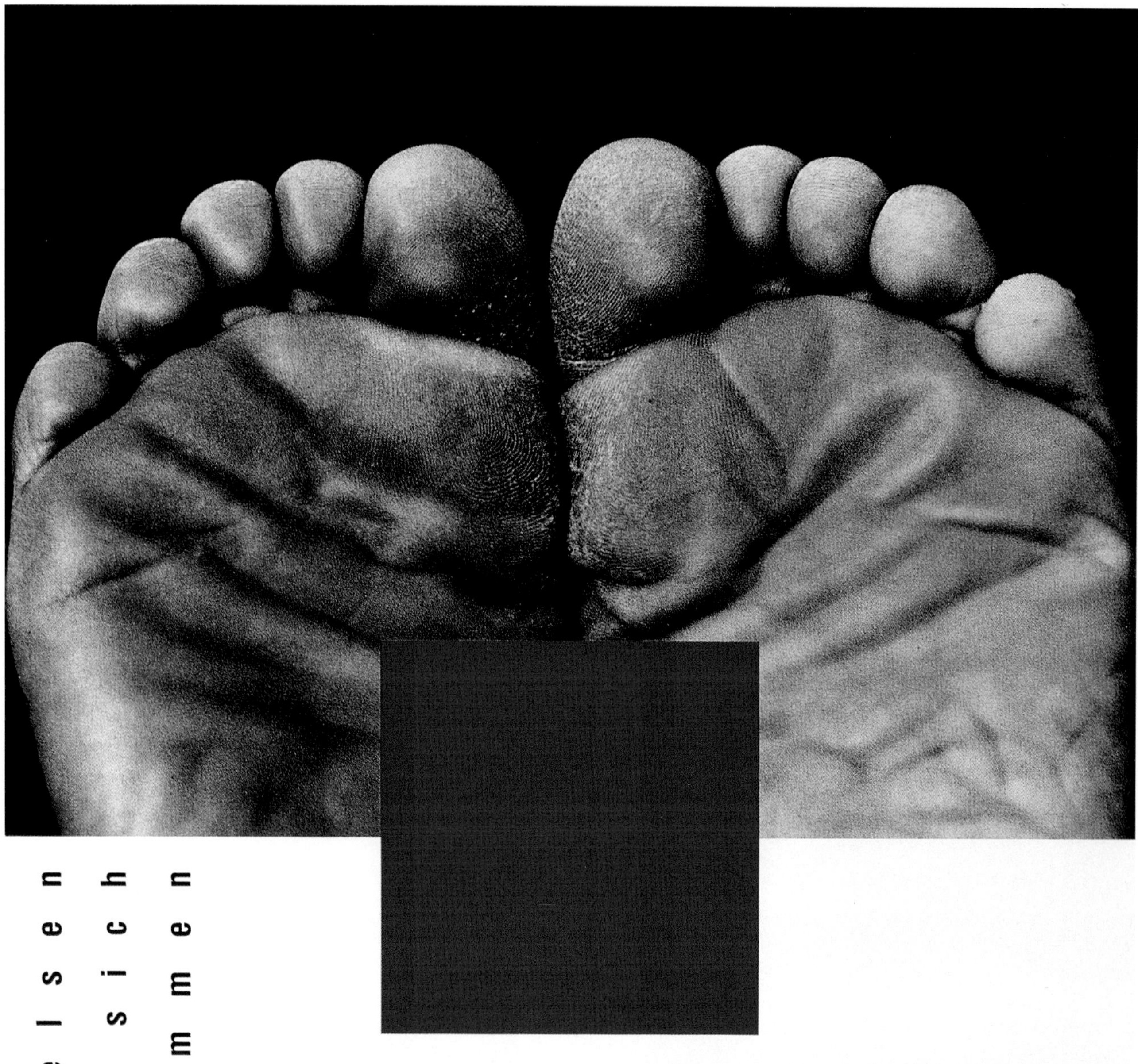

In die Felsen
bohren sich
Zikadenstimmen

Nobuyoshi Araki
George Hashiguchi
Naoya Hatakeyama
Kou Inose
Miyako Ishiuchi

Yoshiko Kamikura
Kozo Miyoshi
Toshio Shibata
Hiroshi Sugimoto
Chie Yasuda

Zeitgenössische japanische Photographie
2. Mai - 4. Juli 1993 Öffnungszeiten : Di-Do 10-21 Uhr, Fr-So 10-17 Uhr, Montag geschlossen
Pfingstmontag 10-17 Uhr, Pfingstsonntag und 1. Mai geschlossen

Schweizerische Stiftung für die Photographie
im Kunsthaus Zürich, Erdgeschoss

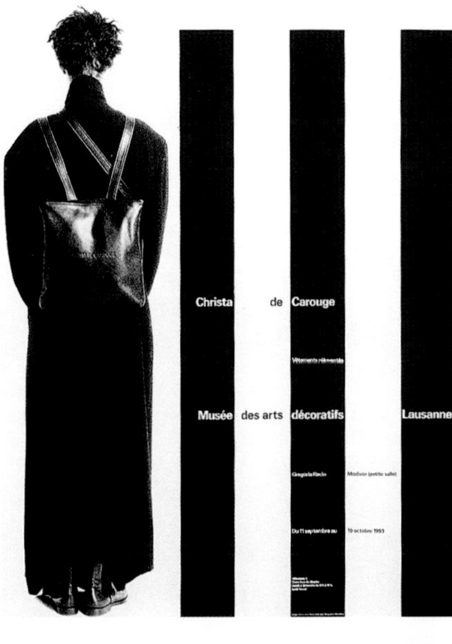

First Choice
Poster for the Zeitgenossische Japanische Photgraphie (Contemporary Japanese Photography) exhibition for the Swiss Foundation for Photography

'The project was a poster for a group exhibition of ten contemporary Japanese photographers. The main difficulties lay in: choosing an image to represent ten individuals each having a very different sensitivity and approach and extremely diverse themes; having to integrate, at the curator's request, a Japanese haiku; and in the context of a Japanese week in Zurich, finding a way to differentiate this poster and make the public sensitive to this particular exhibition. I chose to express Japanese photography through my own language and not an imitation of a Japanese style, the combination of simple elements translates the passion I experienced in discovering these photographers'

Poster for 'Christa de Carouge' for the Musée des Arts Décoratifs, Lausanne

Poster for 'Arles 89' for the Musée de l'Elysee, Lausanne

Poster for 'Brazil by Brazilians' for the Swiss Foundation for Photography, Zurich

Poster for 'Aaron Siskind' Musée de l'Elysee, Lausanne

Poster for 'Man Ray' for the Musée de l'Elysée, Lausanne

Poster for 'Brecht Baal' for the Théâtre de Vidy, Lausanne

PER STRÖM DESIGN/ASPEQT

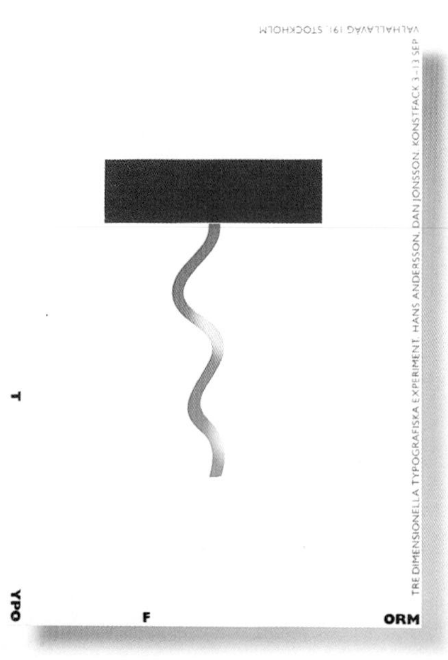
VALHALLAVÄG 191 STOCKHOLM
TRE DIMENSIONELLA TYPOGRAFISKA EXPERIMENT. HANS ANDERSSON, DAN JONSSON. KONSTFACK 3–13 SEP
T
YPO
F
ORM

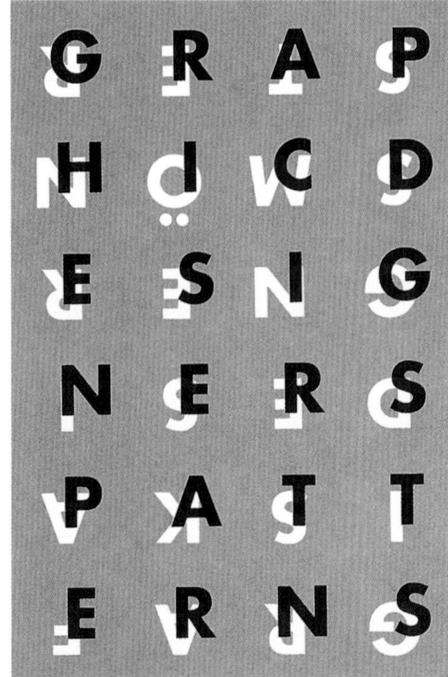
GRAP
HICD
ESNG
NERS
PATT
ERNS

First Choice
Illustration and cover design for catalogue for MIX, the work of eleven illustrators

'The reason why MIX (myself and ten other illustrators) is my first choice, is that this piece of work represents myself in a very pronounced way, a combination of graphic design and fine art. Typographically, the catalogue in its entirety is a balance between the modern and the classical with Bodoni (as typos). It is always difficult but also a challenge to make the design for a group of colleagues which is the case with the MIX catalogue'

Programme and catalogue design for PEO Ström Design, lighting company

Design for Typography Exhibition invitations

Poster and invitation for a graphic designers exhbition entitled 'Patterns'

Poster for a jazz concert, held annually in a small fishing village

Illustration and poster for the magazine 'Z'

Illustration for the exhibition 'Patterns'

NORD
SUD

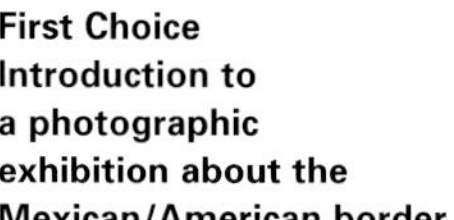

First Choice
Introduction to a photographic exhibition about the Mexican/American border

'This is not a poster as such but a generic introduction to a photographic exhibition of the Mexican/American border, which was first shown in Arles during the photo festival in 1991. The exhibition was designed as a real-life construction of what the photographers really saw when they went 'down there' to both sides of a 'wall' which still seems fairly solid'

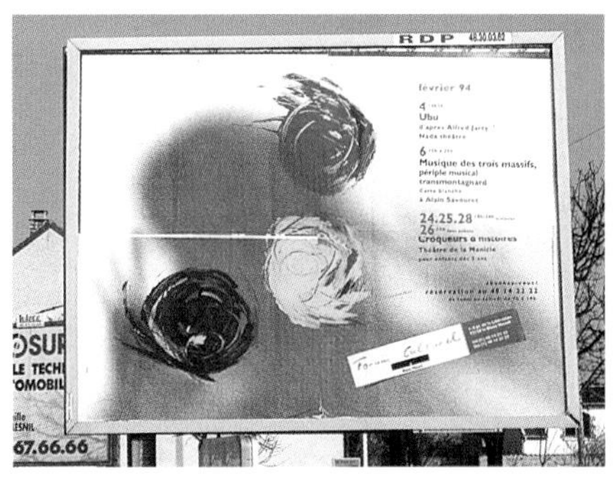

Poster for Local Associations Festival, Aubervilliers

Poster for the season at the Cultural Forum, Blanc Mesnil

Poster for the International Kites Festival, Dieppe

Poster announcing the opening of the Cultural Forum, Blanc Mesnil

Poster for the opening of 'Les Silos' at the 'Maison du livre et de l'affiche', Chaumont

Poster promoting the town of Montluçon

SYMPOSIUM-2
超高層都市と環境
Environment and
Skyscraper Cities
1994年10月3日月…7日金 会場…G8ホール 主催…Q&Aの会

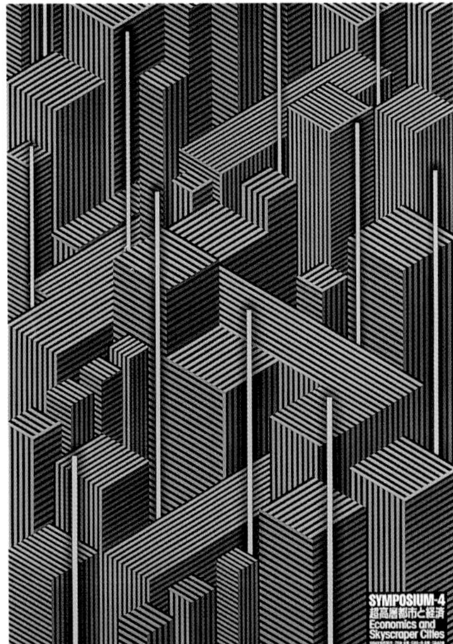

First Choice
Poster for Symposium-2 Environment and Skyscraper Citites

'Both in Japan and other Asian countries, they are now developing high-rise buildings with unusual rapidity. Are there ever any problems in the form of skyscraper city? These are the posters for the series of symposium on the topics culture, environment, life, economics and the future in the skyscraper cities. The panelists are scholars, philosophers, architects and inhabitants. I designed these posters pursuing the nature of the expression of graphic design'

Poster for Symposium Number One, 'Culture and Skyscraper Cities'

Poster for Symposium Number Five, 'The Future and Skyscraper Cities'

Poster for Symposium Number Four, 'Economics and Skyscraper Cities'

Poster for Symposium Number Three, 'Life and Skyscraper Cities'

Poster for IBM Personal Computers entitled 'Speed'

Poster for IBM Personal Computers entitled 'Quality'

勇
Creativity:
破
Breaking
成
the Rules
規
靳埭強
Kan Tai-keung
北京設計教學
Lectures in Beijing
中央工藝美術學院
Central Academy of
Arts & Design
一九九二年九月
September 1992

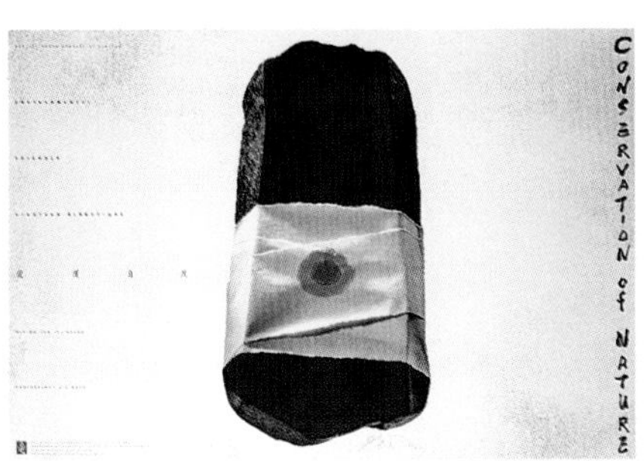

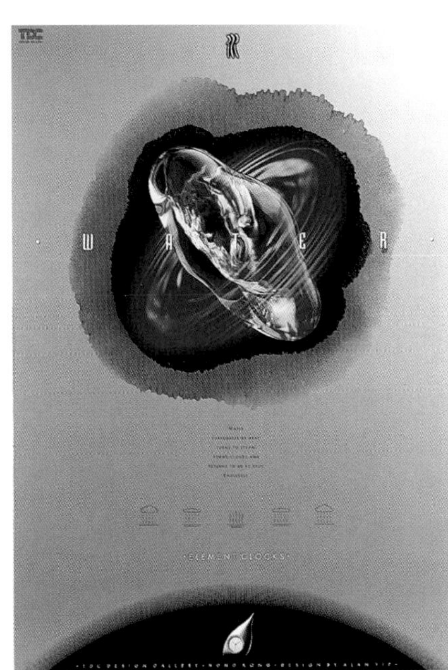

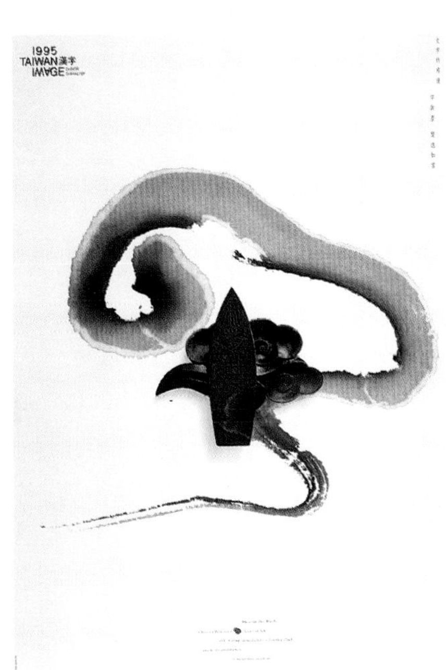

First Choice
Poster design for Tai-Keung Kan lectures held in Beijing entitled 'Creativity, Breaking the Rule'

'I think that teaching should enlighten students to the creation of something unprecedented. After giving students basic knowledge and guidelines, they should be left to explore alone. Of course, a solid foundation of aesthetics is essential to every designer. It can be done by learning knowledge and technique from the past, both traditional and modern design. Then we must free our minds from fixed ideas and be ready to break old rules, establishing new concepts. I used a Chinese wooden ruler and a piece of perfect round golden paper, symbolizing traditional thinking, breaking them in two then expressed a breakaway from constraints. The broken parts constitute a great visual impact resembling the letters B & J, the initials of Beijing, where the lecture takes place'

'IDEA' magazine special feature on Tai-keung Kan

Lecture in Graphic Design in China entitled 'Eastern Philosophical Thinking & Design'

Poster for Taiwan Image Design Association entitled 'Cloud and Ink '

Poster for Quality Paper Specialist Ltd entitled 'Conservation of Nature'

Poster for the Hong Kong Trade Development Council Design Gallery entitled 'Element Clock Water'

Poster for Taiwan Image Design Association entitled 'Water and Paper'

Rilke
AHMET CEMAL

ERDAL ALOVA
LORCA

özel tiyatro
DORMEN TIYATROSU
WOODY ALLEN
TANRI
GÜLAY KUTAL
ALİ YENEL
MIGIRDİÇ DÖNDÜYAN

Inge-borg Bach-mann
MET CEMAL

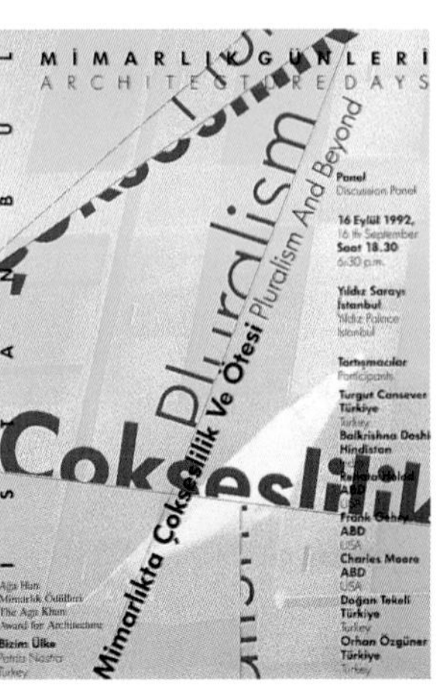
İSTANBUL
MİMARLIK GÜNLERİ
ARCHITECTURE DAYS
Pluralism
Mimarlıkta Çokseslilik Ve Ötesi
Pluralism And Beyond
Çokseslilik
Panel
Discussion Panel
16 Eylül 1992,
16 th September
Saat 18.30
6:30 p.m.
Yıldız Sarayı
İstanbul
Yildiz Palace
Istanbul
Tartışmacılar
Participants
Turgut Cansever
Türkiye
Turkey
Balkrishna Doshi
Hindistan
Frank Gehry
ABD
USA
Charles Moore
ABD
USA
Doğan Tekeli
Türkiye
Turkey
Orhan Özgüner
Türkiye
Turkey
Bizim Ülke
Patria Nostra
Turkey

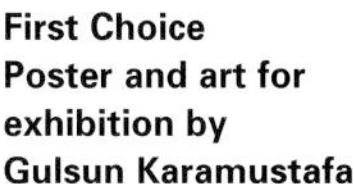

Gülsün Karamustafa Sergisi

19 Mart - 6 Nisan 1993
Kadın Eserleri Kütüphanesi
Fener, PTT yanı (tarihi bina)
Haliç İstanbul
Tel: (1) 534 95 50

First Choice
Poster and art for exhibition by Gulsun Karamustafa

'It is not because the little girl on the poster is my wife. I also don't think that being chosen for some international exhibitions and publications is the reason this poster is my 'first choice'. What attracts me is the tension between the baby-face and the semi-militaristic pose and the potential chauvinism in the text, which was written on a schoolbook by the girl. The text and the images were the main objects of the exhibition. All I did was superimpose them and put the text upside down'

Book jacket for Rilke Poems

Book jacket for Lorca Poems

Poster for Woody Allen's play 'GOD'

Book jacket for Bachmann Poems

Poster for a panel discussion on architecture

Book jacket for Marge Piercy's 'The Woman on the Edge of Time'

70 JAHRE RUNDFUNK
IN DEUTSCHLAND
HESSISCHER RUNDFUNK
hr

Hessischer Rundfunk hr
25. Deutsches Jazz Festival Frankfurt '94

MUSIK & SCHOTT

EXIL
Freitag, 20. Mai, 19.00 Uhr Palas der Wartburg
„Der Autor Hans Sahl". Elisabeth Raabe, Verlegerin des Luchterhand Literaturverlages.
Dr. Ulrich Fickel, Minister für Wissenschaft und Kunst des Landes Thüringen.
20. Mai, 19.30 Uhr Palas der Wartburg
Konzert. Philharmonia Quartett Berlin. Werke von Mendelssohn, Hindemith und Schulhoff.
Aufzeichnung durch Deutschlandradio.
Sonnabend, 21. Mai, 16.00 Uhr Wartburgsalon
Das Exil nach dem Exil. Vortrag. Edita Koch, Frankfurt/Main.
21. Mai, 17.00 Uhr Kaminzimmer
Hans Sahl, 1902–1993. Lesung und Gespräche. Edita Koch, Herausgeberin der Zeitschrift „Exil", Herbert Grenien, Schauspieler.
21. Mai, 20.00 Uhr Wappensaal
„Wir sind die letzten. Fragt uns aus." Gespräch mit Anja Lundholm, Erwin Leiser, Ernest Borneman, Hans Keilson. Gesprächsleitung: Lea Rosh.
Sonntag, 22. Mai, 11.00 Uhr Wartburgsalon
Die selbstgemachte Kultfigur und der Moralist. Anmerkungen zu Bertolt Brecht und Hans Sahl. Vortrag und Gespräch: Dr. Wolfgang Jaske, Frankfurt/Main.
22. Mai, 17.00 Uhr Kaminzimmer
Lesung mit Anja Lundholm und Hans Keilson.
22. Mai, 19.00 Uhr Wappensaal
Lesung und Gespräch mit Ernest Borneman und Erwin Leiser.
22. Mai, 20.30 Uhr Wappensaal
Als Gott das Los der Gefangenen Zions wendete. Jüdische Lieder als Spiegelbild jüdischen Lebens von König David bis heute. Mit Daniel Kempin, Gesang und Gitarre.
Eine Veranstaltung des Eisenacher Kulturkreises in Zusammenarbeit mit der Zeitschrift „Exil".
20. Mai bis 22. Mai 1994 Wartburg, Eisenach.
EXIL. „Wir sind die letzten. Fragt uns aus." Eine Hommage an Hans Sahl.
Projektvorbereitung: Edita Koch, Reinhard Lorenz.
Kartenvorverkauf und Informationen: Kulturamt der Stadt Eisenach (0 36 91-67 04 19) Wartburg-Information (0 36 91-7 70 72)

Landesmuseum Mainz
Ursachen und Auswirkungen
Goethe: »Die Belagerung von Mainz 1793«

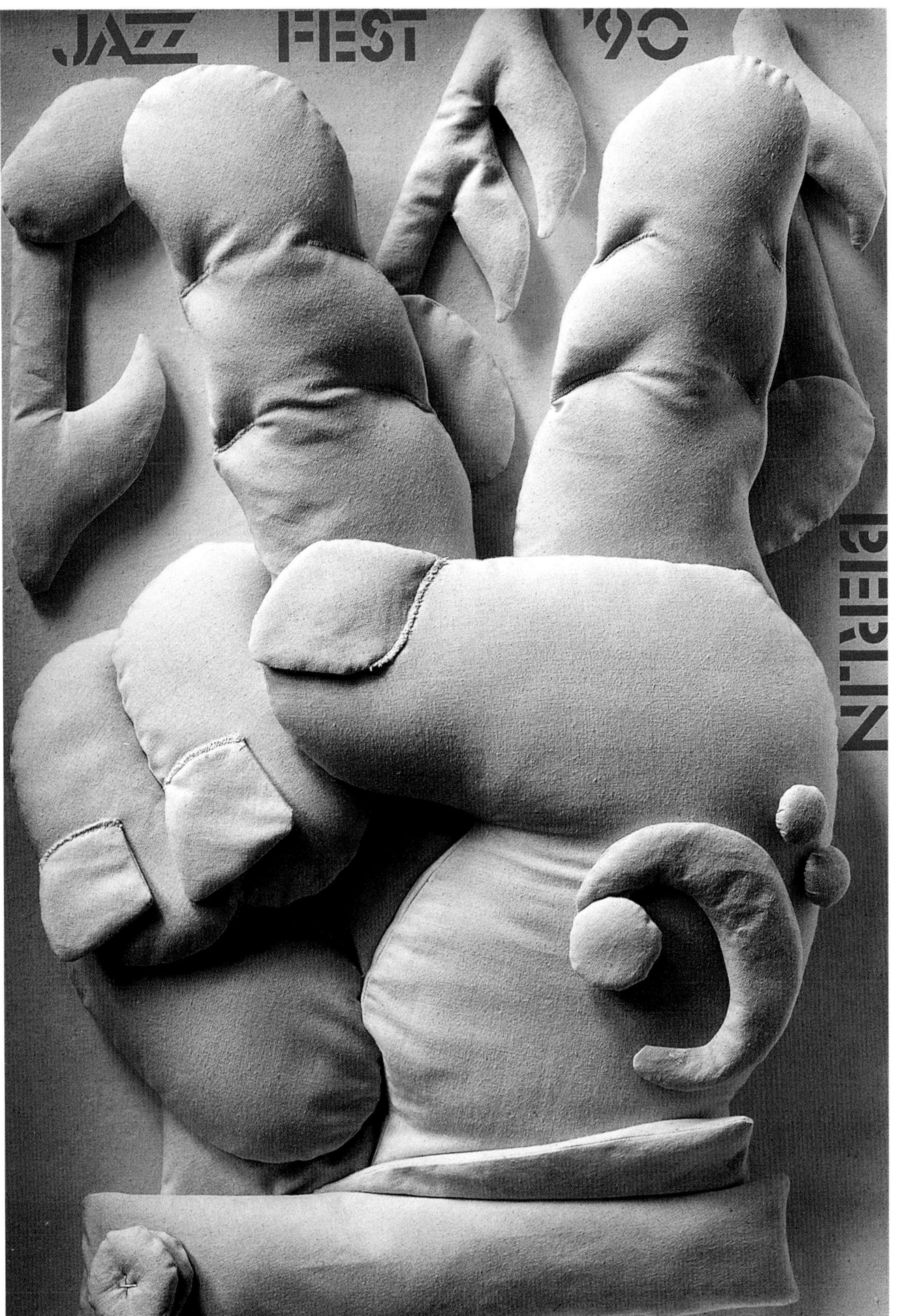

First Choice
Poster for Jazz Fest Berlin, 1990

'It uses an image that has a test mission and contain various 'services' made by artists. These artists do not spare themselves from demanding design, they master skillfullness in the tradition of image art in new ways. They address people in an impressive and assuming way, and do not pursue mediation for every subject and at any price. These artists explore the meaning of their task and in keeping with the theme, then imagine for themselves and for others. This work, in a time of image abundance (of all kind) is a constant witness for artistic imaginative imagery. It uses the information about the image and produces with sensual power suggestive images for messages'

Poster for Jazz Fest Berlin, 'Traditional Jazz Songs'

Poster for 70 years of Radiotime

Poster for the Jazz Festival, Frankfurt

Poster for a Music Notes publisher 'Schott Mainz'

Poster for Kulturell Department for the exile of people away from Nazi Germany

Poster for Exhibition Landesmuseum, Mainz

GLORY
TO THE
NEW
BOOK
Typography : Alan Kitching
Printed letterpress at The Typography Workshop

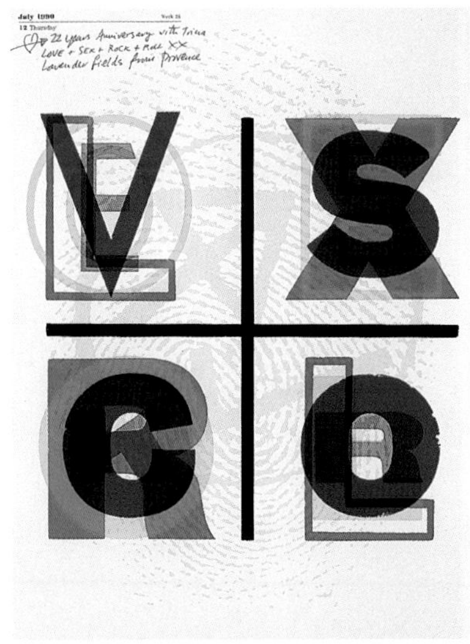

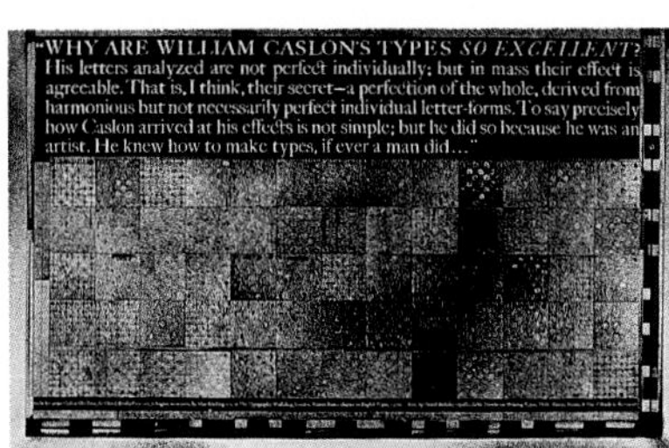

First Choice
Detail of a large window display, one of a series of six for Music Sales, London

'I chose this because it says something about the way I design. On the press, direct with the material, letter form, colour, paper, ink; with its purpose always in mind. This is not 'art' , it has a reason to be the way it is. In this case the purpose was for a window. It had to allow light to pass through it and be read from a distance as well as close up. It had to convey something of the spirit of the event, that is the joy of Christmas, a celebration of birth'

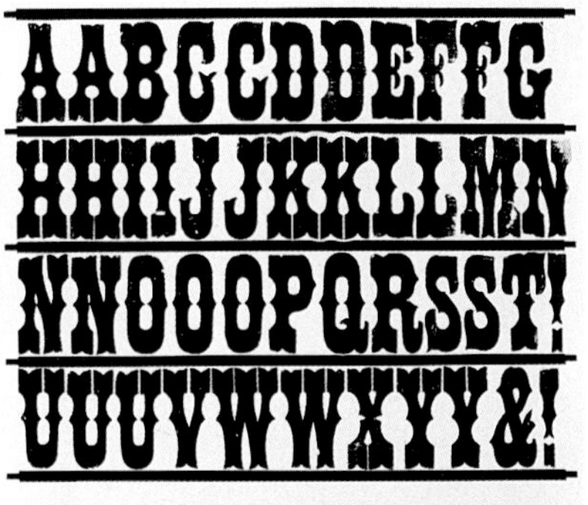

A page from 'Picabia', a project produced in collaboration with Terry Jones

Another detail from the Music Sales window

Poster for Caslon's Types, a limited edition print

Page from the edition folio 'Typecases'

Prospectus for the Typography Workshop featuring a map of London and Clerkenwell showing the location of the Workshop and other places of interest

Small poster for the Typography courses at the Royal College of Art, London

SEASON'S
GREETINGS
HAPPY
ZOOMIT
REMOTE
LINK
PLUS
Barry McPeake

First Choice
Design for computer software packaging for Zoomit International Inc

'This computer software packaging project for Zoomit International allowed us to explore and incorporate a wide range of graphic and production techniques to help reinforce the product identity and KDA-generated 'visual style' of the company. We were able to develop an extremely tactile use of vinyl appliqué (both printed and non-printed) with full colour elements, developed in 3-D software. Since the inception for Zoomit, we have created their logo, stationery, exhibitions, packaging, print and multi-media materials. Zoomit International has grown and developed, achieving rapid recognition through its coordinated and energetic graphic style'

Corporate Identity for Vincor International, a group of Canadian wineries

Corporate Identity for CBC Broadcast Centre

Corporate Identity for Canadian Pavilion / Expo

Signage for the Ford Centre for The Performing Arts, Ontario

Design based on the theme, 'New York, the apple of my eye'

Packaging design for a commemorative label for Vincor International

MONDAINE
SWISS

MONDAINE
SBB CFF FFS
SWISS MADE

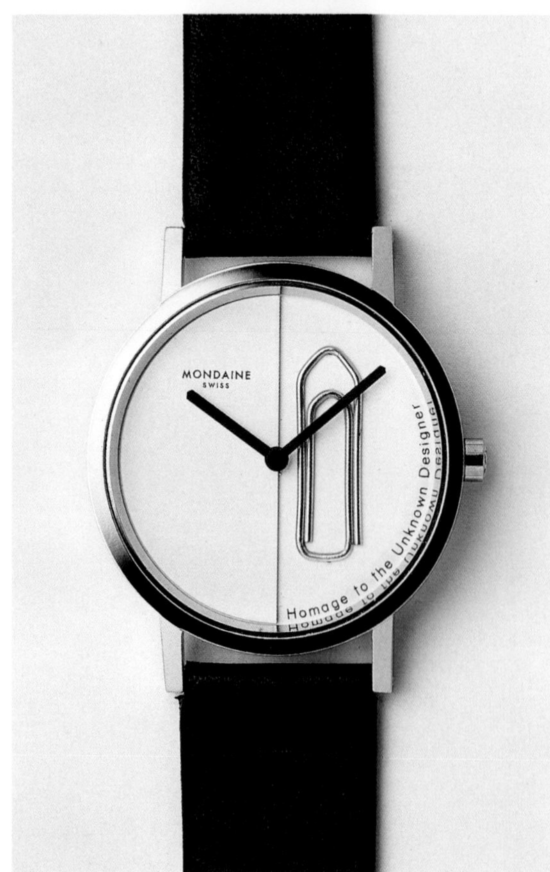
MONDAINE
SWISS
Homage to the Unknown Designer

MIN
SEC
1/10
SEC
MONDAINE
SWISS

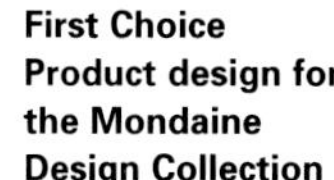

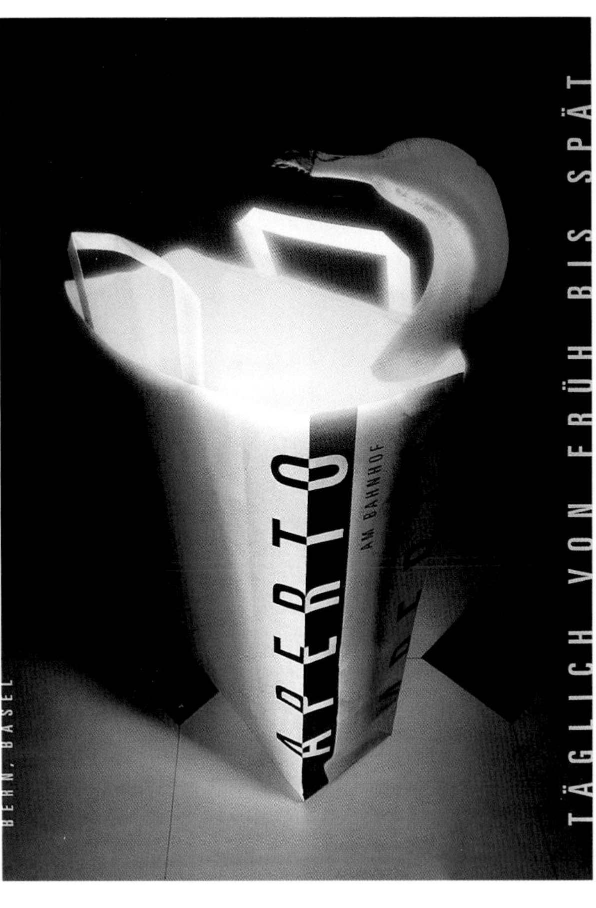

First Choice
Product design for the Mondaine Design Collection

'The Mondaine watch company's focus had been exclusively on traditional and classic timepiece design. Külling + Partners created the Design Collection. This new watch line appealed to totally new customer segments and gave the company access to new distribution channels. The Mondaine Design Collection won the Designer Prize awarded by the London Design Museum'

Poster design for Aperto, a 24-hour grocery outlet

Corporate Identity for Emil Hirt, a painter

Corporate Identity for the Widder Hotel

Poster for Fernet Branca, an aperitif

Corporate Identity for Jelmoli, a large warehouse in Zurich

Corporate Identity for Fédération Internationale de Ski

VIOLENCE

First Choice
Poster promoting
Anti-violence

''Posters against violence worldwide', with the endorsement of Alliance Graphique Internationale, organised a competition for a poster campaign to motivate people throughout the world to believe they can do something about stopping violence in all its many forms.
In the words of David Bernstein, the judge representing Great Britain
' This poster won the first prize because the judges deemed it so simple, deceptively simple.
It concentrated on the essentials and ignored the traps. You almost want to take part in the erasing''

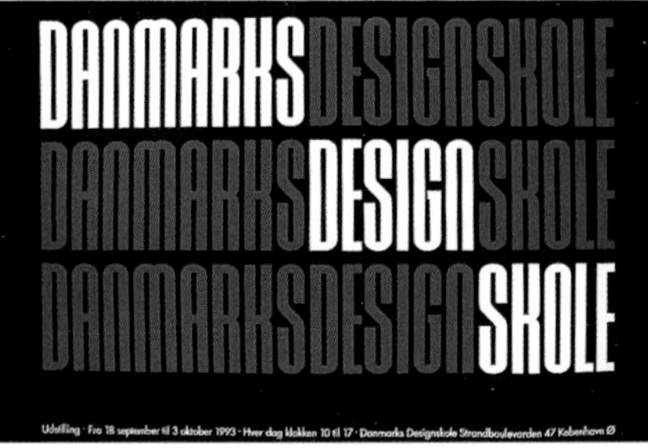

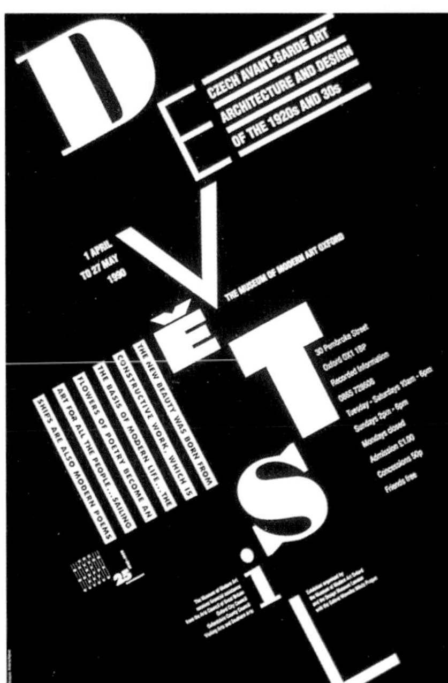

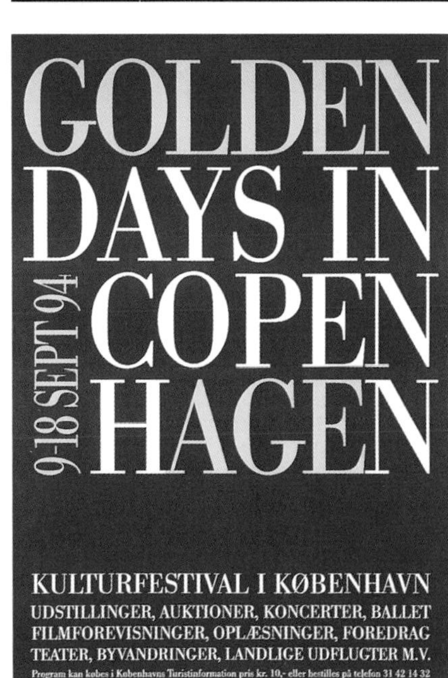

Poster for the Observatoire International des Prisons, a body affiliated with Amnesty International on the theme of 'Keeping a watch on the prison environment'

Design based on the theme of The Big Apple, part of a contribution to an auction to raise money for the New York Sculpture Project

Logotype/poster for Danmarks Designskole, a school dedicated to education 'for a changing world'

Flag design for the Polish Pavilion, Expo '92 in Saville, Spain to promote global solidarity

One of a series of posters to promote changing exhbitions, this one for Devétsil, a Czech Avant-garde Art movement at the Museum of Modern Art, Oxford

Logotype/poster for the annual autumn festival, 'Golden Days in Copenhagen' a celebration of the Golden Age of Danish Culture (1800-1850)

First Choice
A page from the Dalton Fine Paper FACES A1 promotion

'The promotion's theme was faces, the similarities and the endless differences of the human face. Having a fascination with typefaces I chose to paint in gouache so as to give the image the quality of the hand rather than the computer. The overall promotion was a great success'

SEVEN SPIRIT BAY

Paper collage originally created by David Lancashire to feature in a Dalton Fine Paper promotion and featured here on a self promotion poster

Symbol and logotype created for Seven Spirit Bay, Cobourg Peninsula

Symbol and logotype created for Cobourg Marine, Cobourg Peninsula

Packaging design for one of David Lancashire Design's self promotional bottles of wine

Front and back of a letterhead for C & P Julien, furniture designers

Display for the Warradjan Aboriginal Cultural Centre, Kakadu National Park

Logotype for the Warradjan Aboriginal Cultural Centre featuring the Warradjan pig-nosed turtle

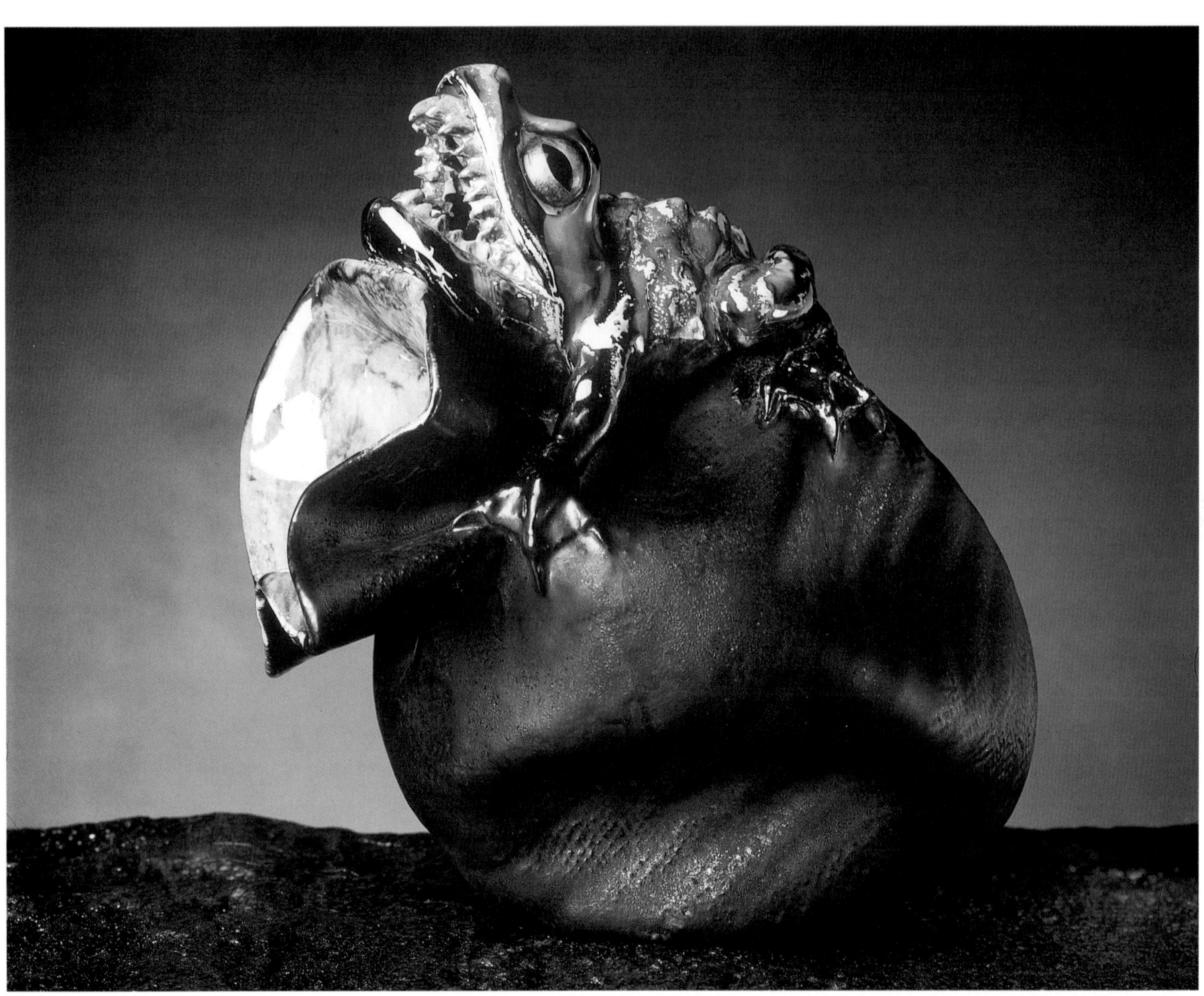

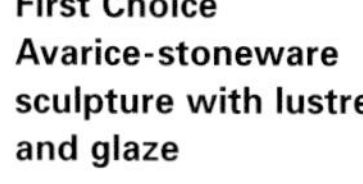

First Choice
Avarice-stoneware sculpture with lustre and glaze

'A series of pieces illustrating the seven deadly sins was created by myself in collaboration with our head caricaturist Pablo Bach and the ceramicist Janice Tchalenko. 'Avarice' features a toad at the throat of a mediaeval money bag. This stoneware pot was exhibited, along with the other six deadly sins, as part of the Seven Deadly Sins Exhibition at the Victoria & Albert Museum in 1993. In the event the V & A bought the entire set. 'Avarice' is my favourite because although grotesque, it is strangely beautiful'

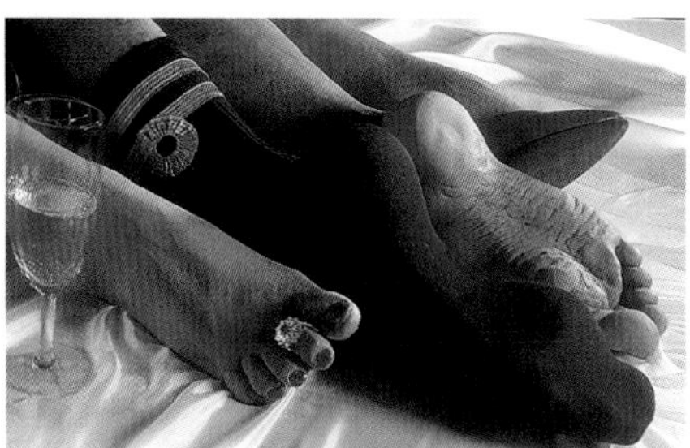

3D caricature of Rupert Murdoch created for Spitting Image

3D caricature of Mrs Thatcher as Marilyn for a Spitting Image publication

Exhibition of 3D satirical caricatures staged at the Barbican Arts Centre, London entitled 'The Last Supper'

3D caricature of a 1792 James Gillray portrait of the Duke and Duchess of York

Poster of a caricature of the Queen for a publication

Set design for 'Peter and the Wolf' for a Christmas production

1943
Auschwitz
Omarska
Bosnie 1993
Ne dites plus "Je ne savais pas"

ELEMENTS
MOINS
PERFORMANTS
THEATRE DE L'INSTANT

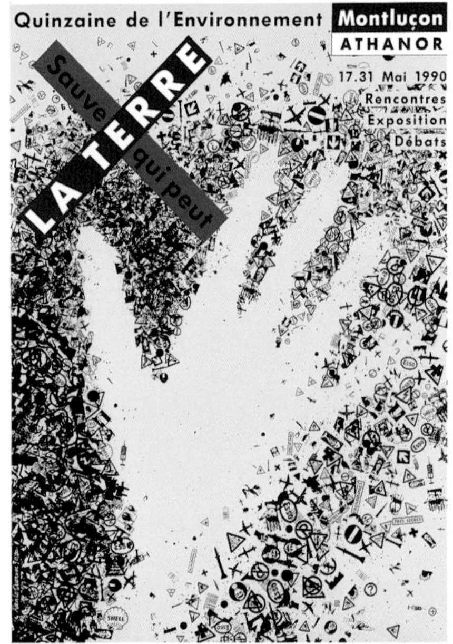
Quinzaine de l'Environnement Montluçon
ATHANOR
17.31 Mai 1990
Rencontres
Exposition
Débats
LA TERRE
Sauve qui peut

ETATS DE SIEGES
Exposition Château de Kerjean
Saint-Vougay
9 avril-31 mai 1993

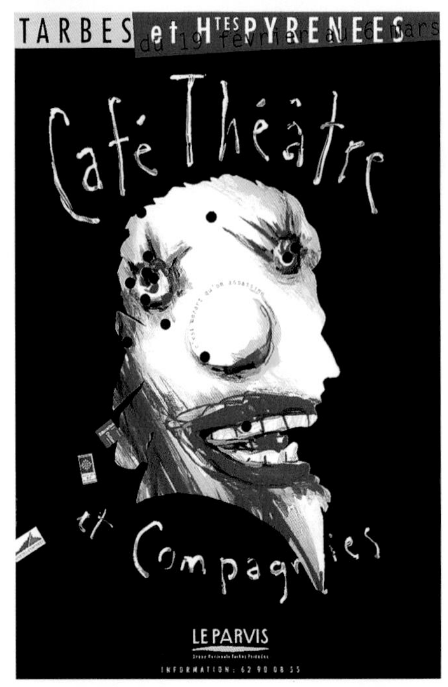
TARBES et H^TES PYRENEES
Café Théâtre
et Compagnies
LE PARVIS

Cinéma
au service des libertés
Quimper
13-19 Décembre
Studios du Chapeau Rouge
Journée Cinéma
France Libertés
Gros-Plan
16 Décembre
Libertés
au service du cinéma

First Choice
Poster for the Graphic Design Month of Echrolles entitled 'La Pub Tue (Advertising Kills)'

'I selected this poster because I was lucky with it. First of all I was lucky with the client who allowed me to do what I wanted. It was not so easy for him to accept such a provocative anti-smoking poster to illustrate a graphic design month.
I decided not to try to illustrate what graphic design is but rather to show the power of graphic design. This poster appeared a few months before the law which no longer allows cigarette advertising in France.
It was a good opportunity to say advertising kills, that is to say there are no ethics in advertising, just money. I am not an ayatollah trying to make advertising disappear or even change, I just wanted to comment on one of its dark sides'

Political poster against war in Bosnia, Auschwitz/Omarska

Theatre poster for a play about unemployed people in factories in a time of industrial crisis

Poster for an ecological symposium, 'Sauve qui peut La Terre'

Poster for an exhibition about chair and seat design

Festival poster on the theme of music for the Centre Culturel Le Parvis à Tarbes

Poster for a film festival about human rights in the world, 'Cinéma et Libertés'

Forty-four settlers
from Mexico
establish the pueblo
of Los Angeles—
twenty-six have
African ancestors,
1781.

**First Choice
Design for Community Redevelopment Agency of Los Angeles entitled 'Biddy Mason Time & Place'**

**'Like all graphic designers, my work has been to give form to ephemeral communications.
But now I most often do permanent graphic design works like this, projects that use worlds and images to communicate to a broad audience about a particular place and its people, and try to make a lasting contribution to society. This project publicly tells the story of a citizen who lived at this site, a story that could reflect and sustain present and future populations'**

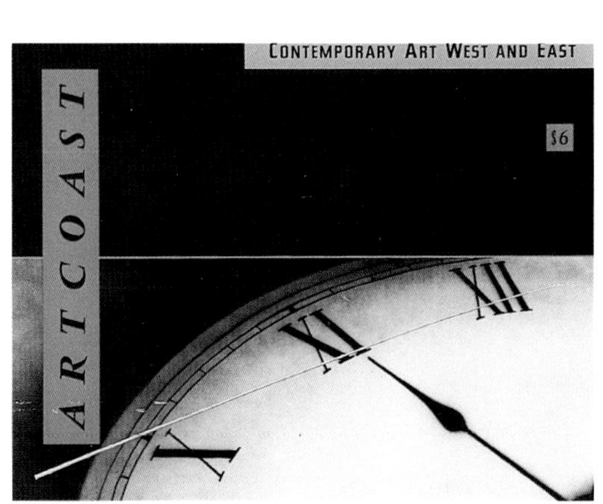

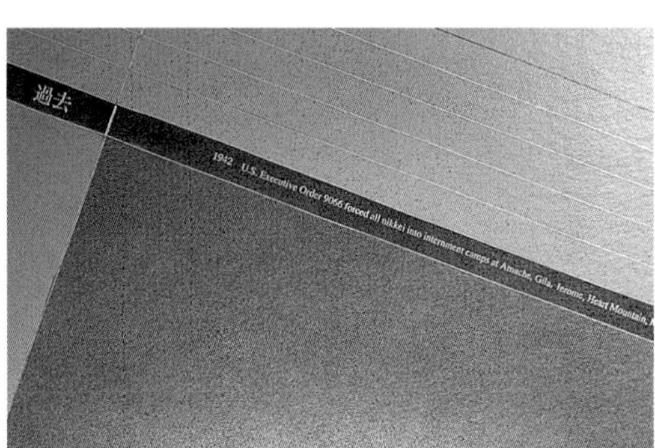

Environmental design for McCormack Baron & Associates/The Related Companies entitled 'Path of Stars in the Square'

Book design for 'The Motown Album' for Martin's Press

Catalogue design for 'The Art of Betye and Alison Saar' for the Wright Gallery

Magazine design for Artcoast, Robert Crothers and Kay Larson

Environmental design for Community Redevelopment Agency of Los Angeles Japanese American Cultural Center 'Memories of Old Little Tokyo'

Exhibition design for Moving Introductions for the Otis Exhibition Center

OBAN
1794
WEST HIGHLAND MALT

OBAN
'Little Bay of Caves'
Along the shores of Lorn lies a record of man far more ancient than that of any city in the land. The first settlers arrived on the mainland in 5,000 BC and sheltered in the natural caves of the land then known as 'An Ob'. The 'Distillery Cave' was one such shelter hidden in the Creag a' Bharrain cliffs which rise dramatically above the
'OBAN DISTILLERY'
Producers of a Delicate
SINGLE
MALT
WEST Highland MALT
SCOTCH WHISKY
OBAN DISTILLERY OBAN ARGYLL SCOTLAND
75 cl

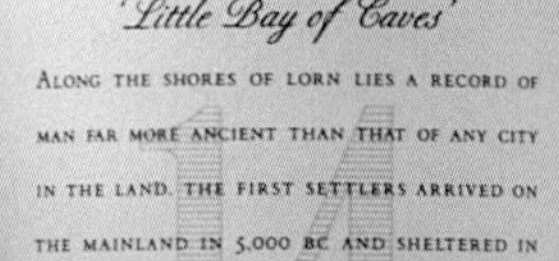
OBAN
'Little Bay of Caves'
Along the shores of Lorn lies a record of man far more ancient than that of any city in the land. The first settlers arrived on the mainland in 5,000 BC and sheltered in the natural caves of the land then known as 'An Ob'. The 'Distillery Cave' was one such shelter hidden in the Creag a' Bharrain cliffs which rise dramatically above the
'OBAN DISTILLERY'
Producers of a Delicate
SINGLE
MALT
WEST Highland MALT
SCOTCH WHISKY

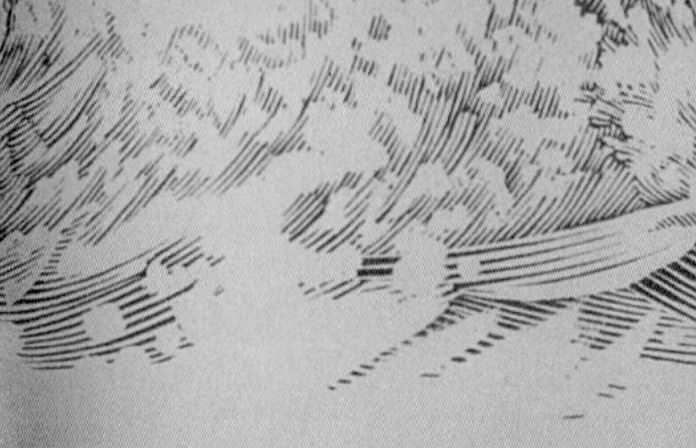

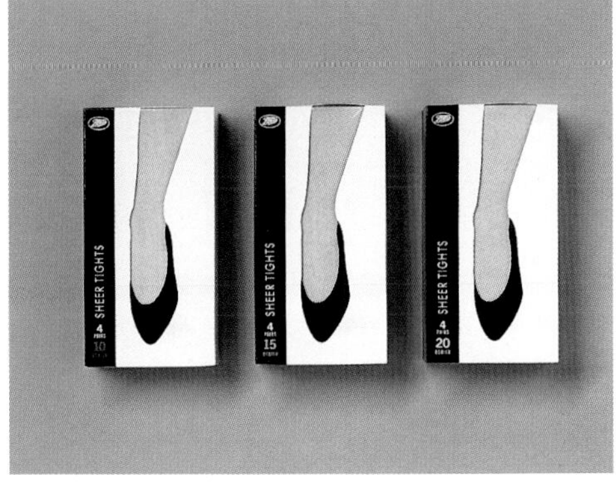

First Choice
Packaging Design for Oban Malt Whisky

'Creating a brand image and defining its personality is the challenge I most enjoy. I wanted to achieve a design which was rich in visual imagery and typographic detail. The pace between bottle and carton presented the opportunity. Oban is a 14-year-old malt whisky. The packaging needed to embody authenticity, heritage, quality and distinction. Time was spent at the distillery researching the history of the area in order to build a story around the product. The graphics aim to reflect the bleak, rocky coastline with its squawking gulls and bracing winds. The long copy label tells the history of the region and distillery and aims to create a 'bookish' feel for the brand and the discerning whisky drinker'

Packaging design for Bahlsen's Family Biscuits

Design for Heal's carrier bag

Packaging design for Boots hosiery

Packaging design for Boots laundry products

Packaging design for Dettling

Logotype design for Heal's

HEAL'S

„Little boy " –

First Choice
Poster for Images for peace, Hiroshima entitled 'Little Boy'

''Little Boy', was the name of the bomb that destroyed Hiroshima. The French 'Movement for Peace' asked me for a poster 50 years after Hiroshima. I looked for an idea, that expressed the speechlessness. ' Little Boy' is a message to all the 'little boys' in our world. A rose is a rose is a rose, a little boy is a little boy - Ce n'est pas une pipe! Not every poster is a poster. I am interested in the language after the language, the image as the place. I think it is one of my best posters, because it is far from any poster we expect'

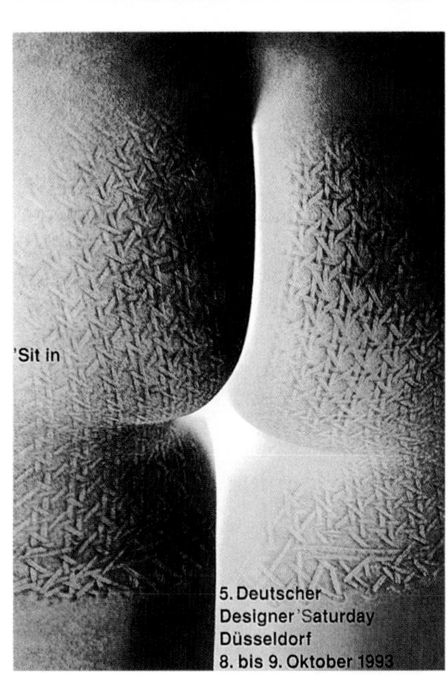

Poster for Museum für Angewandte Kunst, Cologne

Poster for VIVA! 'Don't talk it to death' 2nd United National Conference for Environment and Development

Poster for Migration of Nations, the Political Theatre

Poster for 'Sit in-5th German Designers' Saturday' for the Design Centre NRW

Poster for Vis-a-vis, German and French Photographers for the Ruhrlandmuseum, Essen

Poster for Aids, 'Let's talk open about it', Artis, Paris

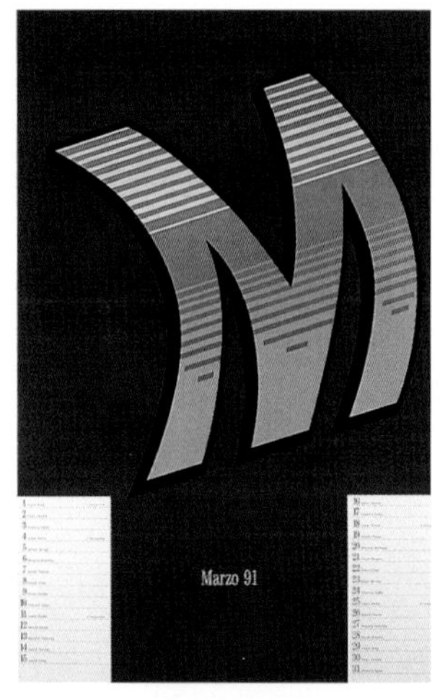

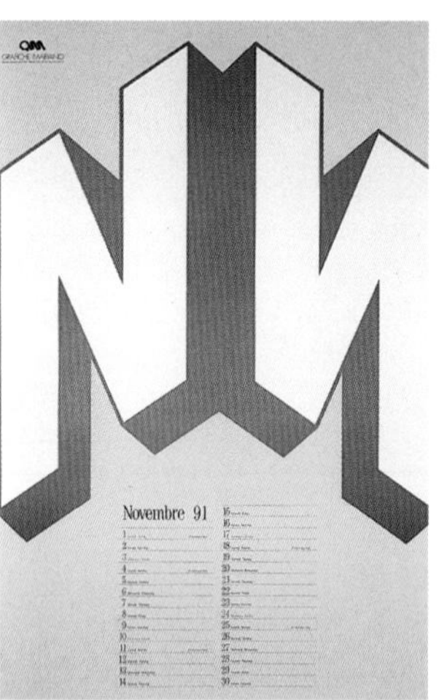

Guardare al passato per vedere il futuro

First Choice
Cover Design for 'Domus' magazine and a poster for 'De Pedrini', colour separation, with natural alphabet made of stones

'My project of First Choice is not one, but two. The first, a series of 4 posters for the magazine 'Domus', where the faces of 4 'masters' of architecture (Mies, Ponti, Les Corbusier, Aalto) are covered by a very coloured mask, which is in contrast with the B&W portrait; printed on 3 metre high posters they had a great effect, affixed in the streets of Milan. The second is a promotional poster for my favorite colour separation company: 26 stones represent, without tricks, the whole alphabet. Every stone has a sign which resembles a letter; every stone was found in a month of happy research on the beach in Tuscana by my son's girlfriend'

Poster for 'De Pedrini' a colour separation company

3 pages from the Calendar, 'Grafiche Mariano'

Cover for 'Abitare' magazine

Poster for 'La festa della Repubblica'

On 8 September 1664 New Amsterdam was renamed New York.

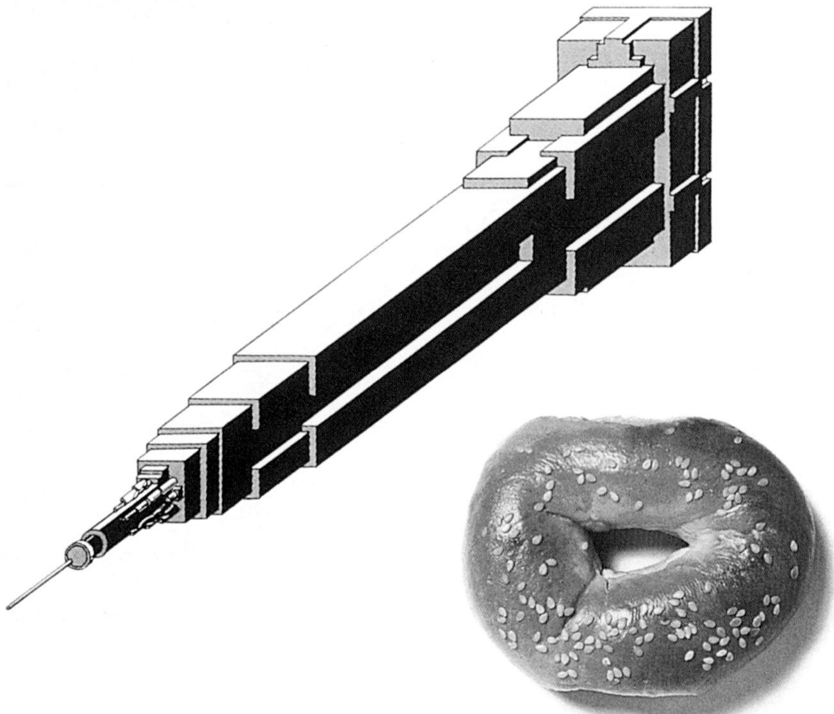

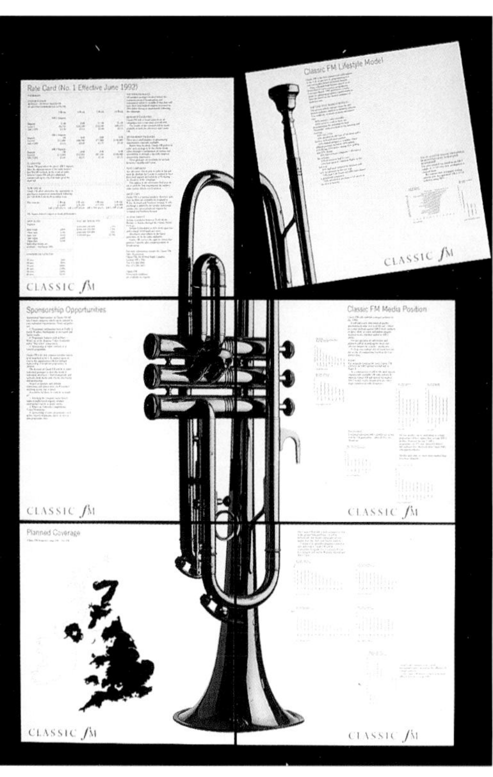

**First Choice
Calendar for Applied
Graphic Technologies**

'US printers and typesetters Applied Graphics Technologies invited twelve international designers to design a page each for their 1992 calendar. The given theme of 'famous personalities' was an opportunity for me to indulge a pleasure in found objects and the graphic equivalent of word play. For the face of 'Manhattan' a bagel mouth seemed quite apt, offset by the Empire State Building as its most prominent feature, with two airmail letters, complete with views of the Big Apple providing the finishing touches for 'Ol blue eyes''

Advertisers' pack for Classic FM radio station

Corporate Identity programme for Galleria Colonna, shopping mall and business centre, Rome

Catalogue design for Spink goldsmiths, London

Corporate Identity and Bookjackets for Editions de l'Olivier, a French publishing house

Design scheme for Faber & Faber, publishers

Design for an Earth Flag for the Polish Pavilion, Expo '92 Spain

Jocs de la XXVa Olimpíada
Barcelona 1992

Juegos de la XXV Olimpíada
Barcelona 1992

Jeux de la XXVe Olympiade
Barcelona 1992

Games of the XXV Olympiad
Barcelona 1992

First Choice
Poster of the symbol and logotype for the Barcelona Olympic Games '92

'It is a dream come true. Since I was very young I wanted to be the designer of the graphic of such a relevant and special event as the Olympic Games, and there you have it. Furthermore, there was also an unbelievable accumulation of coincidences in the sense that Barcelona, the city of my birth, presented its candidacy to host the Games; that it won; that a design competition limited to six professionals was held; that I was one of them; and most importantly, that I won almost unanimously. Finally, I believe it was one of those cases where reason, function and emotion were truly there at the time of creating the design'

Label design for 'Cava Chandon'

Poster for Barcelona Olympic Games '92

Sports Pictogrammes for Barcelona Olympic Games '92

Logotype for TV3, Televisió de Catalunya, S.A.

Packaging design for Spectromatic Paints

Symbol and logotype for Parque Espana

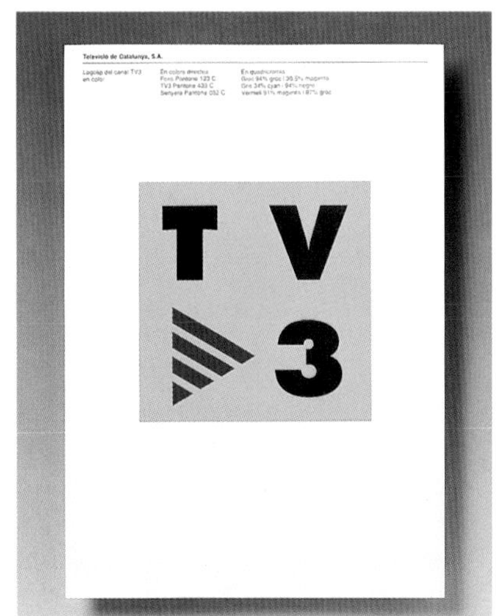

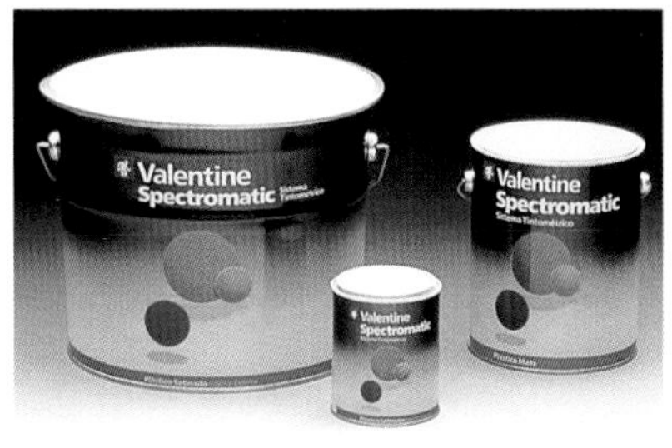

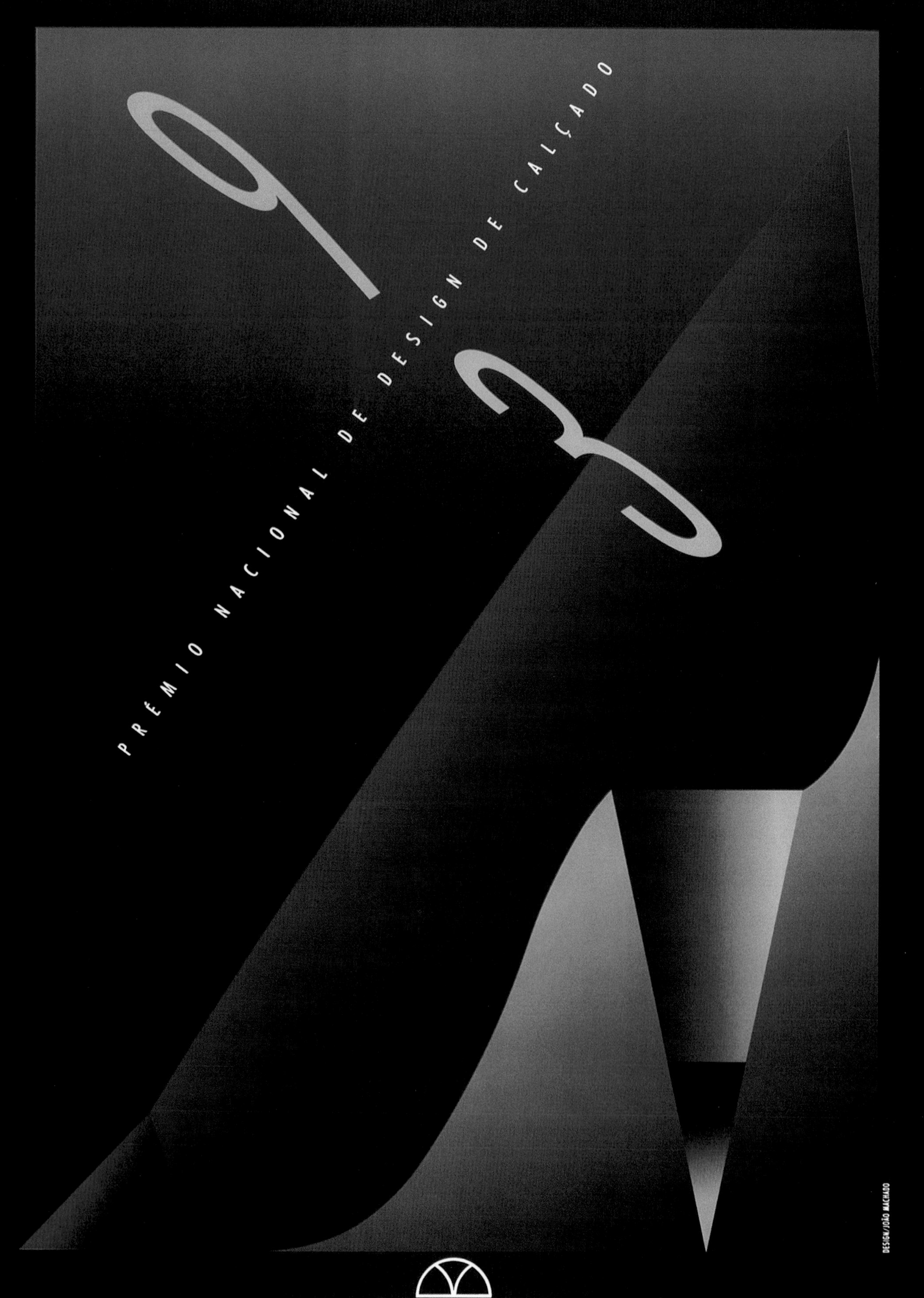
93
PRÉMIO NACIONAL DE DESIGN DE CALÇADO
DESIGN/JOÃO MACHADO
CENTRO DE ARTE DE S. JOÃO DA MADEIRA

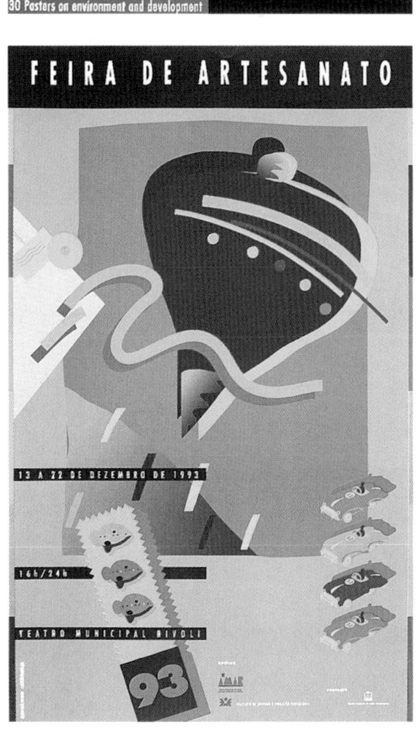

First Choice
Poster for Design Calçado '93

'My choice may be attributed to my personal taste which I sum up with other considerations, such as the aesthetic and semiotic nature that belong to any plastic creation and especially to the poster. In the first place I detach the 'Premio Nacional de Design de Calçado '93'. In this poster I have employed a computerised technique for the first time and obtained vibrant colours and great luminosities, defining the ground of the design in this way. What I meant to show was design, not footwear'

Poster for Jazz Festival '93

Poster for Jazz Festival '94

Poster entitled 'Caring for the earth and its people'

Poster for Eco '92

Poster for Design Calçado '94

Poster for Feira de Artesanato

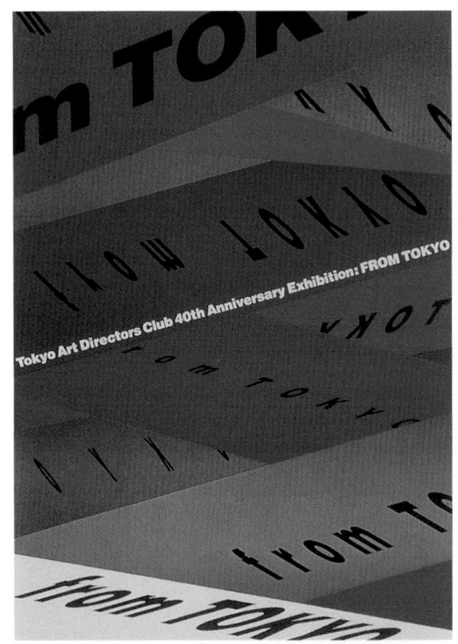
Tokyo Art Directors Club 40th Anniversary Exhibition: FROM TOKYO
from TOKYO

Everything must have a beginning.
I'm here.

PEACE

gom

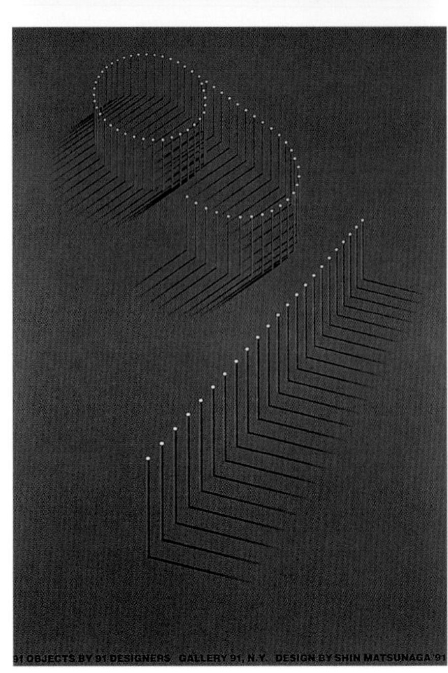
91 OBJECTS BY 91 DESIGNERS GALLERY 91, N.Y. DESIGN BY SHIN MATSUNAGA '91

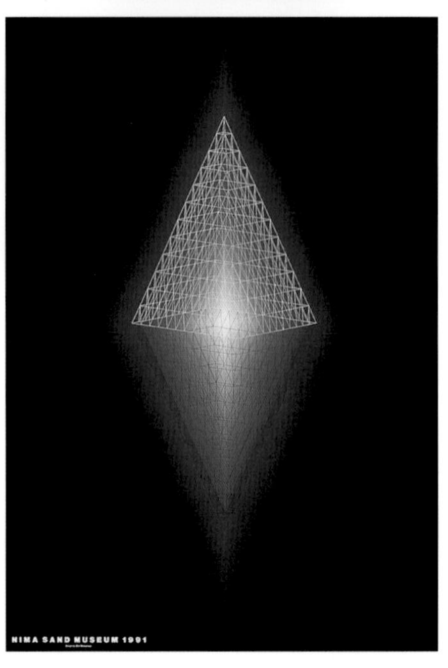
NIMA SAND MUSEUM 1991

First Choice
Poster for an exhibition - LIFE, Japan Design Committee '94

'This is one of my works from a new drawing series which was created as an entry for the exhibition featuring a theme of 'The Life'. The drawing has a symbolic meaning, more than being a simple, new creative design. The eyes staring in the face symbolise 'Thinking', five fingers 'The Technology', and the foot firmly standing on the ground symbolises 'Action'. This very trinity composes the design itself. This is one of the most important and impressive works for me'

Poster for an exhibition 'From Tokyo' for the Tokyo Art Directors Club '93

Poster for a peace and environmental campaign 'I'm Here' for the Japan Graphic Designers Association

Poster for a peace campaign 'Peace '91' for the Japan Graphic Designers Association

Poster for a tableware series 'GOM' for Fuso Gum Industry

Poster for an exhibition entitled '91 Objects by 91 Designers' for the 91 Gallery

Poster for a sand and sandglass museum 'Nima Sand Museum'

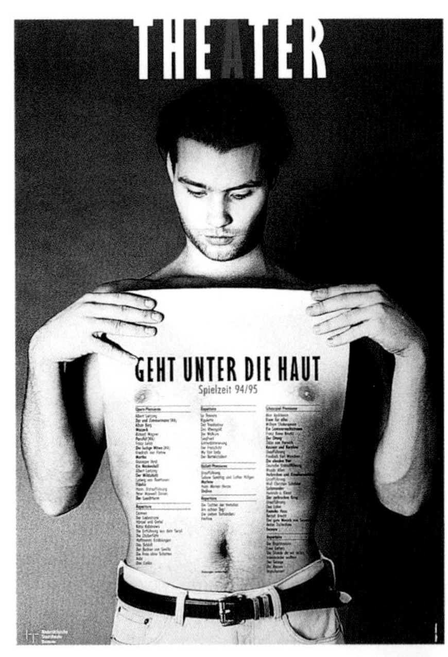
THEATER
GEHT UNTER DIE HAUT
Spielzeit 94/95

Don Carlos
Giuseppe Verdi
Ab 5. Dezember 1992
Niedersächsische
Staatsoper
Hannover

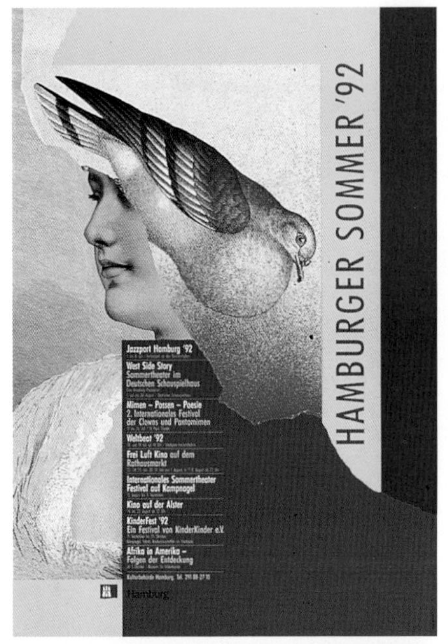
HAMBURGER SOMMER '92
Jazzport Hamburg '92
West Side Story
Sommertheater im
Deutschen Schauspielhaus
Mimen – Possen – Poesie
2. Internationales Festival
der Clowns und Pantomimen
Weltbeat '92
Frei Luft Kino auf dem
Rathausmarkt
Internationales Sommertheater
Festival auf Kampnagel
Kino auf der Alster
KinderFest '92
Ein Festival von KinderKinder e.V.
Afrika in Amerika –
Folgen der Entdeckung
Hamburg

HAMBURGER
SOMMER 1994
Hamburger Architektur Sommer
Meisterwerke aus dem Guggenheim
Museum
XX. Hamburger
Ballett Tage
WestPort Hamburg '94
Freiluft Kino
Musicals in Hamburg
11. Intern. Sommertheater Festival
Der Hamburger Jedermann
Musikfest Hamburg
Welt Kultur Sommer
Vietnam Tage

Die
Entführung
aus dem
Serail
Oper von
Wolfgang
Amadeus
Mozart
Ab 18. Juni
1994
Nieder-
sächsische
Staatsoper
Hannover

Theaterplakate Holger Matthies Ausstellung vom 5. bis
30. Juni im Schauspiel Hannover (Foyer), Prinzenstraße 9.
Geöffnet: Montag bis Freitag 15.00 bis 18.00 Uhr,
Samstag und Sonntag 11.30 bis 18.00 Uhr. Eintritt frei.
Die fetten Jahre sind vorbei.
Alle Macht der Phantasie!

First Choice
Poster for 'Theatre in Bewegung'

'My favourite is the poster 'Theatre in Bewegung' (Theatre in movement). In the same way that the curtain opens, the strips in the blue open too and you can see the program of the theatre. I like it, its reliance on the wind as the main actor. He is a designer and agitator! All the other posters are created for institutes for culture too. Here you have the greatest freedom as a designer'

Poster for 'Theater geht unter die Haut'

Poster for 'Don Carlos '92'

Poster for 'Hamburger Sommer '92'

Poster for 'Hamburger Sommer '94'

Poster for 'Die Entfurrung aus dem Serail'

Poster for 'Die fetten Jahre sind vorbei'

30 POSTERS ON ENVIRONMENT AND DEVELOPMENT THE UNITED NATIONS RIO CONFERENCE '92

First Choice
Poster for the client Design Rio entitled 'The Earth is Our Mother'

'In 1992 I was invited to design a poster on 'Environment and Development' emphasising a positive interpretation of this theme for the Earth Summit Conference in Rio de Janeiro. I chose to develop a theme which, for reasons of mankind's relationship with nature, is common in almost every culture: 'The Earth is our Mother'.
Starting with the idea that the closest link between all living creatures is the bond between a mother and child, the image became clear and obvious.
The rendition and interpretation came from my environment and culture, which although dry and foreboding, sustains all of us and therefore must be respected'

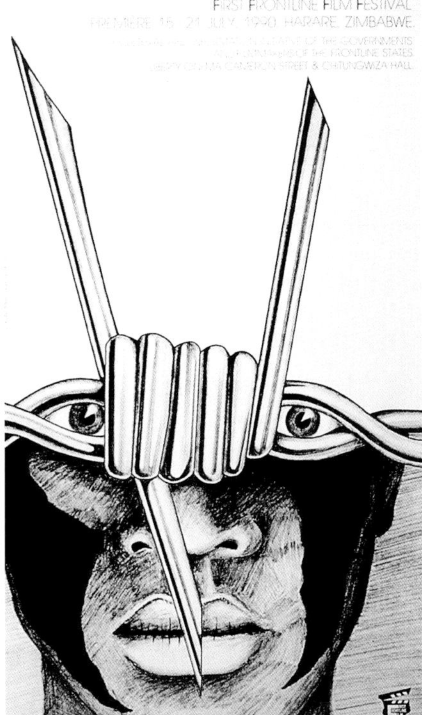

Poster for the British Council to encourage library use entitled 'Knowledge will set you free'

Poster for the African tour of the jazz musician Andy Sheppard

Poster for the First Frontline Film Festival

Poster for the Southern African Film Festival

Poster for the IUCN for the conservation of nature entitled 'Caring for the Earth and its People'

Poster for the Just World Trust, for a seminar on 'Rethinking Human Rights from a Third World Perspective' entitled 'Dominance'

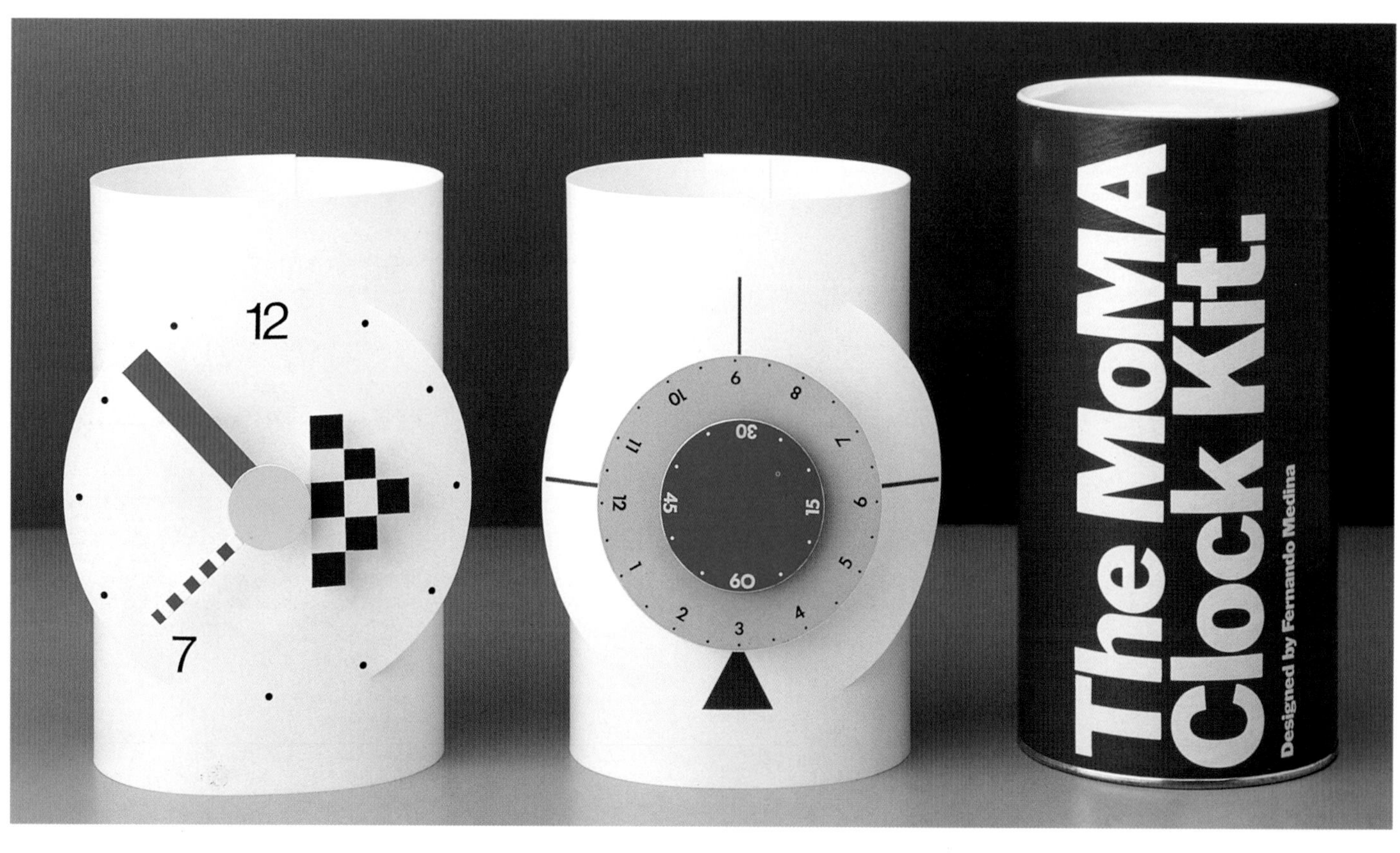
12
7
The MoMA Clock Kit.
Designed by Fernando Medina

$H_2Oh!$

First Choice
The MoMA Clock Kit

'In 1989, I designed a series of products in exclusivity for The Museum of Modern Art of New York (MoMA) which included clocks and lamps, thermometers, mobiles. My idea was to design products not expensive, made of light materials not requiring any moulding to be easily manufactured. I also use the kit concept to interact consumers with the products. Each clock is made of flexible sheets of polyethylene mixed with snaps, wood and metal elements to be assembled by consumers'

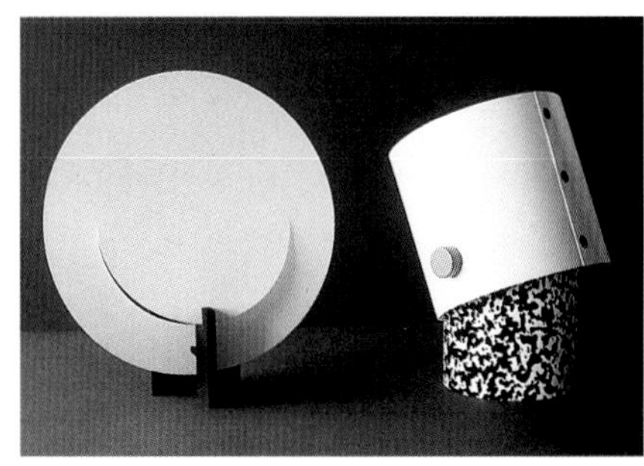

A design for the competition Fax Art with the theme 'Just Now' focusing consciousness on the water

Poster for the annual Chicago World Congress on Environmental Planning and Design

A design to feature on a T-shirt for the First International Conference of Design in Ixtapa, Mexico

A personal piece entitled 'TV or not to be', one of a series of graphic concepts and images drawn on shopping bags which forms part of an exhibition

A sculpture based on the theme 'Earth' for the 5th International Design Competition held in Osaka

Product design for The Museum of Modern Art in New York, The MoMA Lamp Kit

Goethe Institut

Danilo
Silvestrin
Design im
Raum
Villa Stuck
24.7.–27.9.
1992

Quilts der
Amischen
17.4.–2.6.91
Die Neue
Sammlung

Buchgestaltung
in der Schweiz
20.7.-18.9.1994
Die Neue
Sammlung

Japanische
Plakate
1960 bis
heute

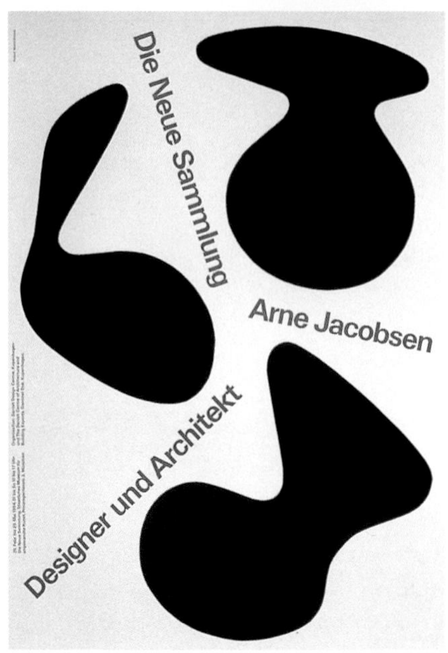
Die Neue Sammlung
Arne Jacobsen
Designer und Architekt

First Choice
Poster for 'Don Giovanni' at the Bavarian National Opera

'This poster is my first choice because to a conservative audience it is however slightly shocking. So is Don Giovanni'

Poster for the Goethe Institut

Poster for an exhibition of the designer and architect Danilo Silverstrin

Poster for an exhibition of quilts

Poster for an exhibition of Swiss bookart

Poster for an exhibition of Japanese posters

Poster for an exhibition of the designer Arne Jacobsen

Istituto Italiano di Cultura New York **Ottagono**

Less is More or More is Less?

Society and Design

Il dibattito "Design e società" vuole centrare l'attenzione sulle relazioni che intercorrono tra il design e l'evoluzione del gusto, in contesti sociali diversi, degli ultimi decenni, attraverso contributi di relatori che operano in ambiti differenti con l'obiettivo di mettere a fuoco il tema da diversi punti di vista.

The debate "Design and Society" is intended to concentrate attention in the relationships that exist between Design and the changes in taste in diverse social contexts over the last ten years. Speakers who work in different areas will contribute to the debate with the aim of focusing on this theme from different points of view.

Furio Colombo
Direttore dell'Istituto Italiano di Cultura di New York, moderatore.
Director of the Italian Cultural Institute of New York, moderator.

Aldo Colonetti
Direttore di Ottagono, trimestrale di Disegno Industriale.
Editor of Ottagono, quarterly of Industrial Design.

Carl Gustav Magnusson
Senior Vice President,
Direttore del Design per Knoll Group, New York.
Senior Vice President,
Director of Design for the Knoll Group in New York.

Cara McCarty
Museo d'Arte di Saint Louis, curatore delle Arti Decorative e del Design.
The Saint Louis Art Museum, curator Decorative Arts and Design.

Lella Vignelli
Vice Presidente della Vignelli Associates e Presidente della Vignelli Design.
Executive Vice President of Vignelli Associates and President of Vignelli Designs.

6 maggio 1993
May 6 1993
6 - 8 pm

686 Park Avenue, New York, N.Y. 10021
Rel. 212/879-4242

MORE
LESS

Design: Armando Milani

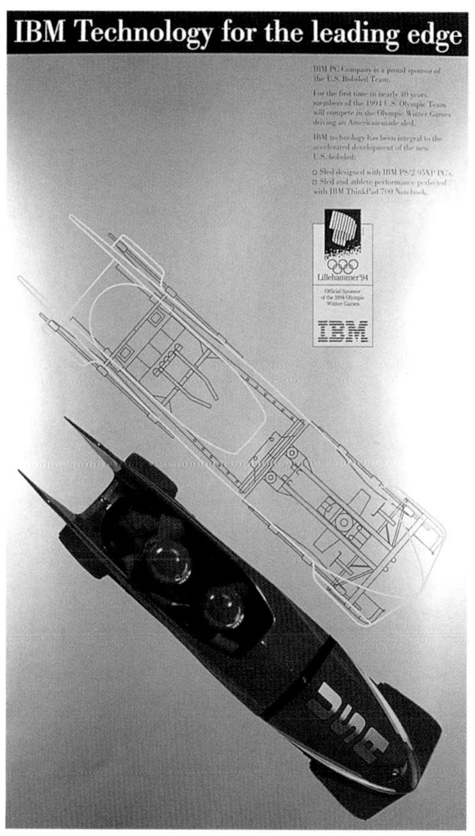

First Choice
Poster 'Design and Society, less is more or more is less?'

'This poster is about the debate on the relationship that exists between design and the changes in taste in different social contexts over the last ten years. The poster was designed for the Italian Culture Institute of New York and highlights the theme of this very controversial period of design. I am particularly satisfied with this poster because it is an answer to the components that I am always searching for in the process of my work: synthesis, directness, and ambiguity, and because this solution reflects my beliefs that less is more'

Poster for IBM sponsoring the US Bobsled team at the Lillehammer Olympic Games

Symbol for Bottega Veneta, a fine leather goods company in New York, Tokyo and Milan

Poster for Altos de Chavon, Santo Domingo (a school of design affiliated with Parsons School, New York and Paris)

Poster for Observatoire International Des Prisons

Logotype for Espresso Bar Chain, New York

Symbol for Promexa Publishing Company, Mexico City

MON
1872
MONDR
ARTI

First Choice
Cover design for 'Mondrian' a book published by Parana State Library

'The 'Mondrian' piece is my first choice because it is a recent piece and transmits very well the intention of its use. It is a cover of the paperback-monograph the third and final edition of a series dedicated to Mondrian. The information was resumed with a photo of the artist and only a part of his name. The piece has transformed into a poster of great success and recall'

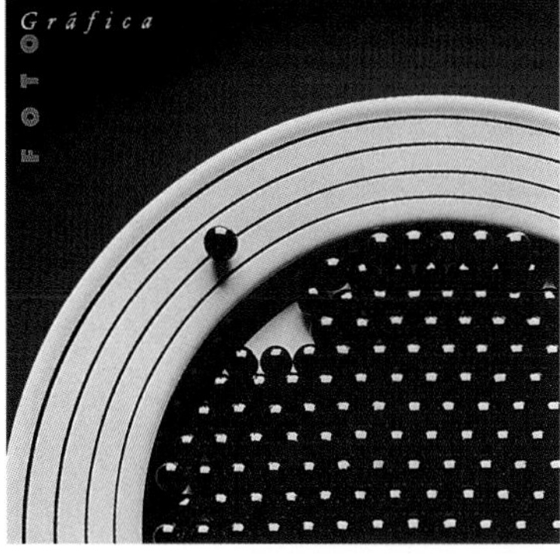

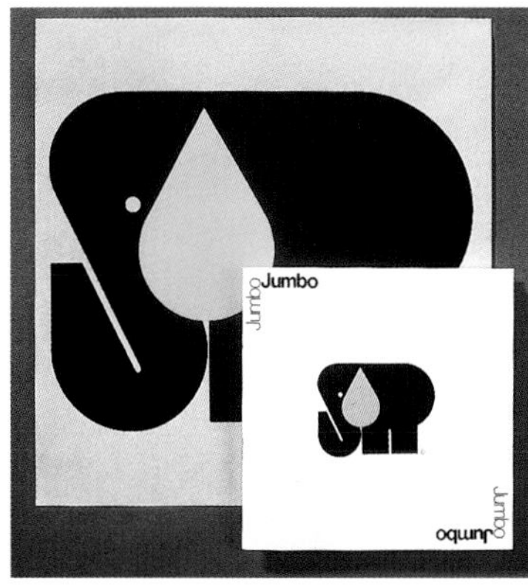

Cover design for 'AdD' an Art Direction and Design magazine

Cover design for 'Foto-Gráfica' special issue

Page design for 'Gráfica', in hommage to El Lissitzky

Corporate Identity for 'Jumbo', gas station network

Cover design for 'Gráfica'

Symbol for 'Pro-Music a childrens' music school

Museo Cantonale d'Arte
BOTTA
CUCCHI
ZURICH 3. JUNI 30. JULI 1989
KUNSTHAUS
SCHWEIZERISCHE STIFTUNG FUR DIE PHOTOGRAPHIE
PHOTOGRAPHIE AUS DER SOWJET UNION
Museo Cantonale d'Arte via Canova 10 Lugano 16 Dicembre 1989–28 Gennaio 1990
1987–1989
adriana beretta
fotografie '90 '92
luciano rigolini
CARICATURE
caricature
DISEGNI
7 Settembre 10 Novembre 1991
SILOGRAFIE
lyonel feininger
Museo Cantonale d'Arte
Lugano Via Canova 10

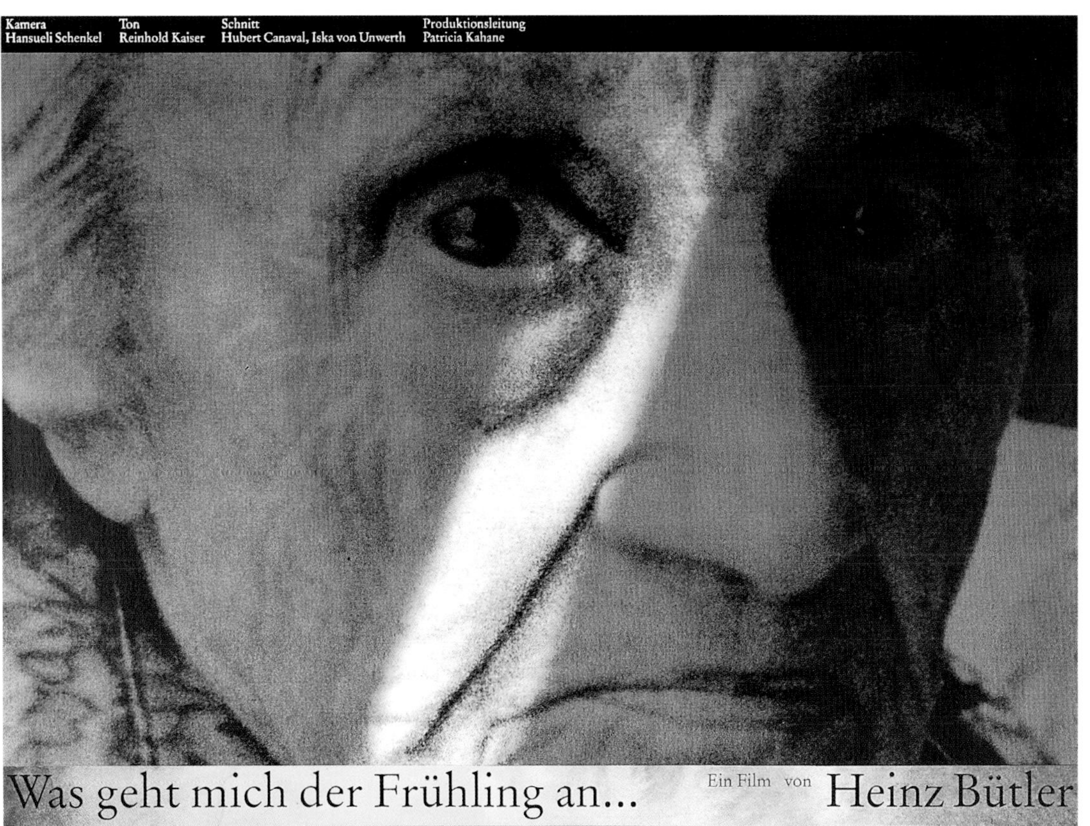

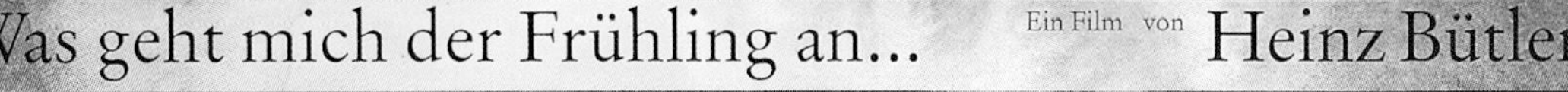

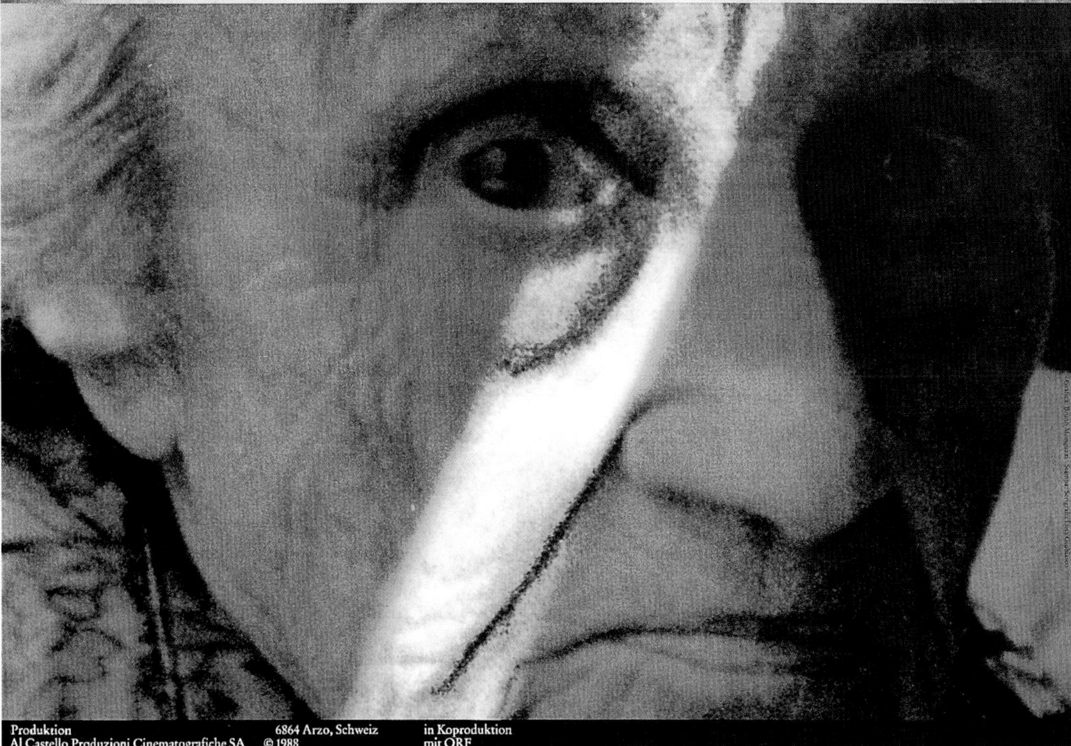

First Choice
Design for a film poster

'I do not really have a favourite piece of work. I have chosen this film poster because the idea to add the stroke of light made the portrait stronger and more meaningful'

Poster for the '80's and 90's in the Panza di Biumo Collection' exhibition

Poster for 'Botta and Cucch, The Monte Tomato Chapel' exhibition

Poster Design 'Before and After the Revolution' photograpy in the Soviet Union

Poster for an exhibition of Nando Snozzi paintings and collages

Poster for an exhibition of Luciano Rigolini photography and Adriana Beretta installations

Poster for an exhibition of Lyonel Feininger wood cuts, drawings, caricatures and paintings

MUSÉE DES BEAUX-ARTS
DE MONTRÉAL

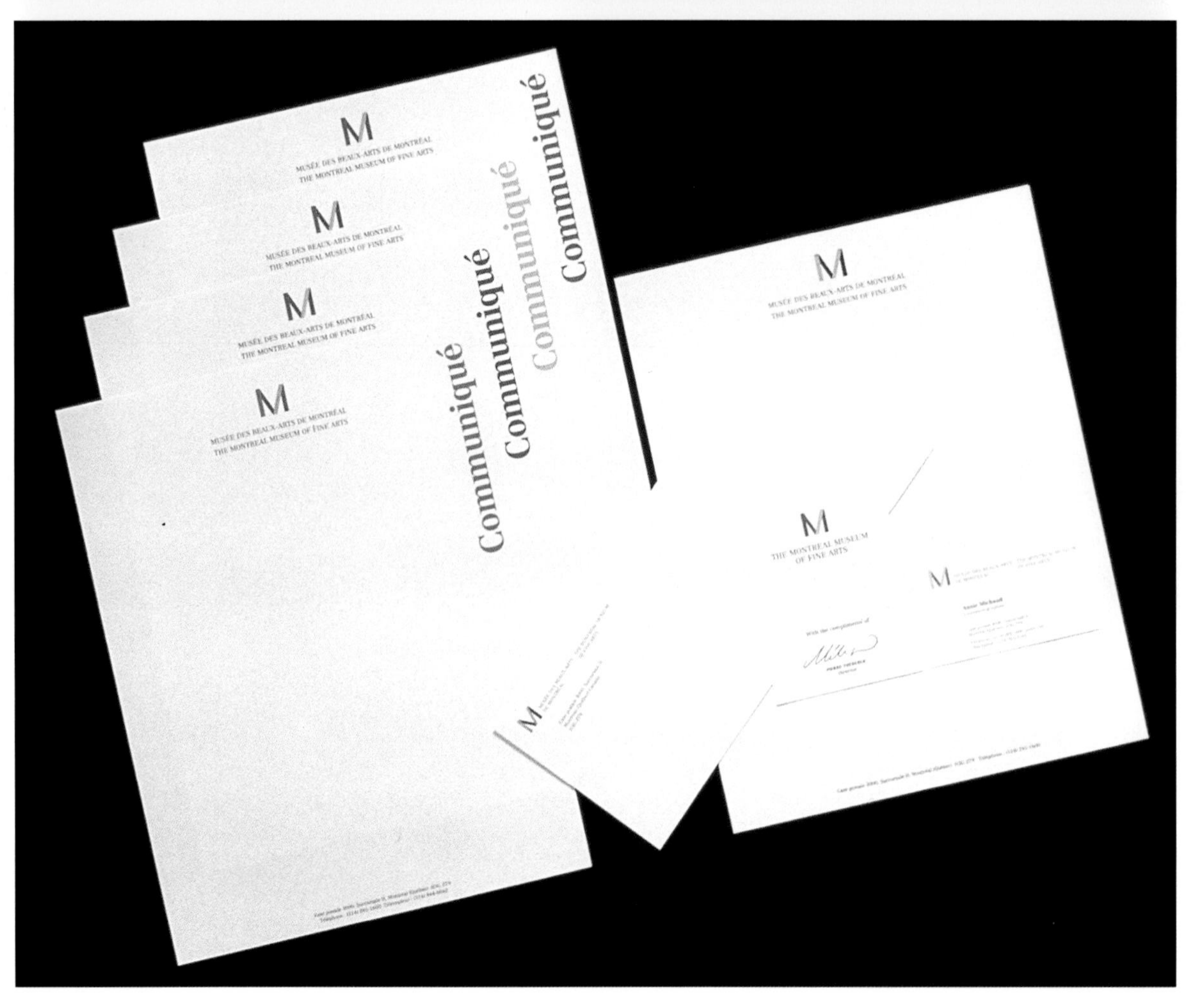

Jean Morin

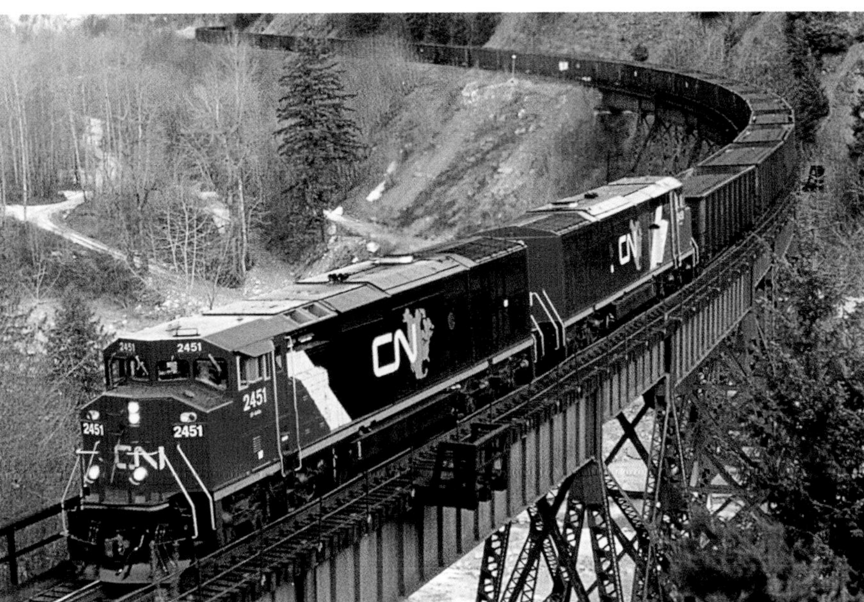

First Choice
Symbol and Logotype for the Montreal Museum of Fine Arts, Québec

'In 1992, the Museum of Fine Arts, a cultural monument in Montreal, added a new wing which sufficiently altered the museum's personality to justify a new identity.
The new identity system had to adapt to corporate needs as well as to intense promotional requirements, and allow for essential, yet subtle, evolution.
The apparent simplicity of the signature is a mastery of equilibrium. It evokes the traditional/dynamic duality of the Museum; both contemporary and dynamic in its promotional activities, and faithful to its traditions and its mission as guardian of Montreal's artistic heritage.
The identity, which extends into the Museum's signage system, contributes to guiding and informing the public without undermining the works of art or the ambience'

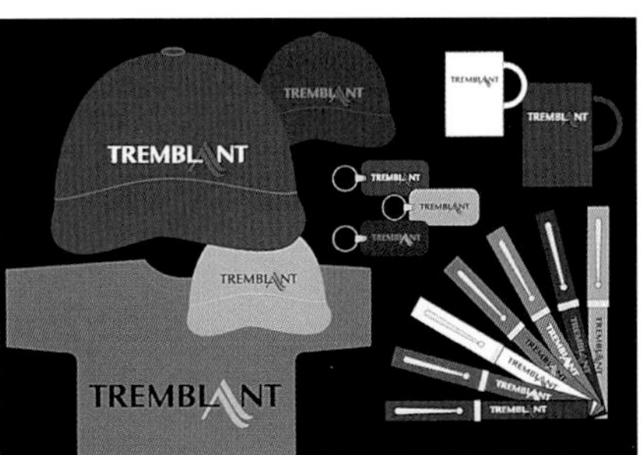

Corporate Identity for Canadian National, North America

Corporate Identity for BC Telecom Inc, Vancouver

Corporate Identity and new brand name for Tremblant, Quebec

Corporate Identity for Hydro-Quebec, Montreal

Design for a postage stamp, Canada

Design for a postage stamp, Canada

San Fran
cisco Mus
eum of
Modern Art
Design Lec
ture Series:
The Radical
Response

First Choice
Poster for SF Museum of Modern Art Design Lecture Series

'My first choice fave has to be the Museum of Modern Art design lecture series poster which I created back in 1991. It was one of the few times that the actual design process has determined the look of the end product. This was due to my relative naivete of 'Illustrator' and 'Photoshop'. Specifically, my hand drawn type and, as originally conceived, continuous tone photograph, both turned more 'radical' as I allowed the computer and software to alter my original design intent. As if by magic, the 'opening' of the type filled in, the photo pixilated, and the polka dots and colour scheme naturally followed suit'

Poster design for the Stanford Conference on Design

Design for Simpson Parchment Paper Promotion

Design for Cocolat retail packaging

Design for the San Francisco International Airport, '93 Annual Report

Design for the book, 'Espresso'

Design for the Capp Street Project Catalogue

KAZUMASA NAGAI DESIGN LIFE
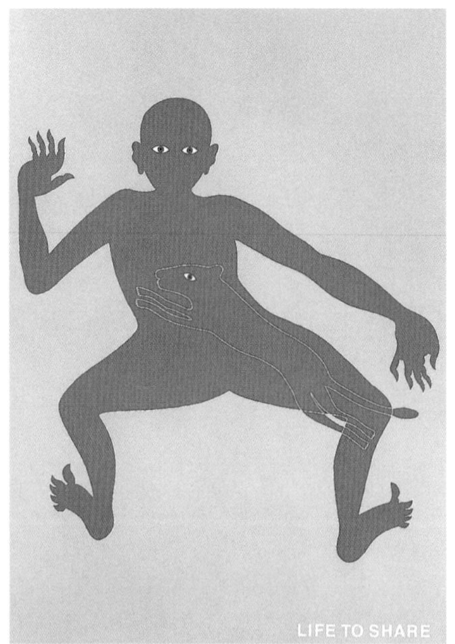
LIFE TO SHARE

KAZUMASA NAGAI DESIGN LIFE

KAZUMASA NAGAI DESIGN LIFE

Save me, please. I'm here.

KAZUMASA NAGAI DESIGN LIFE

First Choice
Poster entitled 'Save me, please. I'm here'
For Peace and Environment Exhibition

'This exhibition, 'I'm here' was organised by the Japan Graphic Designers Association. The eyes of the lion who is driven into a tight corner by environmental destruction are strongly appealing to us for 'help', as he disappears into darkness. I believe that this is a symbolic poster'

Poster series entitled 'Kazumasa Nagai Design Life'

Poster design entitled 'Save me, please. I'm here'

Poster design for Japan Design Committee entitled 'Life to Share'

JAZZ
AARHUS INTERNATIONAL JAZZ FESTIVAL JULY 24-29 1989

First Choice
Poster for Aarhus International Jazz Festival

'My First Choice favourite piece of work is the first of a series of posters I have produced for the Aarhus International Jazz Festival since 1989. I have chosen this because of several reasons. Firstly, the poster is an excellent form for the expression of both illustrative and graphic arts, and the synthesis between the two is of great personal interest to me. Secondly I am a great lover of jazz music, and I believe the poster, picturing Duke Ellington at the piano, captures something of the flavour, smell and sound of jazz'

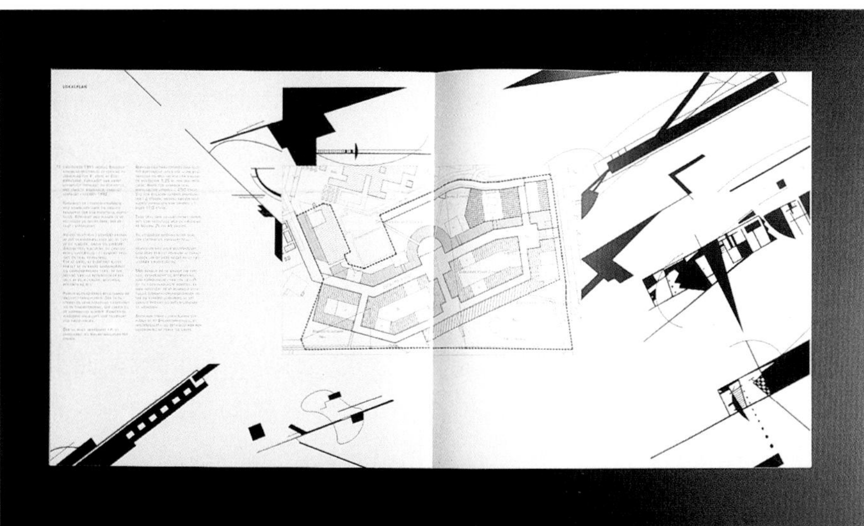

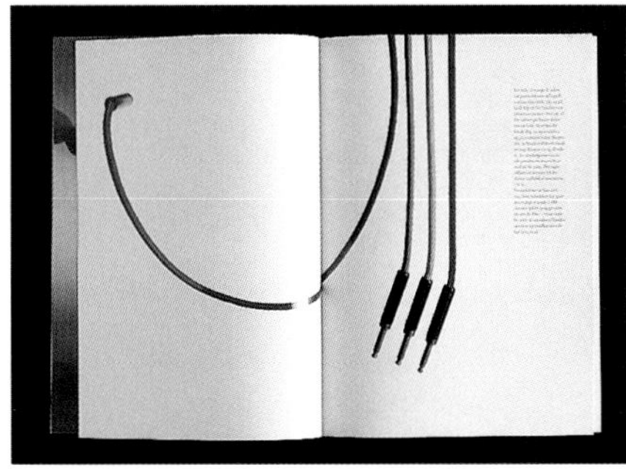

Poster for the Foundation for Parents with Children with Cancer

Poster for the musical 'Magic at 4am Freedom South Afrika'

Design for a brochure 'Bo iby' (Living in the City)

Design for a brochure 'Bøg madsen Blomster' (flower company)

Poster for a Danish cigarette company

Design for a brochure produced for Jydsk Telefon, Denmark

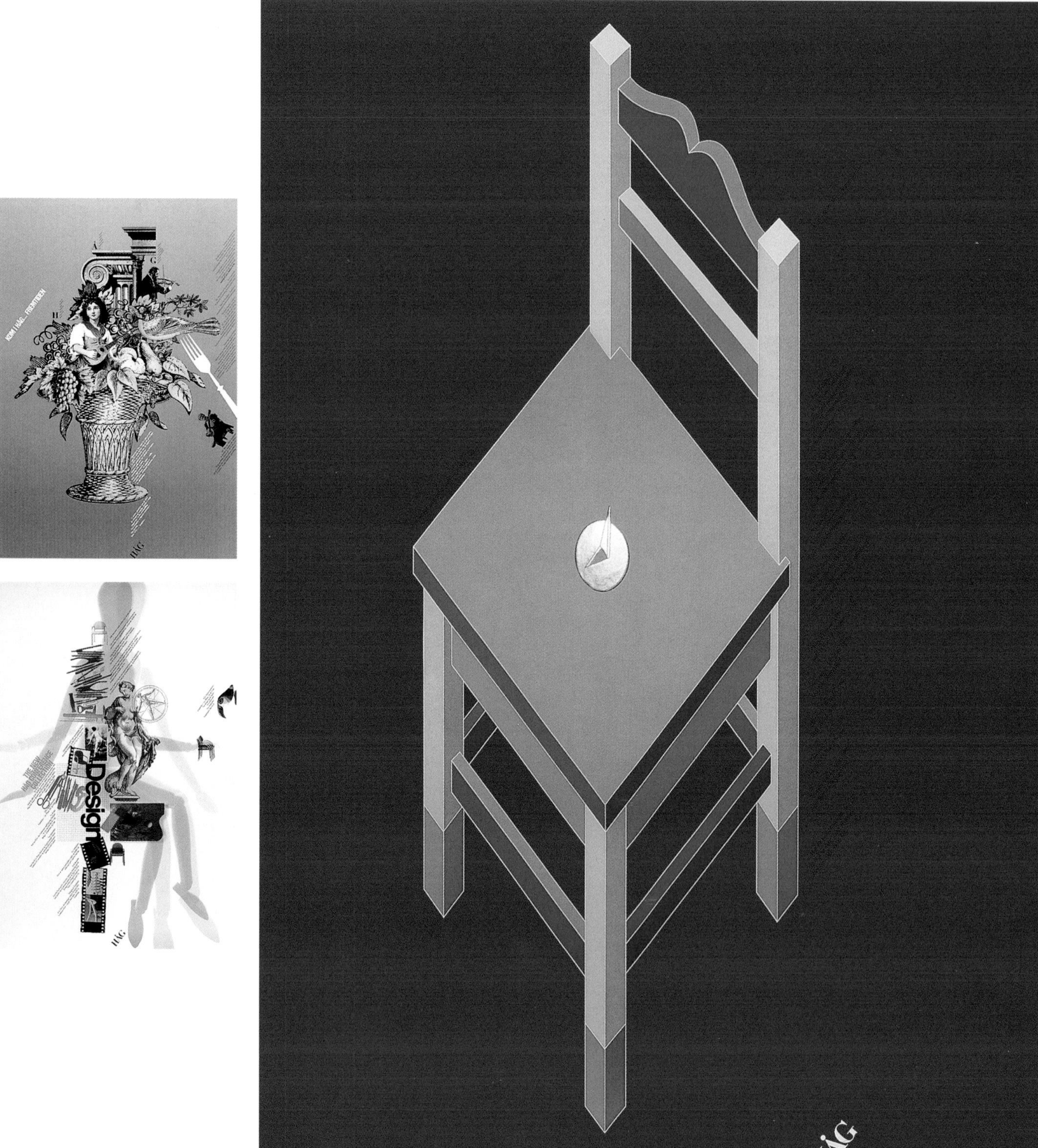
HÅG
Design
HÅG
HÅG

**First Choice
Series of Poster Invitations for HAG as Oslo, manufacturers of office chairs**

'These three posters are equal and a series. The first is an invitation to to vernisage, a party and a presentation of a complete set of new office chairs and the topic that day 'A world that is properly seated, is never at a standstill'. The second is an invitation to a party and presentation of conference chairs and the topic was 'The body should not be forced into a static piece of furniture. Seating should also be be an interface between soft humanity and hard architecture'. The third is an invitation to a party and presentation of office chairs and participation in a nightclub party with a jam session. Architects, designers and friends had to bring their own musical instruments along to play the blues the whole night through!'

Design which was applied to a double page advertisment, poster and T-shirt for A-Z, printers who take care of repro and printing through to delivery

Bookcover for a textbook for visiting orchestral conductors

Bookcover and poster for Tiden Norsk Forlag entitled 'Gategutt' (Street Boy)

Poster for the Gannet Outdoor International Poster Contest Against Violence, 'Stop Violence Now...!'

KAMARASZÍNHÁZ
WILLY RUSSELL
BLOOD BROTHERS
VÉRTESTVÉREK
musical 2 részben
VÁRI ÉVA
MAKRAI PÁL m.v.
ANDAI GYÖRGYI
SZEGVÁRI MENYHÉRT
RÁTÓTI ZOLTÁN
KEREKES JÓZSEF
NEMCSÁK KÁROLY
LÉTAY DÓRA
RENDEZŐ
SZEGVÁRI MENYHÉRT m.v.
a JÓZSEFVÁROSBAN

ÜNNEPI
KÖNYVHÉT
1993. június 4-8.

ТОВАРИЩИ
ADIEU!

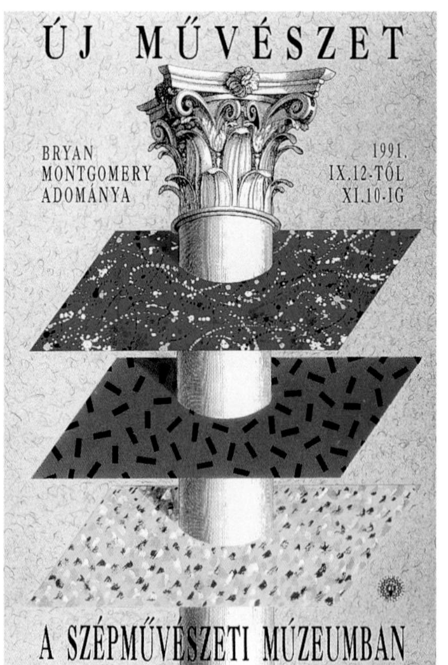
ÚJ MŰVÉSZET
BRYAN
MONTGOMERY
ADOMÁNYA
1991.
IX.12-TŐL
XI.10-IG
A SZÉPMŰVÉSZETI MÚZEUMBAN

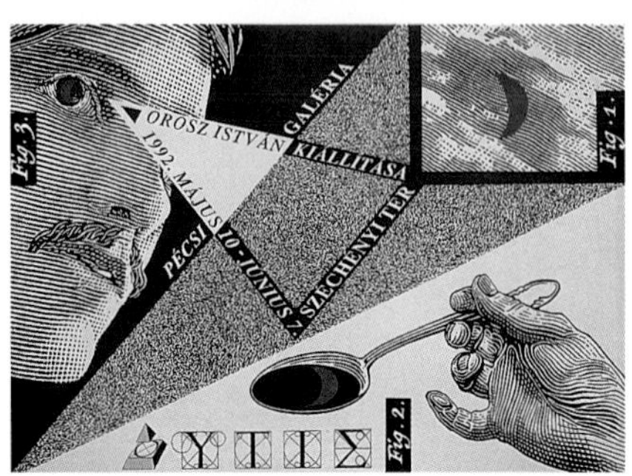
OROSZ ISTVÁN
GALÉRIA
KIÁLLÍTÁSA
PÉCSI
SZÉCHENYI TÉR
Fig. 3
Fig. 1
Fig. 2

First Choice
Poster for OYTIΣ (No one!) An exhibition held at Komarom Gallery

'OYTIΣ, this is the title of my 'first choice' work and this ancient Greek name is nothing else but a pseudonym. It means 'No one'. The poster itself was made to put up in my own exhibition in a Hungarian country town in 1989. Before me it was the most cunning of all Homer's heroes, Odysseus, who used this name in his fight against the Cyclops. As we all know, the monster lost his sight in the battle. As I imagine the good poster itself is an Odyssean attitude as well, an attack against the eye, more gently certainly, being the result not to lose the sight but to win it'

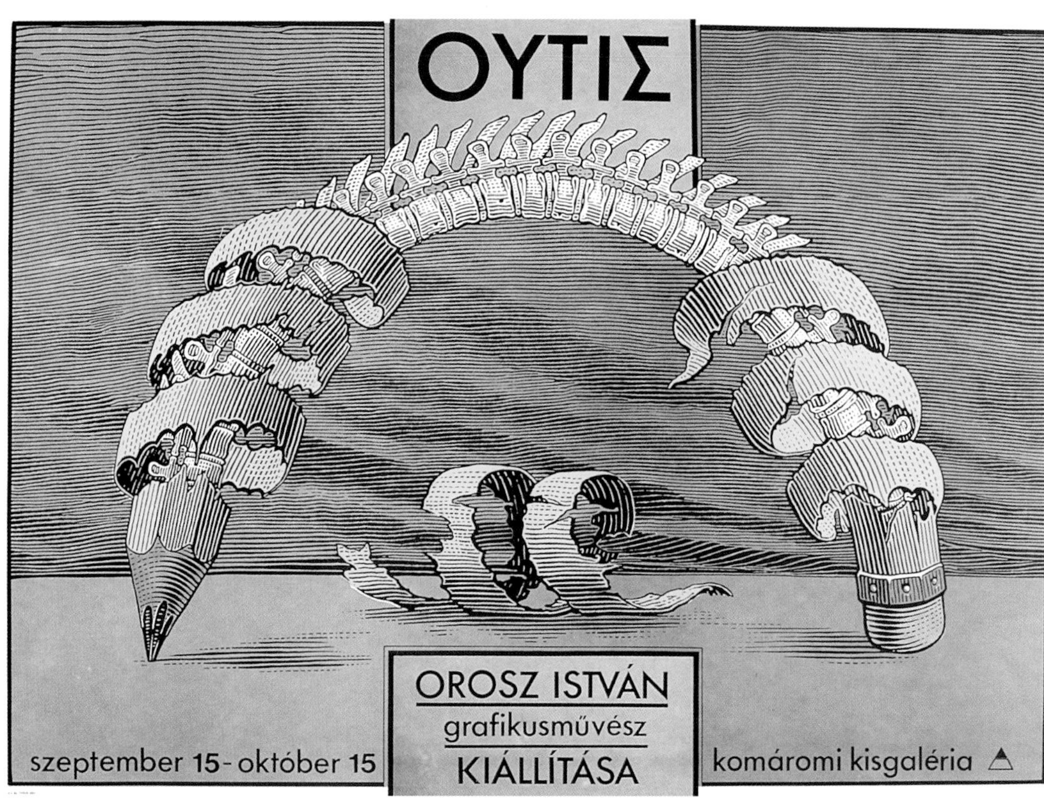

Poster for Vértestvérek ('Blood Brothers'), a theatre poster for a contemporary English musical

Posters for Ünnepi Könyvhét (Festive Book Week) a book festival held in Budapest for the Association of Hungarian Book Sellers

Poster for 'Tovarishi adieu' (Comrades bye bye) for MDF

Poster for 'Új Müvészet' (New Art), an exhibition for the Fine Arts Museum, Budapest

Poster for OYTIΣ made for the Gallery of Pécs

Poster for 'Adriana Lecouvreur', an opera of the Italian composer Francesco Cilea

EINAKTER VON ARKADY LEOKUM

JAZZ + THEATER
MIT
BORIS GURADZE
WERNER SCHUSTER
UND
DER GRUPPE
«SSÄLAWIH»
WERNER SCHULZ
DRUMMS, GITARRE
FRIEDHELM KASPARICK
PIANO, AKKORDEON
VIOLINE
MARTIN LEHMANN
BASS
REGIE
FRANK STROBEL
MIT
UNTERSTÜTZUNG
DES KULTURAMTS
REINICKENDORF
IM RAHMEN
DER DEZENTRALEN
KULTURARBEIT

FEINDE

NICOLAUS OTT + BERNARD STEIN

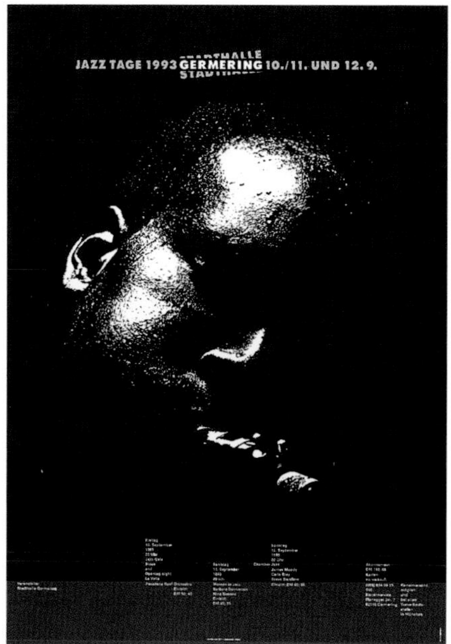

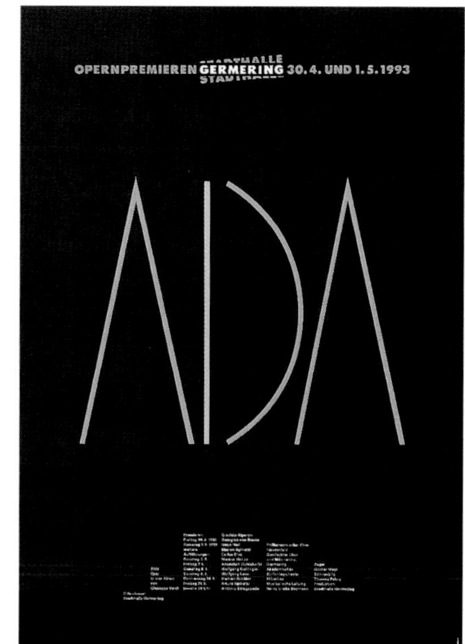

First Choice
Poster for FEINDE

'The poster FEINDE from 1993 shows the pictograms of a knife, a fork and a plate plus the title, which means 'enemies'. It announces a play by Arkady Leokum, in which two people act. They are a guest and a waiter; the waiter has been serving this particular guest every evening for five years. For five years the guest has humiliated the waiter and this is the night the waiter has decided to pay him back. By positioning the four items (knife, fork, plate and title) we formed the pictogramatic illustration of a face, whose expression sums up the contents of the play'

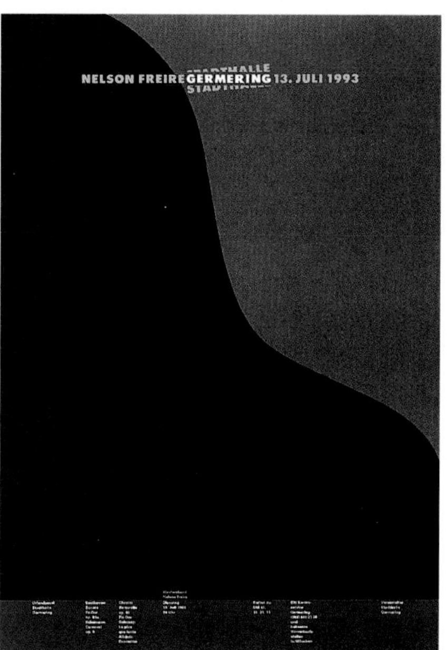

Poster for the festival 'Jazz Tage', Germering City Hall

Poster for the opera 'Aida', Germering City Hall

Poster for an Alan Marks performance of Schubert sonatas

Poster for the Nelson Freire piano concert, Germering City Hall

Poster for a Joseph Beuys exhibition, Berlin Gallery

Poster for the War Requiem Kirchenmusikzentrum Lindenkirche by Benjamin Britten

PRODUCTS
BY DESIGN
GRAPHIS PRODUCTS

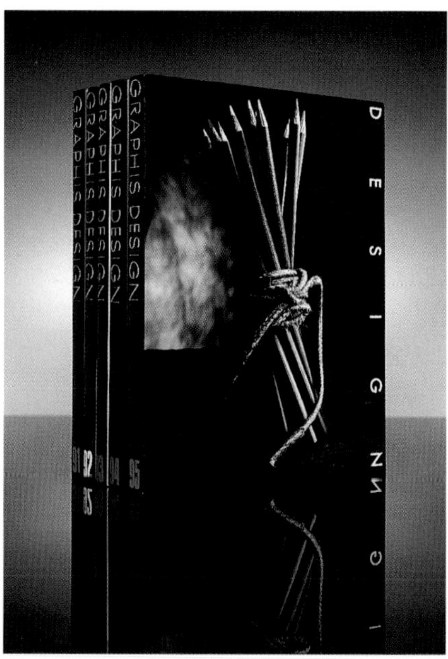

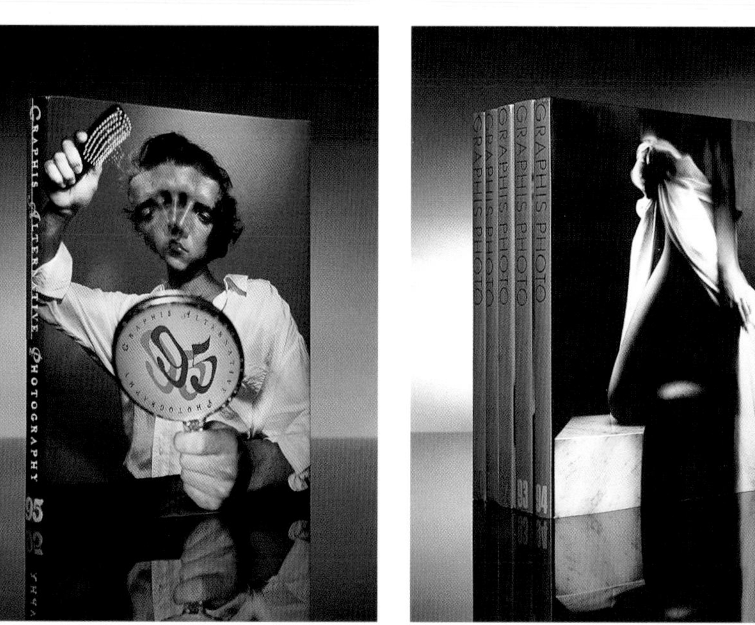

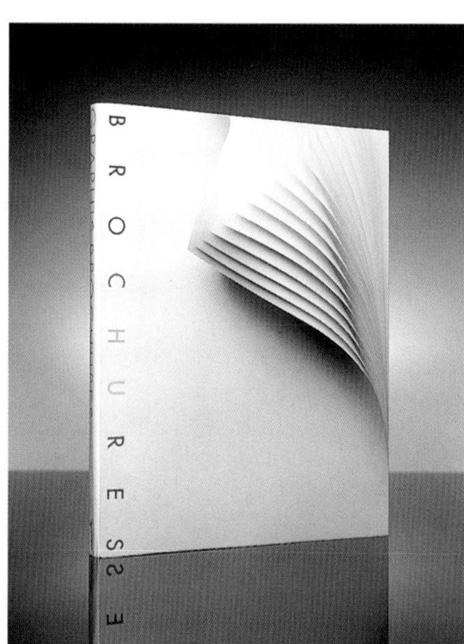

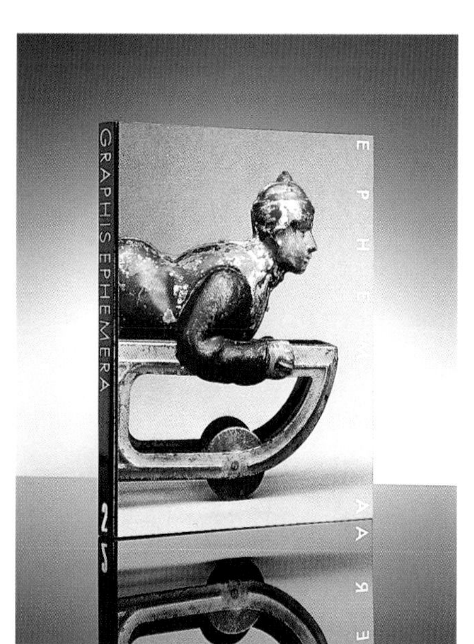

First Choice
Cover design for Graphis 'Products by Design'

'It's hard to pick a favourite, but if pressed I would choose the 'Products by Design' since it was the toughest book to sell to the distributors. Product designers require an enormous amount of education in order to approximately practice their craft, and they seem to be the least appreciated. This book presents some extraordinary work and one that I felt was important to produce to appropriately honour this profession'

Graphis Design Annuals

Graphis Typography Annual

Graphis Alternative Photography

Graphis Photo Annuals

Graphis Brochures Annual

Graphis Ephemera Annual

First Choice
Bill poster for the opera 'L'elisir d'amore' in Zurigo

'It synthesises some subjects on which I have been working recently. The subjects involved are the landscape, the set and the still-life. Futhermore this bill is the conclusion of a long and exacting actitvity as a scene painter and costume designer for an edition of Gaetano Donizetti's 'L'elisir d'amore' staged by the Opernhaus in Zurich'

One of a series of drawings on Robert Louis Stevenson's life and works entitled 'I tavoli di Stevenson' (Stevenson's Tables)

Poster for IBM Europe about the importance of details and planning entitled 'Cono visivo' (Visual cone)

Poster for an exhibition of self portraits at the Galerie Bartsch and Chariau in Munich entitled 'Samuel Beckett'

Drawing for the Italian social and political magazine entitled 'Acqua, aria, terro, fuoco' (Water, air, earth, fire)

Drawing entitled 'Il pittore e la modella' (The painter and the model) published in the Olivetti diary 1994

Drawing for an exhibition at the Kunsthalle of the Deutsche Bank in Frankfurt entitled 'Vaso e Personaggi' (Vase and personages)

JULISTEMUSEO 1975–1990

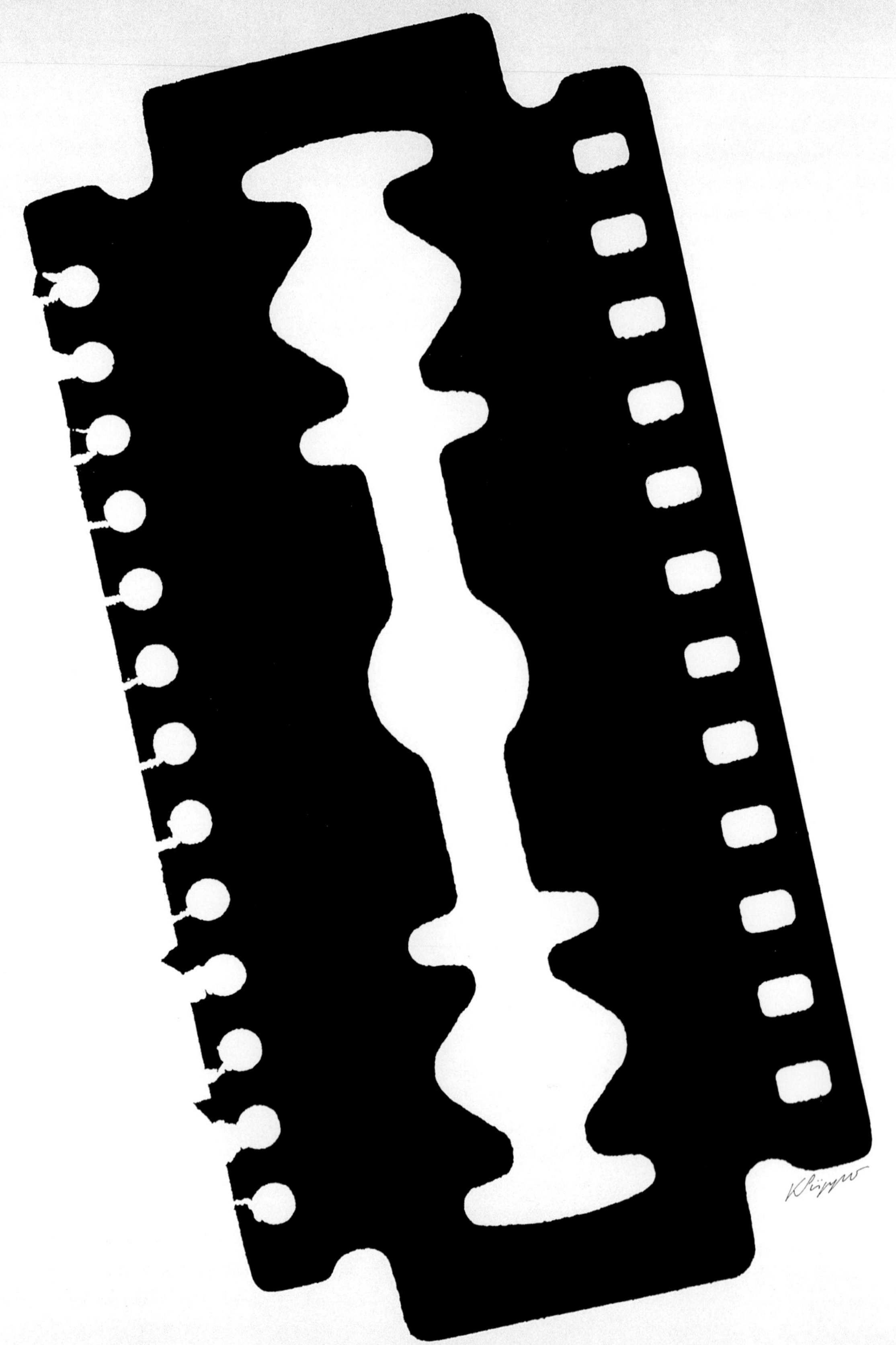

POSTER MUSEUM LAHTI FINLAND

UM-SERI 1990

First Choice
Poster for the Julistemuseo 1975-1990

'Fifteen years of the poster museum in Lahti are celebrated with this poster. A good poster? Simple, strong and sharp'

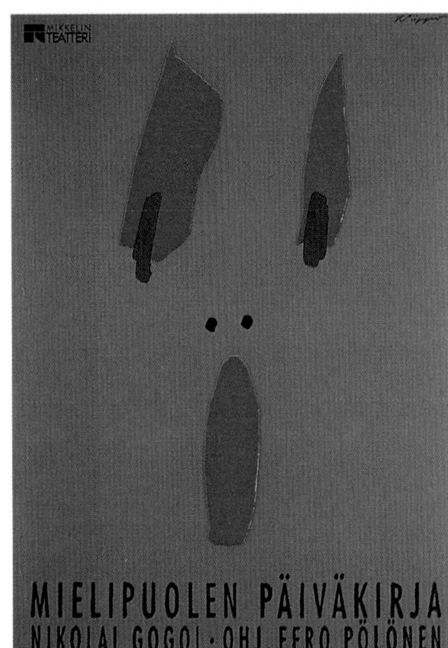

Social poster for Trama Visual entitled 'America Today'

Poster for Mikkelin Musiikkijuhlat, an international music festival in Mikkeli

Invitation poster for Julistekilpailu, an anti-alcohol poster competition

Theatre poster for Mikkelin Teatteri, 'Hamlet'

Theatre poster for Mielipuolen Teatteri, 'The Diary of a Madman'

Exhibition poster for the designer's own exhibition

UCLA
SUMMER
SESSIONS
1989
UNIVERSITY OF CALIFORNIA, LOS ANGELES / LOS ANGELES, CALIFORNIA 90024 / (213) 825 8355

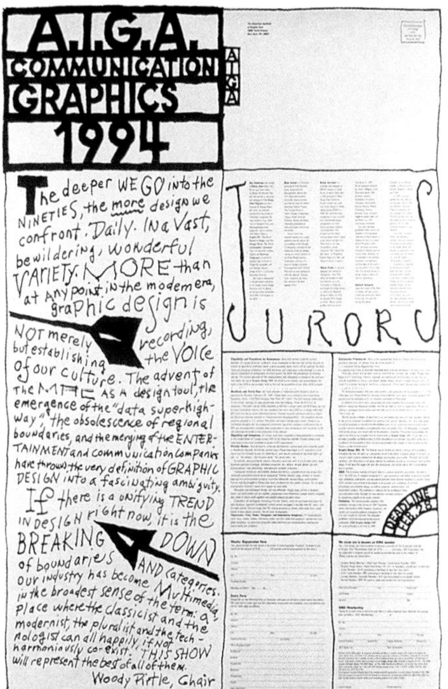

First Choice
Palm Tree poster and catalogue cover for the University of California

'Two textbooks become a familiar Los Angeles palm tree in the promotional image for UCLA's 1989 summer sessions. The warm colours and bold illustration reflect the mood of summer season and the character of the city. The image was applied to the course catalogue cover, poster and T-shirts.
The poster has been published widely and has won awards from 'Communication Arts' and 'Print' magazines and the University and College Designers Association, and was included in New York's 1989 Creativity show, the Brno XIV Biennial of Graphic Design in Czechosolvakia, and the Lahti IX Poster Biennale in Finland'

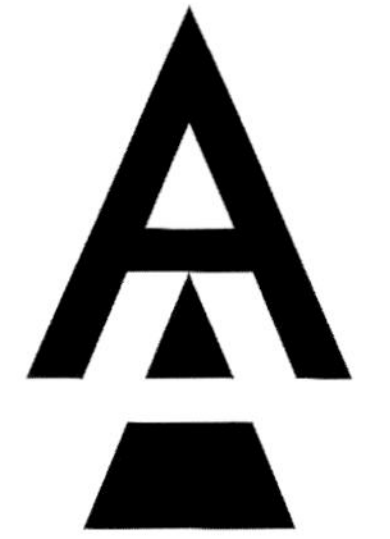

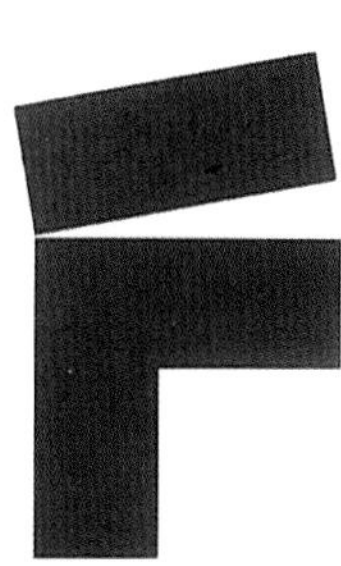

Back and front of a poster for the 1994 Comunication Graphics Show for AIGA

Design for the publication Pentagram Papers entitled 'Skeleton Closet', October 1990 edition

Promotional magazine and poster for Simpson Paper Company's September 1993 Neo

Logotype for the client Noonan Russo Advanced Surgical Inc

Poster promoting the Florida Ringling School of Art

Logotype for the film production company Fine Line Features

Let's Stop Violence

First Choice
Poster against violence worldwide for Gannet Outdoor, New York

'I think the posters with a social message must tune in to the drama which motivates that message. Violence worldwide is of course a personal and social drama. For that reason the picture performing the drama of violence I think can never be a joke neither a poetry, even more if it's conceived to move the looker's conscience. Drama is another thing, and violence (in a generic conception) can never be a lyric anecdote neither an aesthetic game'

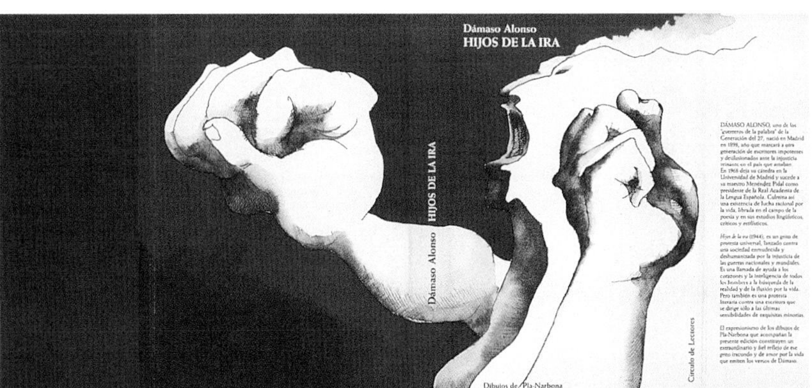

Poster for the Games of the XXV Olympiad, Barcelona 1992

Cover of 'IDEA' magazine No 228, 1991

Cover of the book 'Visual Alphabet' for the Estudio Pla-Narbona

Poster for the 44th Barcelona Book Fair for Gremi de Llibreters de Vell de Catalunya

Cover for the book 'Los hijos de la ira' for Circulo de Lectores

Cover for the book 'San Camilo 1936' for Circulo de Lectores

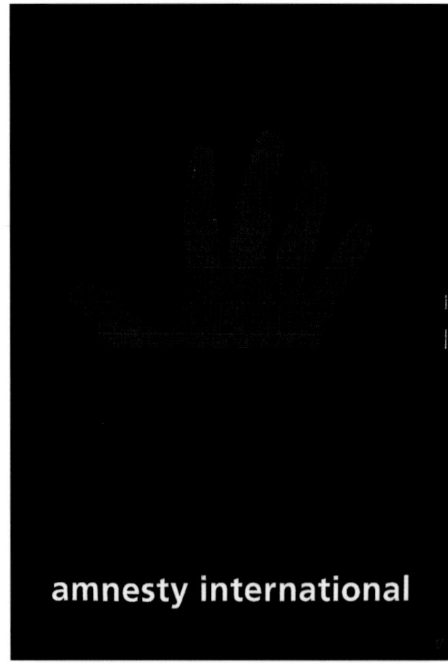

Hochschule für Grafik und Buchkunst Leipzig

work in progress
Rambow

18. Nov. - 19. Dez. '93 HGB Wächterstr. 11

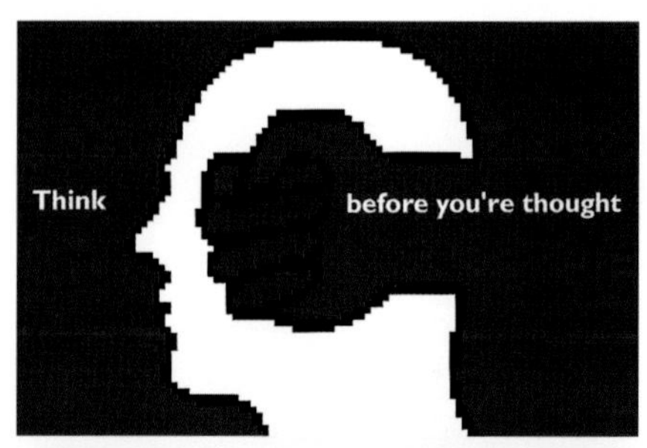

BUGA 97

Gelsenkirchen

First Choice
Poster for the Galerie l'Art et la Paix entitled 'An Image for Peace'

'In a large red area there is a red heart beating. The rhythm is the heart rhythm. And at every beat of the heart one can see some fragments of it...just as long as it beats'

Poster for Wabnitz Editions, Netherlands entitled 'Amnesty International'

Posters for Hochschule für Graphik und Buchkunst, Leipzig entitled 'Rambow-Work in Progress'

Poster for the Gannett Outdoor Group entitled 'Think before you're thought'

Poster for Bundesgartenschau Geisenkirchen entitled 'BUGA '97'

Poster for the Frankfurter Buchändler und Verleger entitled 'Night of books in Frankfurt'

IBM
IBM
IBM
Stage 6
Networking Solutions
for Campus
IBM Networking
IBM Networking Solutions

First Choice

IBM Pavilion at Telecom '95 Geneva, World Exhibition of Telecommunication

'The IBM pavilion at Telecom '95 is a perfect match of engineering and aesthetics. Its structure fully communicates the spirit of the company which is offering to the market 'Solutions for a small planet' creating an ideal atmosphere for the encounter between advanced technologies and people'

IBM Pavilion at Telecom '95 Geneva, World Exhibition of Telecommunication

Exhibition stand design for ZZ Ziegeleien, Swissbau

Exhibition stand design for Silent Gliss, Heimtextii, Frankfurt, Germany

ECOLOGY '05

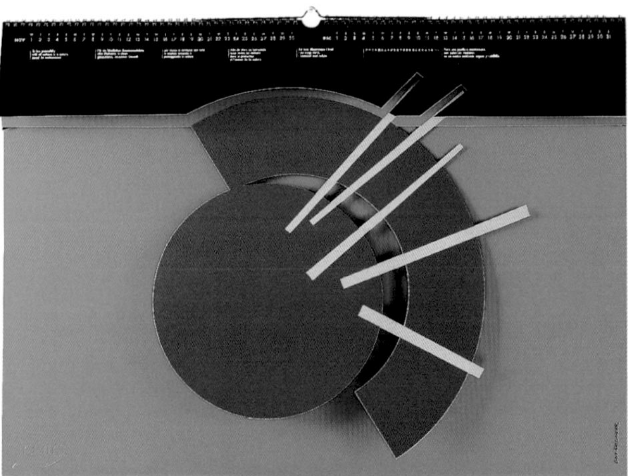

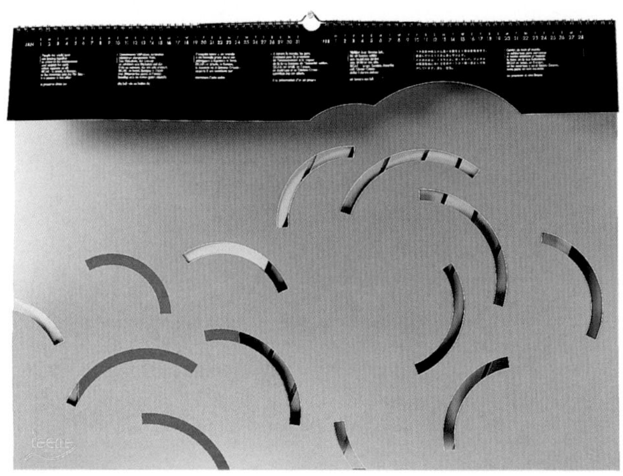

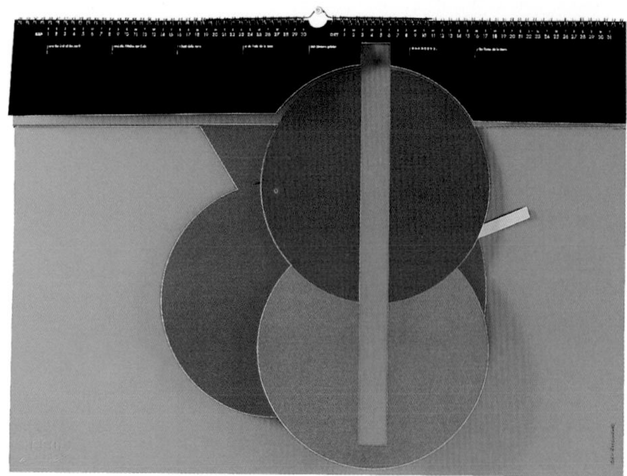

First Choice
1995 Calendar for Iscar Hardmetal Tools Ltd

'People the world over are joining together to preserve the environment and respect the earth which supports us all. ISCAR in Israel, in Europe, in the Americas and the Far East is a partner in this effort to preserve clean air, life-giving rain, fresh water, flourishing trees and fruit of the earth. To live peacefully with all nations in a secure cared for environment'

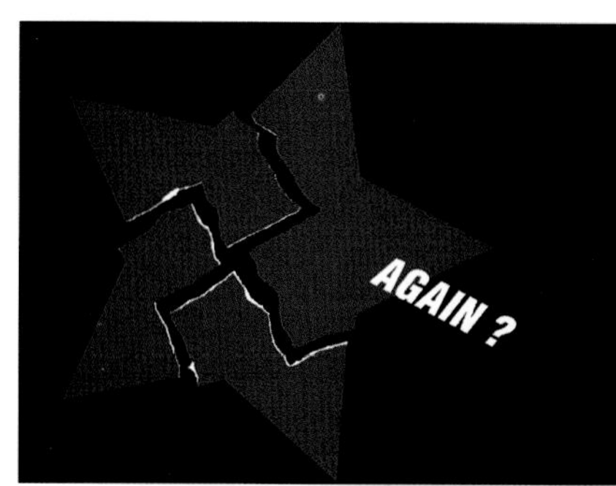

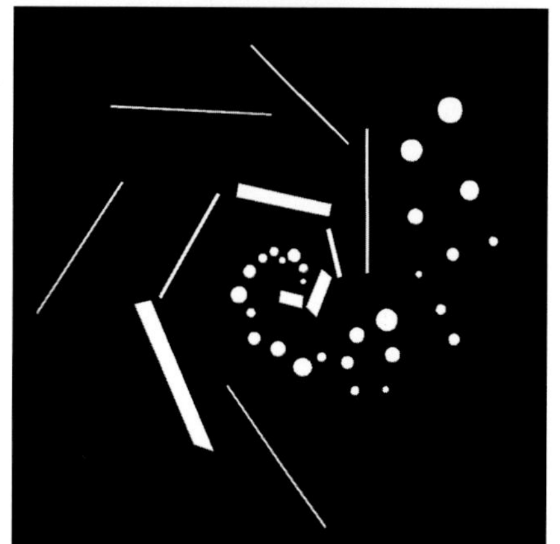

Poster for the Movement for Peace entitled 'Peace after Hiroshima'

Four 3 Dimensional murals/Environmental Art for the library of the Business Administration School at Bar Ilan University

Logotype for the Israel Prime Minister's office as a Peace Treaty symbol

Poster for the Gannett Outdoor Group entitled 'Stop Violence'

Poster entitled 'Again' promoting awareness of the emerging territories of the former Soviet empire

Symbol for Hemda Centre for Science Education

Sutherland Lyall Landscaping and Architecture

Landscaping has regained its importance in architecture over the past two decades. Sutherland Lyall, author of many books on modern British architecture and landscaping, talks about this trend using examples from his latest book, *Designing the New Landscape*. Copies of *Designing the New Landscape* as well as *Rock Sets* will be on sale at the lecture at Pentagram Design, 11 Needham Road, London W11 on Wednesday 27 January at 6.30 for 7.00pm. Admission is free for members, £2.50 for non-members. For further information contact Coralie Langston-Jones on 071 792 3812.

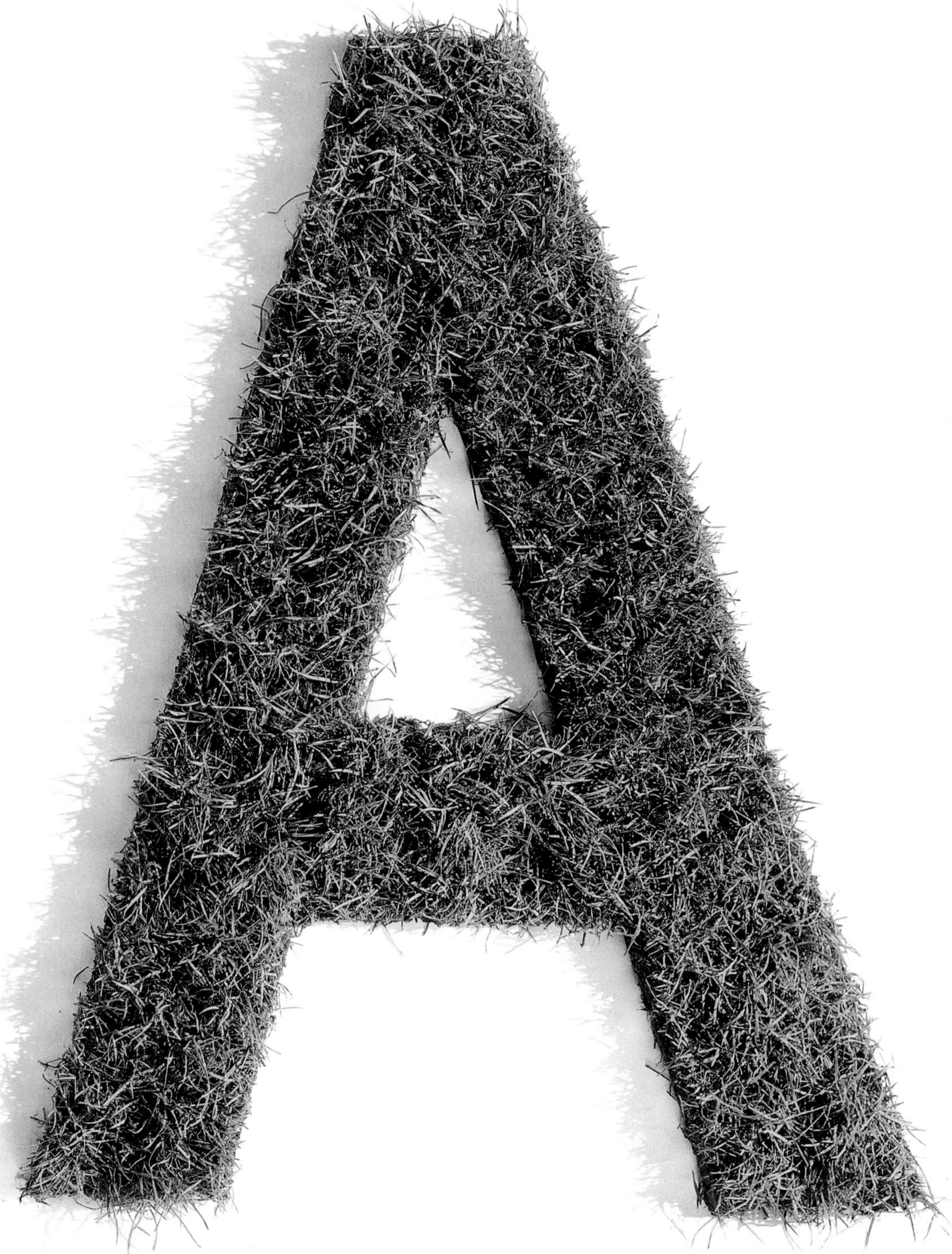

First Choice
Corporate Identity for Art & Architecture Limited, a society which promotes collaboration between artists, craftspeople and architects

'Art & Architecture is a society which exists to promote the widest collaboration between artists, craftspeople and architects in the interest of a more stimulating and convivial built environment. Posters designed to promote the organisation's series of lectures started with the idea of using the letter A, neatly representing 'art' and 'architecture' and illustrating this in a way that suggests the theme of each talk. As the poster designer, the challenge, and the pleasure, has been in seeing how far you can push one idea'

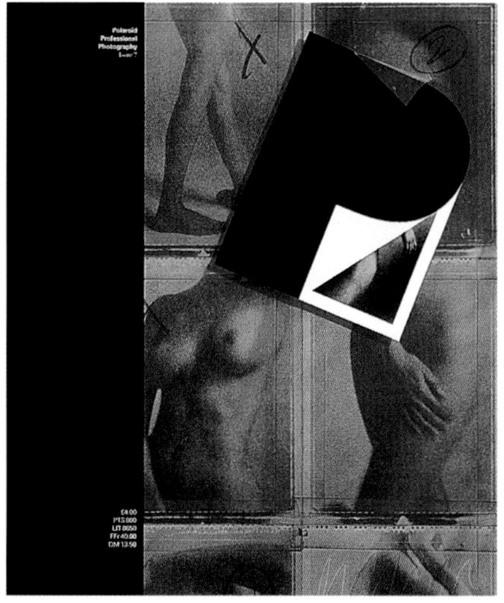

Corporate Identity for Art & Architecture Limited

Brochure for Radford and Ball, Glass Artists

Corporate Identity and packaging for the small independent dairy producers co-operative, The Dairy Farmers Co.

One of the bi-annual professional photographers publications, 'P Magazine' for the Polaroid Corporation

Corporate Identity and design programme for The Crafts Council

Branding development for London Radio for the client, News Radio International

BA-TSU 1994 HARAJUKU

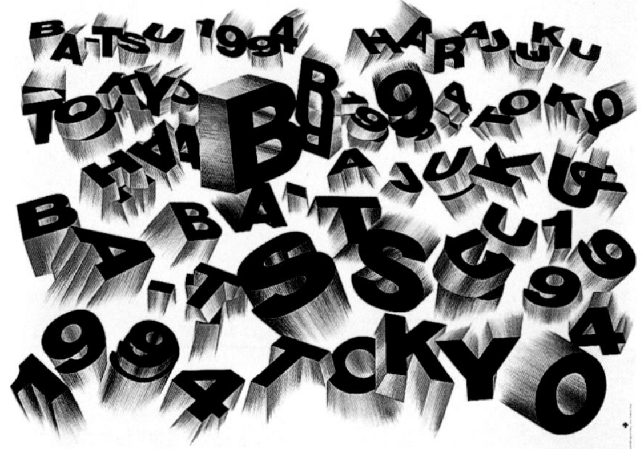
BA-TSU 1994 HARAJUKU

First Choice
Poster for Ba-Tsu Company Ltd

'This is designed for Ba-Tsu, a unique apparel company located in Harajuku, the centre of fashion in Tokyo. The company was founded by Mr Ruki Matsumoto in the mid 70's with his vision to create joyful clothing interweaving contemporary fashion of Harajuku into basic casuals. Harajuku is a most vivid town crowded by youth in their teens and twenties. The poster aims at expressing a vigorous image of the town with the typography, 'Harajuku Tokyo 1994' in combination with a collage of man and woman. Every letter of the typography is designed to portray human energy'

Poster for the Alpha Cubic Apparel Company entitled 'Alpha Cubic Good Face'

Poster for the Alpha Cubic Apparel Company entitled 'Alpha Cubic Bad Face'

Poster for the Dai Nippon Printing Company Trans Art Exhibition Opening at the Ginza Graphic Gallery

Poster for the promotion of Virgin Records 'Soul to Soul'

Poster for the Hasegawa Company Ltd, manufacturers and retailers of home size Buddist shrines

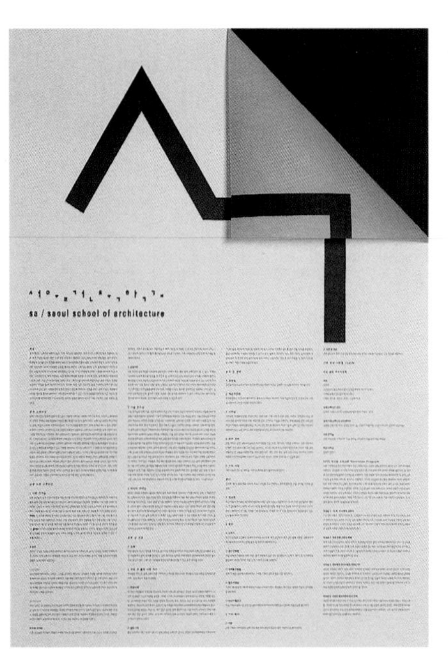
sa / seoul school of architecture

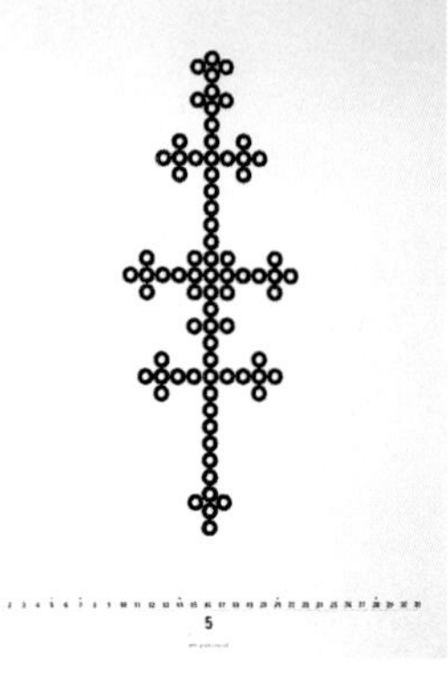

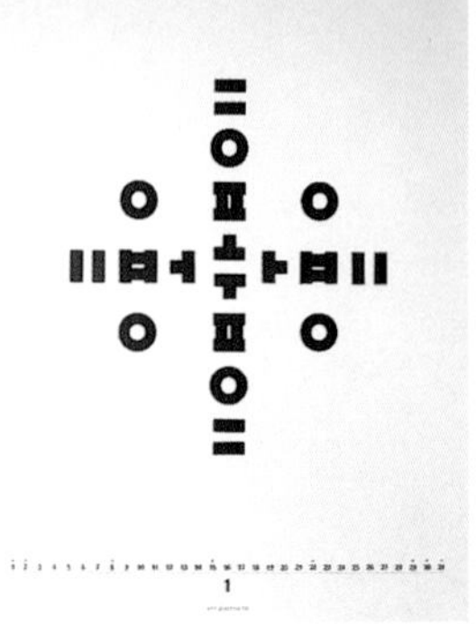

First Choice Logotype for the 50th anniversary of Korean Liberation

'This emblem was selected from among a number of entries submitted in a competition to create a symbol suitable for Korea's significant celebration of half a century since its liberation from the Japanese occupation. The waves and mountain are taken from the first line of the Korean anthem and are also related to the myths of Korea's foundation. The yin-yang symbol, which also appears on the national flag, is here meant to signify harmony between North and South and a future in which a unified Korea can take its proper place in the world'

광복
50

Poster for the Seoul School of Architecture

Poster for the FrontDMZ Cultural Movement

Book cover design for Tal Streeter, sculptor

1995 Calendar for Ahn Graphics Ltd

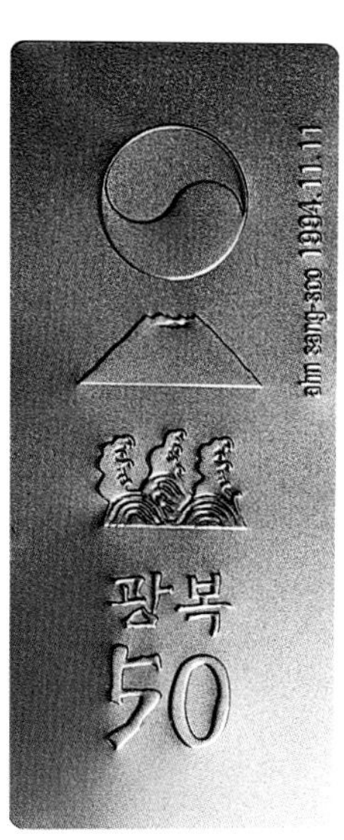

The big A.
Ambassador Arts. Maximum impact. Minimum price.

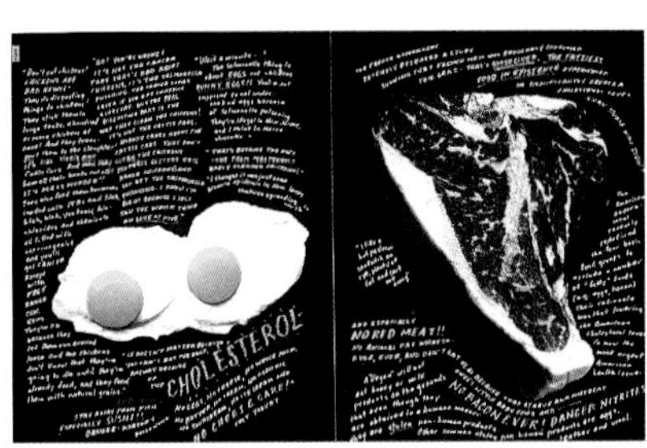

First Choice
Poster for Ambassador Arts Printers

''The Big A' was designed to promote the inexpensive aspect of Ambassador Arts screen printing capabilities. Pentagram made a symbol of gargantuan proportions by enlarging a typewritten character on a photocopier and making a collage of the pieces. This image was printed on oversized sheets of newsprint, a very poor quality stock. The superior quality of the silk screening process is revealed in the subtle differences among the shades of white that appear despite the flimsy paper. This poster has won numerous awards from the American Institute of Graphic Arts, the American Centre for Design, the Type Directors Club, the Lahti (Finland) X Poster Biennale, and 'Print' magazine, and has also appeared in Japan's 'Creation' magazine and 'Graphic Design: New York''

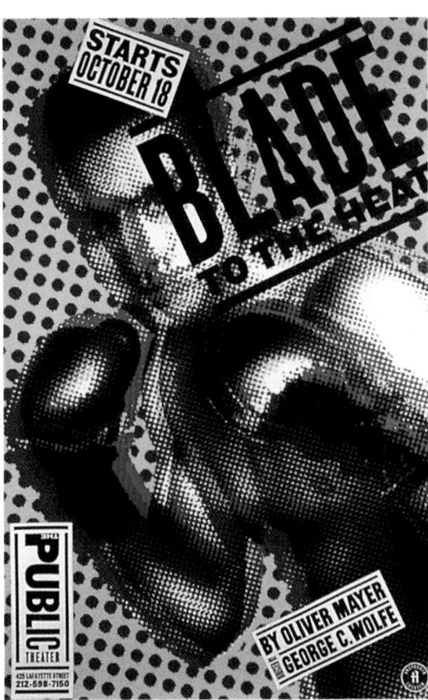

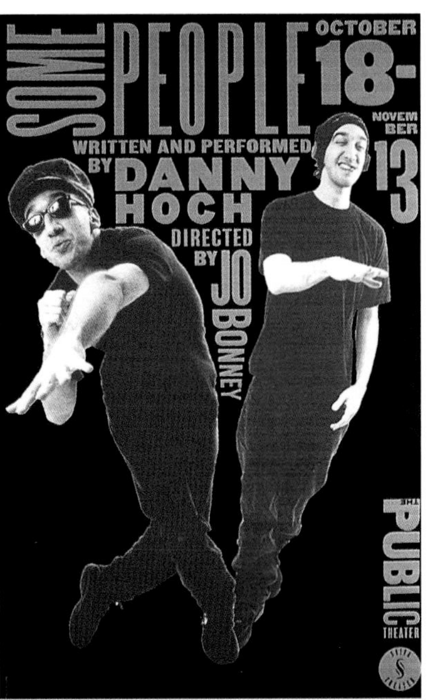

Poster promoting Ambassador Arts Printers and Champion International Corporation's Papers

'Great Ideas' posters for the School of Visual Arts

Publications entitled 'Subjective Reasoning' promoting Champion International's Kromekote line of papers

Poster for the Public Theatre entitled 'Blade to the Heat'

Poster for the Public Theatre entitled 'Some People'

Promotional Programme/billboard concepts for the Sony Corporation

EIN FROHES
WEIHNACHTSFEST
UND EIN GUTES
NEUES JAHR
Die Steirische
Volkspartei

Ein frohes
Weihnachtsfest
und ein gutes
Neues Jahr
Landeshauptmann
Dr. Josef Krainer

miteinander leben
Man muß die Menschen mögen,
um gute Politik zu machen.
Das verlangt ein Herz für
alle Landsleute, für unsere
Nachbarn und für
kommende Generationen
gleichermaßen. Und ein
G'spür für das Zumutbare.

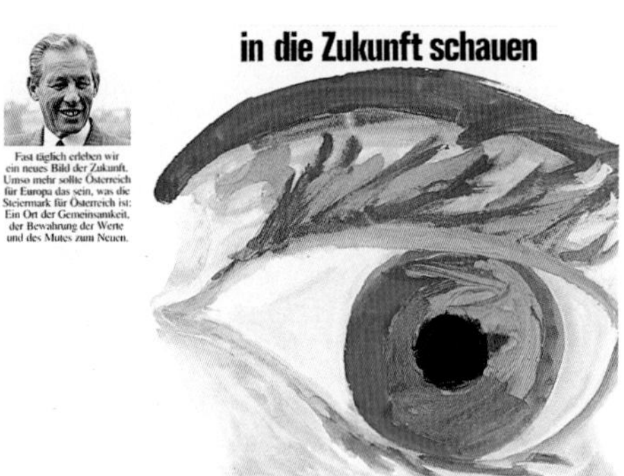
in die Zukunft schauen
Fast täglich erleben wir
ein neues Bild der Zukunft.
Umso mehr sollte Österreich
für Europa das sein, was die
Steiermark für Österreich ist:
Ein Ort der Gemeinsamkeit,
der Bewahrung der Werte
und des Mutes zum Neuen.

miteinander
reden
Besser ein offenes Wort zuviel
als eines zuwenig.
Doch was ausg'redt ist, hält.
So werden wir es auch über
unsere Grenzen hinaus halten:
Miteinander reden –
voneinander lernen.
Steirisches Klima
auf mitteleuropäisch.

B

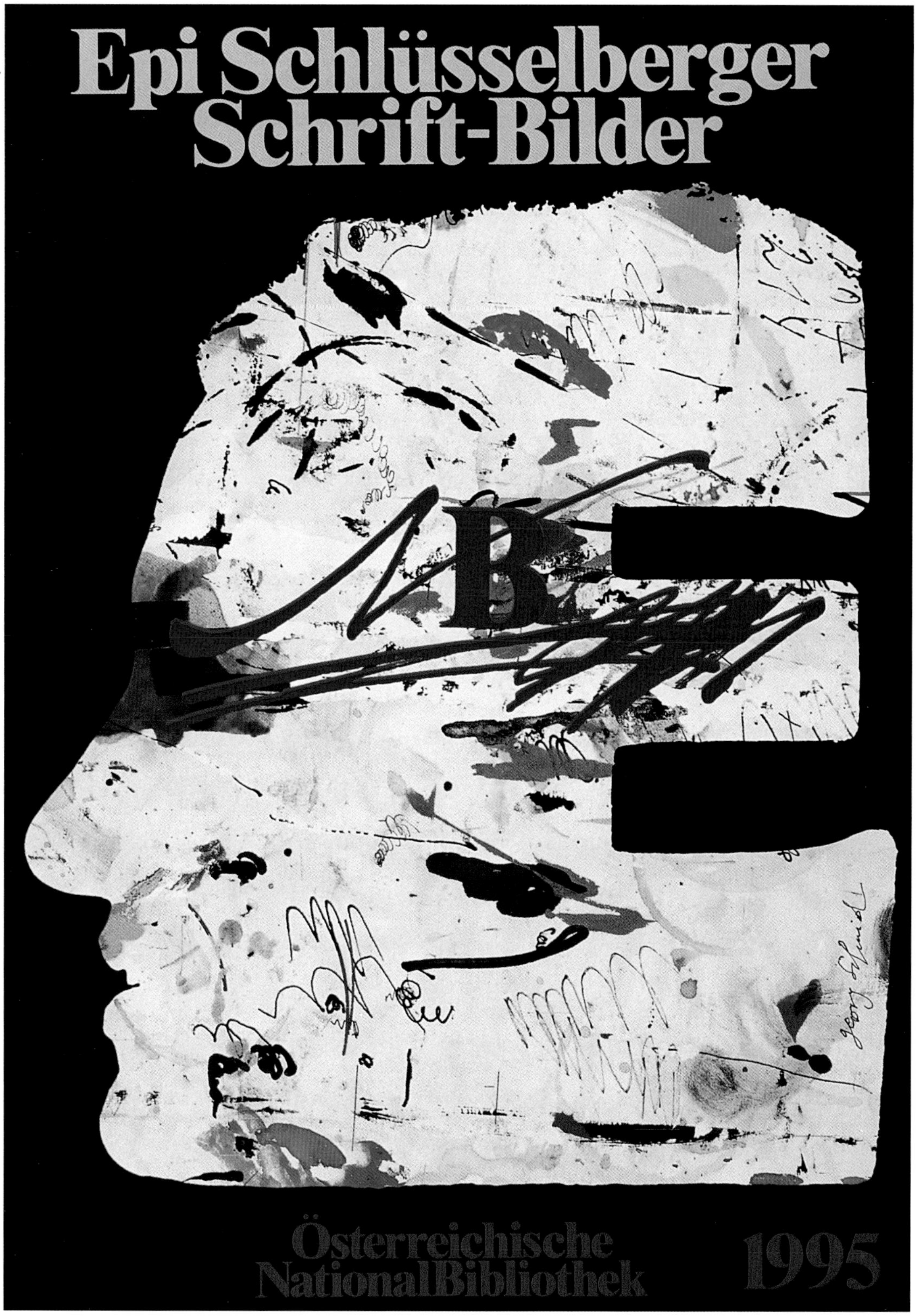

Epi Schlüsselberger
Schrift-Bilder

Österreichische
NationalBibliothek
1995

First Choice
Poster for the Austrian National Library

'This poster is my first choice. It's for an exhibition of Epi's work, using collages of letters. It is the first printing for the Austrian National Library including a new logo, the background is the paper on our table where we did the design for this famous insititution. It is the newest and most important project we are working on. Epi is my partner and my wife, and I tried to make a homage to her'

Poster promoting New Years greetings from the Styrian Peoples Party

Poster promoting New Years greetings from the Governor of Styria

Poster series for election campaign entitled
'Livetogether'
'Lookforward"
'Discuss'

Logotype for Austrian National Library

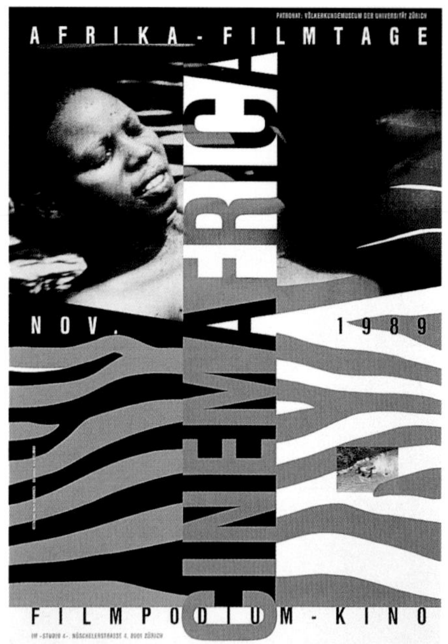

AFRIKA - FILMTAGE
CINEMAFRICA
NOV.
1989
FILMPODIUM - KINO

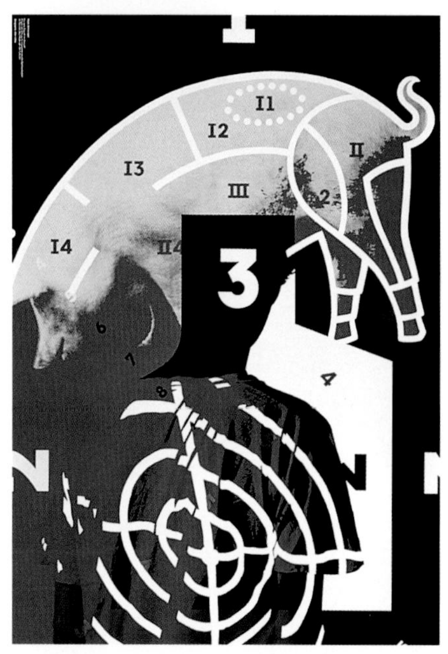

Die Stipendiatinnen des Eidgenössischen Stipendiums für angewandte Kunst 1990
Museum für Gestaltung Zürich
Im Rückenwind

DIE WELT IM KASTEN
VON DER CAMERA OBSCURA ZUR AUDIOVISION
STRAUHOF ZÜRICH
Ausstellung: 31. März bis 18. Mai 1994

HENRY VAN DE VELDE
EIN EUROPÄISCHER KÜNSTLER SEINER ZEIT
MUSEUM FÜR GESTALTUNG ZÜRICH
28. AUGUST BIS 31. OKTOBER 1993

First Choice
Poster for the African Film Festival 1991 'Cinemafrica'

'It is my first choice because firstly there are no clichés, the stripes of the zebra are not really on the poster like they were on the previous one in 1989. But they appear when the newton rings are seen in context with the word 'Africa'. Secondly, It fits perfectly in the series of the posters that I have designed for Cinemafrica, the annual biennal African film festival. My concept is to use only black and white in silkscreen printing. This one is printed black on white paper. It deals with the aesthetics of the interior architecture of the cinema where the festival takes place. The cinema was designed by Roman Clemens, an ex-Bauhaus student in 1949'

Poster for Serigraphie Uldry Printers entitled 'B-4'

Poster for the African Film Festival, Cinemafrica 1985

Poster for the City of Switzerland entitled 'For a Future with Future'

Poster for the scholars of the Swiss Scholarship for Applied Arts 1990 entitled 'With Tailwind'

Poster for the Stranhhof Museum entitled 'The World in the Box'

Poster for the Zurich Museum of Design

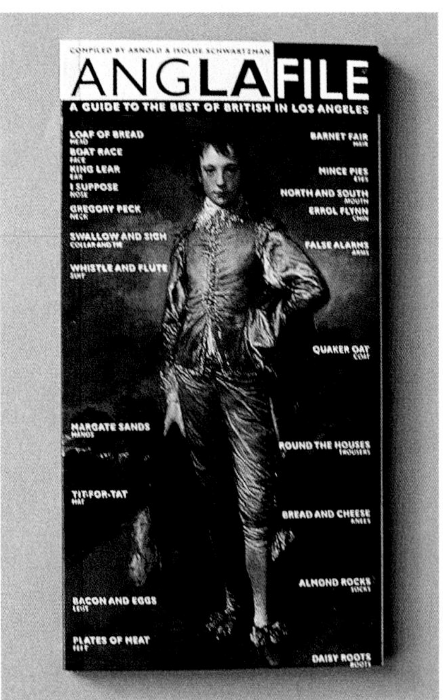
COMPILED BY ARNOLD & ISOLDE SCHWARTZMAN
ANGLAFILE
A GUIDE TO THE BEST OF BRITISH IN LOS ANGELES
LOAF OF BREAD
HEAD
BOAT RACE
FACE
KING LEAR
EAR
I SUPPOSE
NOSE
GREGORY PECK
NECK
SWALLOW AND SIGH
COLLAR AND TIE
WHISTLE AND FLUTE
SUIT
BARNET FAIR
HAIR
MINCE PIES
EYES
NORTH AND SOUTH
MOUTH
ERROL FLYNN
CHIN
FALSE ALARMS
ARMS
QUAKER OAT
COAT
MARGATE SANDS
HANDS
ROUND THE HOUSES
TROUSERS
TIT-FOR-TAT
HAT
BREAD AND CHEESE
KNEES
ALMOND ROCKS
SOCKS
BACON AND EGGS
LEGS
PLATES OF MEAT
FEET
DAISY ROOTS
BOOTS

MOTION PICTURE CENTENNIAL
USA
29
- Edison Kinetoscopic Record of a Sneeze -
Taken & Copyrighted by W.K.L.Dickson
Orange N.J. Jan. 7th/94

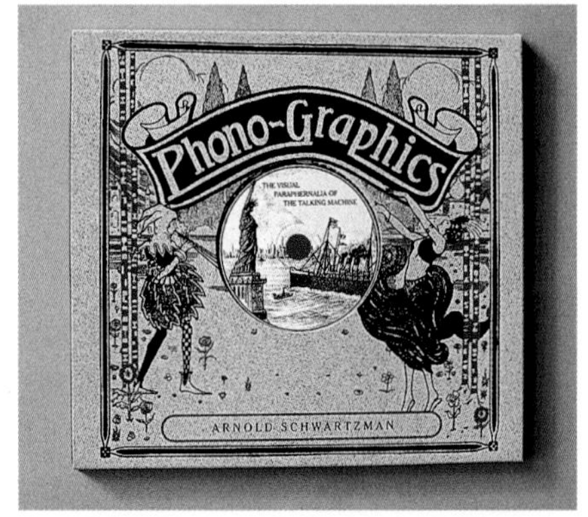
Phono-Graphics
THE VISUAL PARAPHERNALIA OF THE TALKING MACHINE
ARNOLD SCHWARTZMAN

GRAVEN
ARNOLD SCHWARTZMAN
FOREWORD BY CHAIM POTOK
IMAGES
GRAPHIC MOTIFS OF THE JEWISH GRAVESTONE

1992 Cabernet Sauvignon
TO BE
FOR
RNOT
TO BE

007

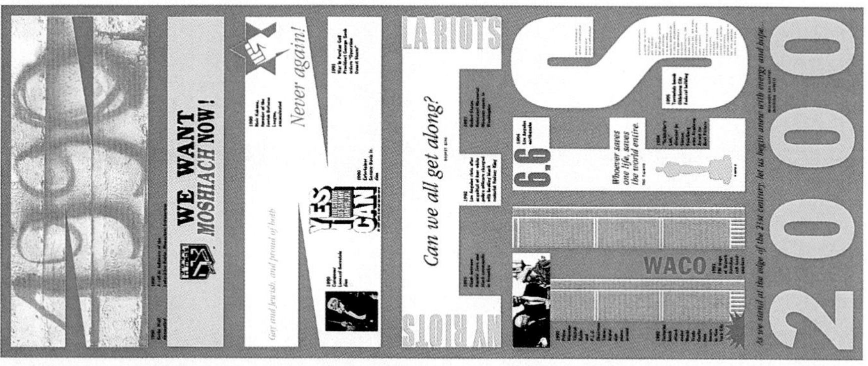

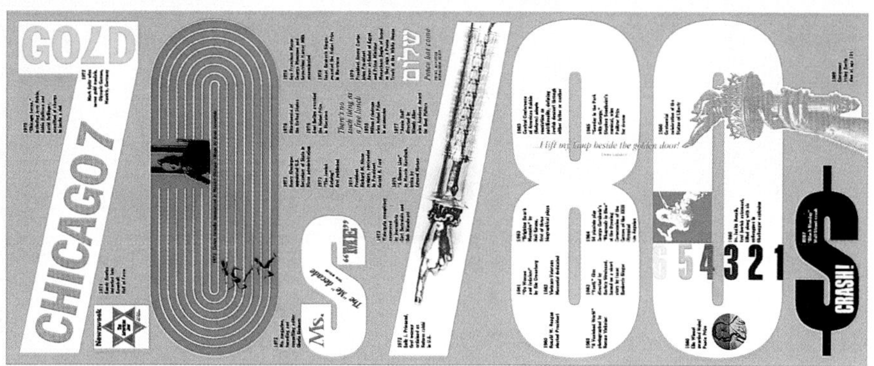

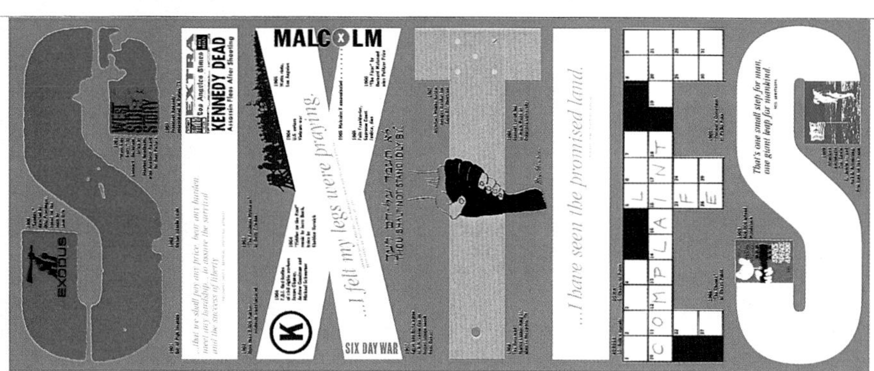

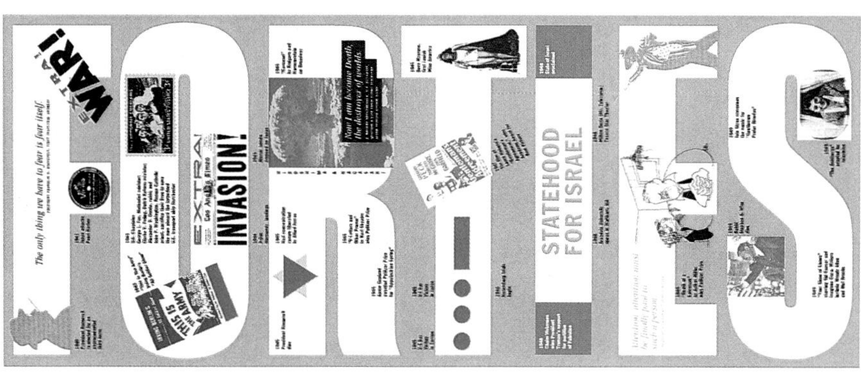

First Choice
A time line mural commissioned by the Skirball Cultural Centre, Los Angeles

'My first choice invariably is my most current work. This 24 x 10 time line mural is adjacent to the eight screen video 'kaleidoscope' permanent exhibit that I created for this museum.
The time line covers the last fifty years of Jewish American history, each panel depicting a decade. I enjoyed the research as much as the design process, my wife Isolde took care of the production and its thirteen complex silkscreen workings.
In a climate of political correctness, I was first asked to remove the red nail polish I had added to the silver Torah pointer representing the first woman rabbi!'

Cover of a guide book published by Schwartzman and his wife to coincide with a major British Arts Festival in Los Angeles

Postage stamp design for the Motion Picture Centennial Committee

Book cover and slipcase for 'Phono-Graphics, The Visual Paraphernalia of the Talking Machine'

Book jacket for 'Graven Images, Graphic Motifs of the Jewish Gravestones', a photographic essay which Schwartzman has been compiling for the last twenty years

One of a series of wine labels used for fundraising for Shakespeare's Globe Playhouse, London

Design for an invitation honouring 'Cubby' Broccoli, the producer of the James Bond films

First Choice
Corporate Identity for Mowhawk Paper Mills entitled 'Things are going to get ugly'

'This promotion for unique imported papers alerts designers to expect the unexpected and warns that their perceptions may be altered. The deliberately ironic interplay of familiar landscapes as precious miniatures, 'ugly' text, and printing techniques demonstrates the exquisite beauty in the commonplace while focusing attention on practical virtues as well as the extraordinary beauty of the papers themselves'

Announcement for a legal practice, Nottage and Ward entitled 'Gentle Peace'

Announcement for the merging of two photo libraries, Fade AllStock and Tony Stone Images, Seattle

Self promotional piece for Concrete Publishing

Promotional piece for The American Centre for design for Ace Lithographers entitled 'No Suprises'

Self promotional piece for Concrete slide presentations entitled 'Inside' and 'Outside'

Design for a lingerie catalogue for artist Sarah Schwartz, New York

A TRAVELING FELLOWSHIP IN ARCHITECTURE
the blues
LYCEUM
competition
93

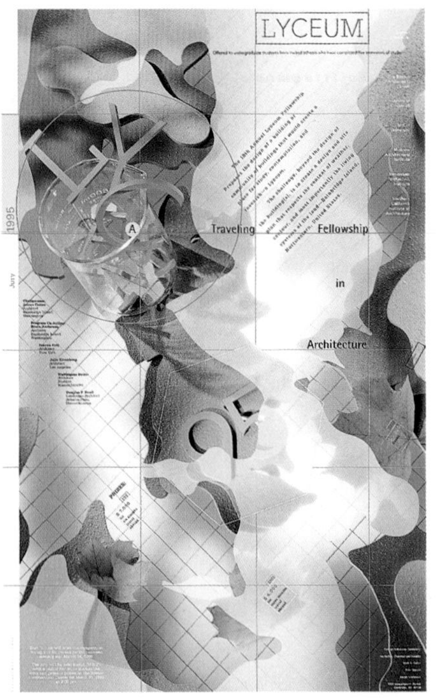
LYCEUM
1995
Traveling Fellowship in Architecture

electronic
IMAGING
Reynolds-DeWalt Printing, Inc.

Berkeley Typographers
Agfa Compugraphic

A TECHNICAL
NIGHTMARE
BROUGHT TO YOU BY
LASERSCAN

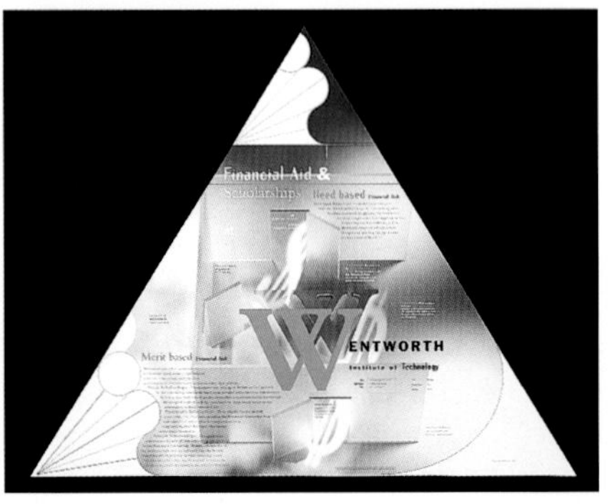
Financial Aid &
Need based
Merit based
WENTWORTH
Institute of Technology

First Choice
Book designed for
Ferrington Guitars

'The book's asymmetric shape maturally evolved as a reaction to the off-centre shapes of Danny's guitars. We photographed each guitar before we did any layouts because we wanted the forms of the guitars to be the driving visual force. Because guitars aren't objects that have to sit on the ground or a surface like a chair or a vase, we had freedom to photograph them from every angle without making them look too frenetic. The forms of the guitars were so harmonious to begin with, the various views nestled effortlessly into each other and the layouts designed themselves. The beauty and excitement of the guitars was unusually rich. This project taught us how to have tremendous reverence for the subject material and that is a lesson we have carried forward'

Poster for a Travelling Fellowship in Architecture '93

Poster for a Travelling Fellowship in Architecture '95

Poster for Reynolds DeWalt Printing

Poster for Laserscan Inc

Poster for Berkeley Typographers

Scholarship Poster for Wentworth Institute of Technology

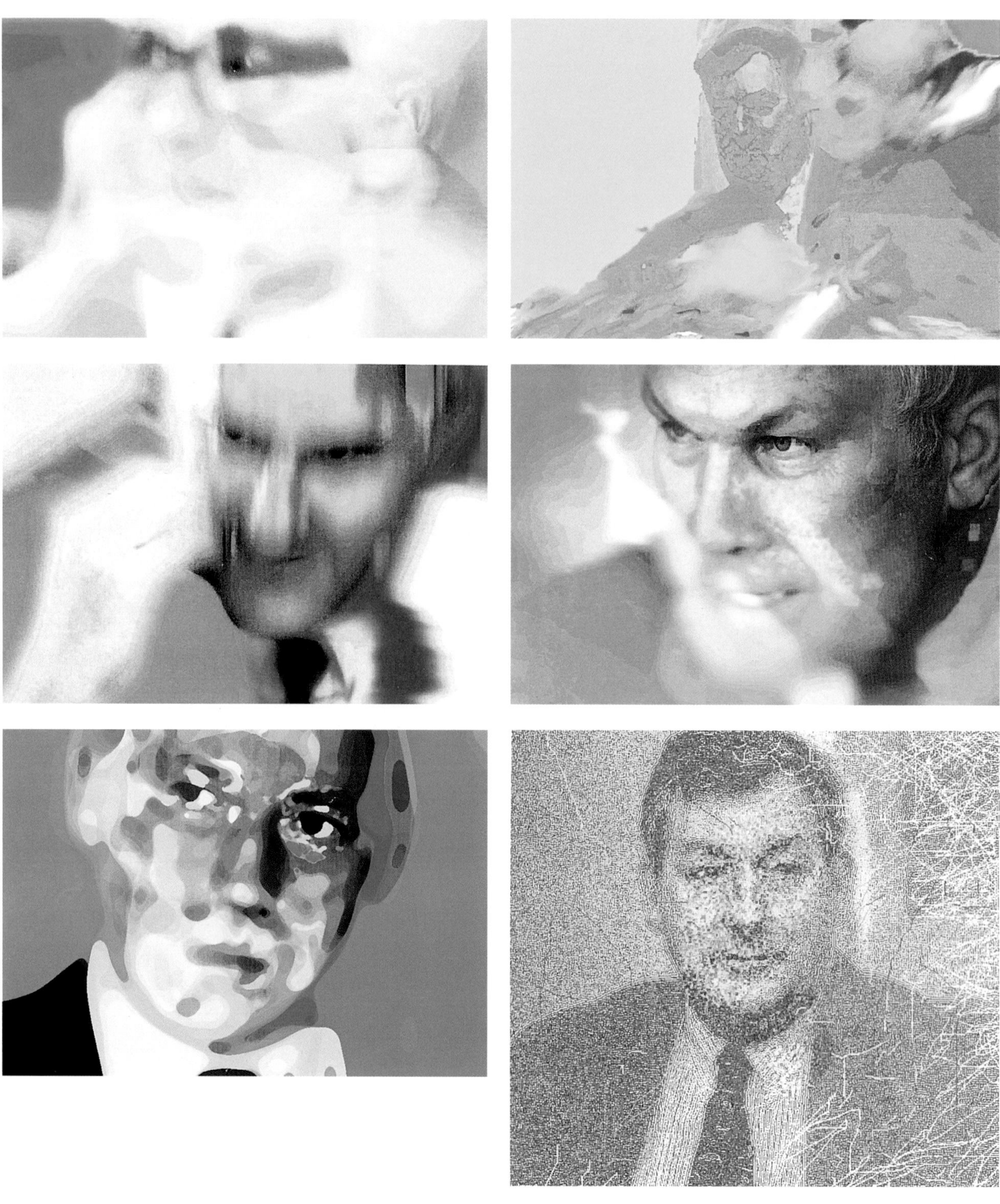

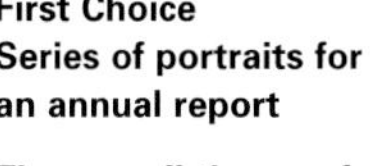

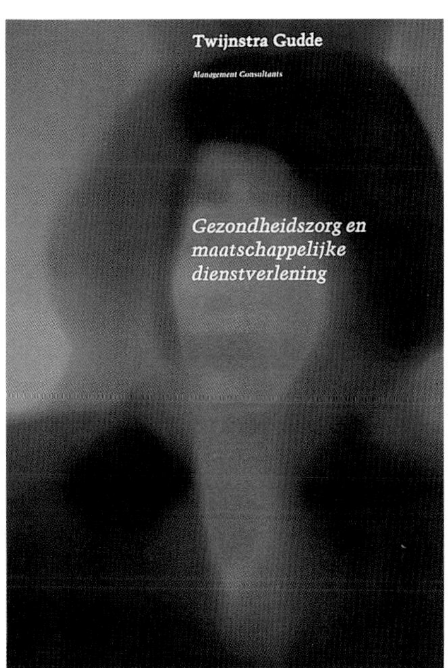

First Choice
Series of portraits for an annual report

'The overall theme of all the annual reports of Twijnstra Gudde, a management consultancy firm, is 'interaction between people'. Every year a variation on this theme is made. With the limitation that the conventional category of 'smiling idiots' will be avoided.
My first choice is the year when the idea was to paraphrase on 'officially painted portraits'. Modern technology makes it possible to do now what was impossible in the past: produce over fifty 'painted' portraits within fourteen days. Using 'Photoshop' in an unconventional way, fifty lively and dynamic portraits were used'

Series of corporate brochures for Twijnstra Gudde

Cover featuring symbol and logotype for the society of Health Insurance, Netherlands

Cover for the Twijnstra Gudde annual report with the theme 'Faces of Things'

Sculpturistic variation of the Ministry of Transport, Public Works and Water Management logo

Corporate Identity for the Ministry of Justice

Logo for the refuse incinerator of Amsterdam

モリサワ

十 Y

P 三

DESIGN: HENRY STEINER © 1991

First Choice
Poster for Morisawa & Company Limited, Japan entitled TYPE

'Over dinner after the 1990 Morisawa judging, Mitsuo Katsui referring to some ancient characters in a Chinese almanac asked me what were the archetypical letter forms for a Western designer. On reflection I realised that both the Latin and Chinese writing systems are inspired by stone incriptions. This poster confronts examples of both and synthesises them into the word 'TYPE'. It exemplifies my continuing interest in the contrast and fusion of iconography from East and West'

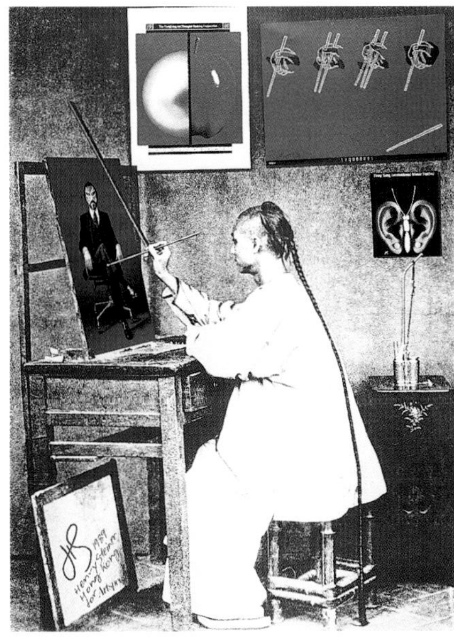

Poster entitled 'Self-portrait'

Cover design for 'IDEA' magazine, No 226 entitled 'Fung Shui'

Poster for Ginza Graphic Gallery

Poster for Northern Telecom Asia/Pacific entitled 'The Joy Luck Club'

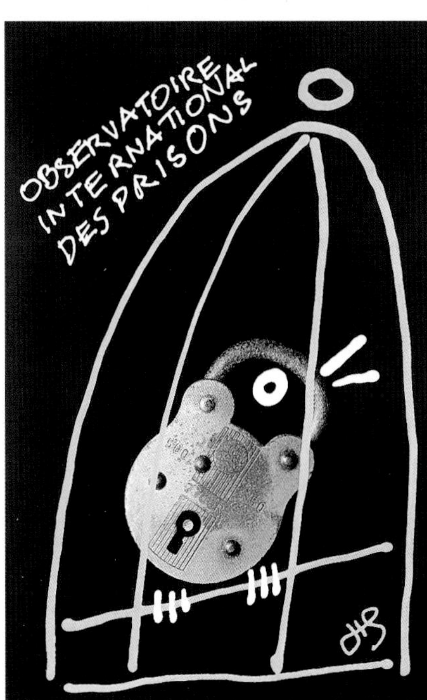

Poster for Observatoire International des Prisons entitled 'Prisoners Rights'

Poster for Quality Paper Specialist Ltd, Hong Kong entitled 'Conserve Nature'

REVCO
CAVS
GUND ARENA
CAVS

Glad to be of service
The Gas Company

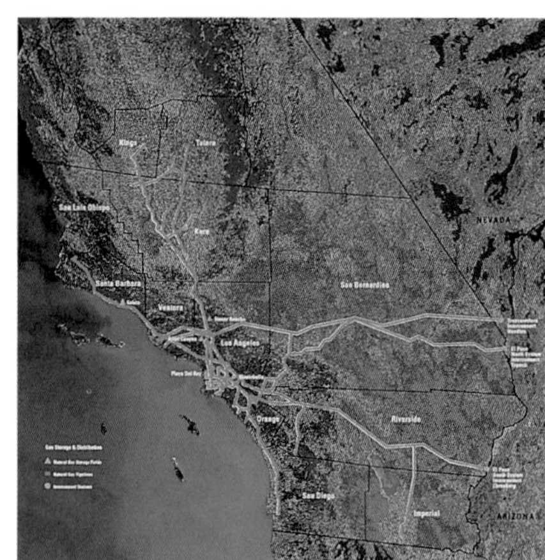

Kings
Tulare
San Luis Obispo
Kern
NEVADA
Santa Barbara
San Bernardino
Ventura
Los Angeles
Playa Del Rey
Orange
Riverside
San Diego
Imperial
ARIZONA

DS+S/P@NY!
THE MASTERS SERIES: DEBORAH SUSSMAN
MARCH 20 - APRIL 7, 1993

First Choice
AIGA Call for Entries

'After concentrating energy for a long time on big environmental projects, I found creative release in going back to one of my early great loves: the pleasurable act of cutting paper or 'drawing with scissors'. The American Institute of Graphic Arts 'Call for Entries' was reasonably complicated, so it got to be a team effort on the part of Robert Cordell, Holly Hampton and me. We all ended up cutting some paper, having fun and combining type set on computer with the hand-wrought images. This all inspired me to continue and rediscover the power of the hand. Drawing was my first passion: one which I plan to indulge in lots more'

Corporate logo for Euro Disney Information Kiosk 'i point'

Graphics and Interior design for Gund Arena/Cleveland Cavalier Basketball Court

Corporate Identity Programme and Uniforms for Gas Company Energy Resource Centre

Map design for Gas Company Energy Resourse Centre Lobby

Poster for a Visual Arts Museum Exhibit, New York

Development and design of Apple Computer's new Research and Development Campus

ASDA
ASDA
Chocolate
Smooth Milk
Chocolate
200g
BEST BEFORE END:
SEE REVERSE

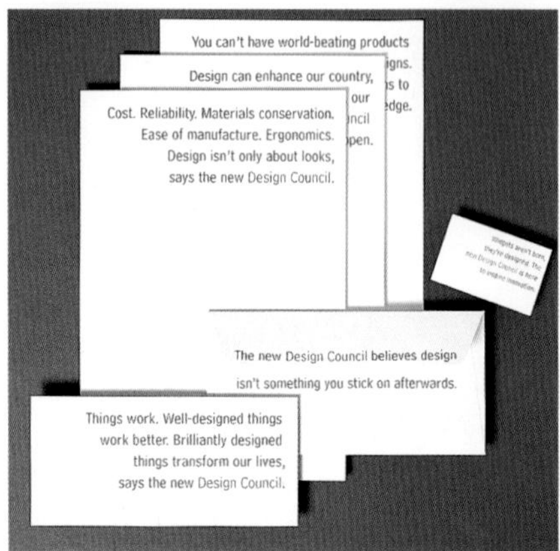
You can't have world-beating products
Design can enhance our country,
Cost. Reliability. Materials conservation.
Ease of manufacture. Ergonomics.
Design isn't only about looks,
says the new Design Council.
The new Design Council believes design
isn't something you stick on afterwards.
Things work. Well-designed things
work better. Brilliantly designed
things transform our lives,
says the new Design Council.

mencap
mencap
mencap
mencap
mencap

BODDINGTONS
BITTER
BODDINGTONS
BITTER
BITTER
BITTER

First Choice
The Partners 'Time Capsule of the Future'

'A tin 'time capsule' which takes a light-hearted look at what everyday life might be like in the near future to celebrate The Partner's 10th anniversary. Every year, a 'book' to celebrate our anniversary has been sent to clients and friends, based on the material associated with that year. The time capsule includes a transatlantic bridge linking Europe and the USA; a 10-hour decimalised watch; an instant knowledge patch; tobacco-tipped cigarette; sugar sachet from Buckingham Palace Motel; a travel card for travel in the Northern Hemisphere...and so on. The reason the time capsule is our favourite is that it exemplified what we (try to!) do best for our clients: the intelligent and effective application of creativity to design, often with a twist of wit, and with great attention to detail'

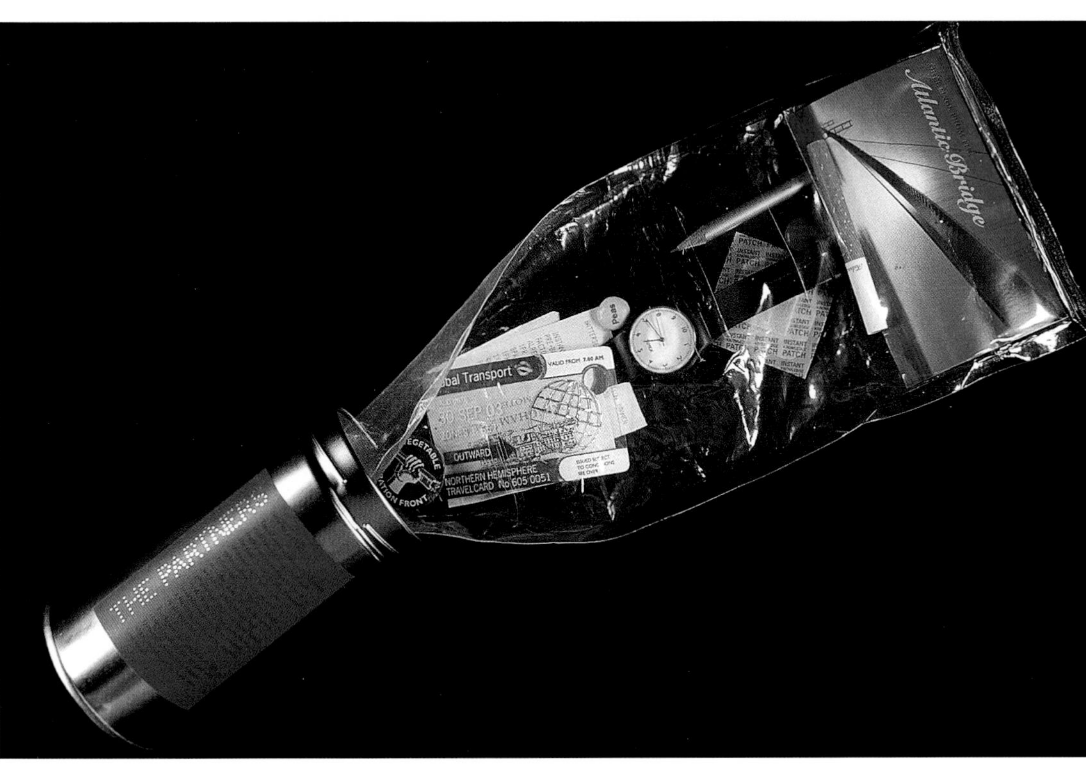

Packaging design for ASDA supermarkets' home brand

Corporate Identity for the Design Council of Great Britain

Corporate Identity for Mencap, The Royal Society for the Mentally Handicapped

Corporate Identity for Boddingtons Brewery

Design for Thrislington (94 calendar)

Annual Report design for BSO/Origin

Gary Baxter
James Beveridge
Aziz Cami
Shaun Dew
Stephen Gibbons
Mark Lee
David Stuart

THE PARTNERS

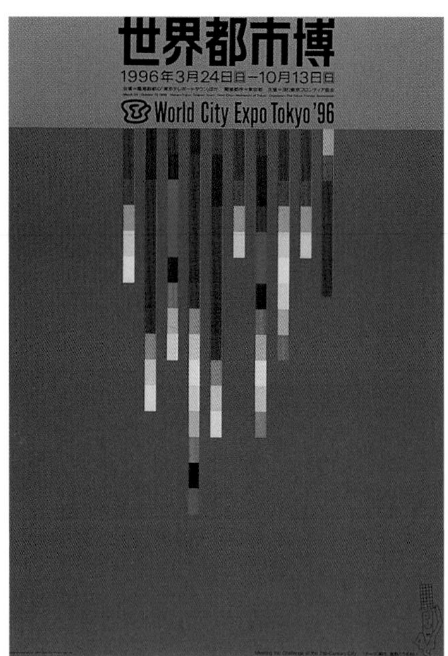
世界都市博
1996年3月24日日–10月13日日
World City Expo Tokyo '96

Internationale Musikfestwochen 17.8.–10.9. 1994
Luzern

1993
Cartelloni Svizzeri premiati
Affiches Suisses primées
Prämierte Schweizer Plakate
Placats Svizzers premiads

domus

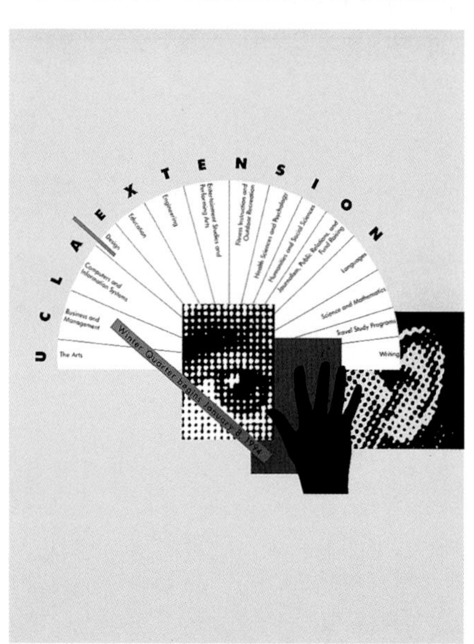
UCLA EXTENSION

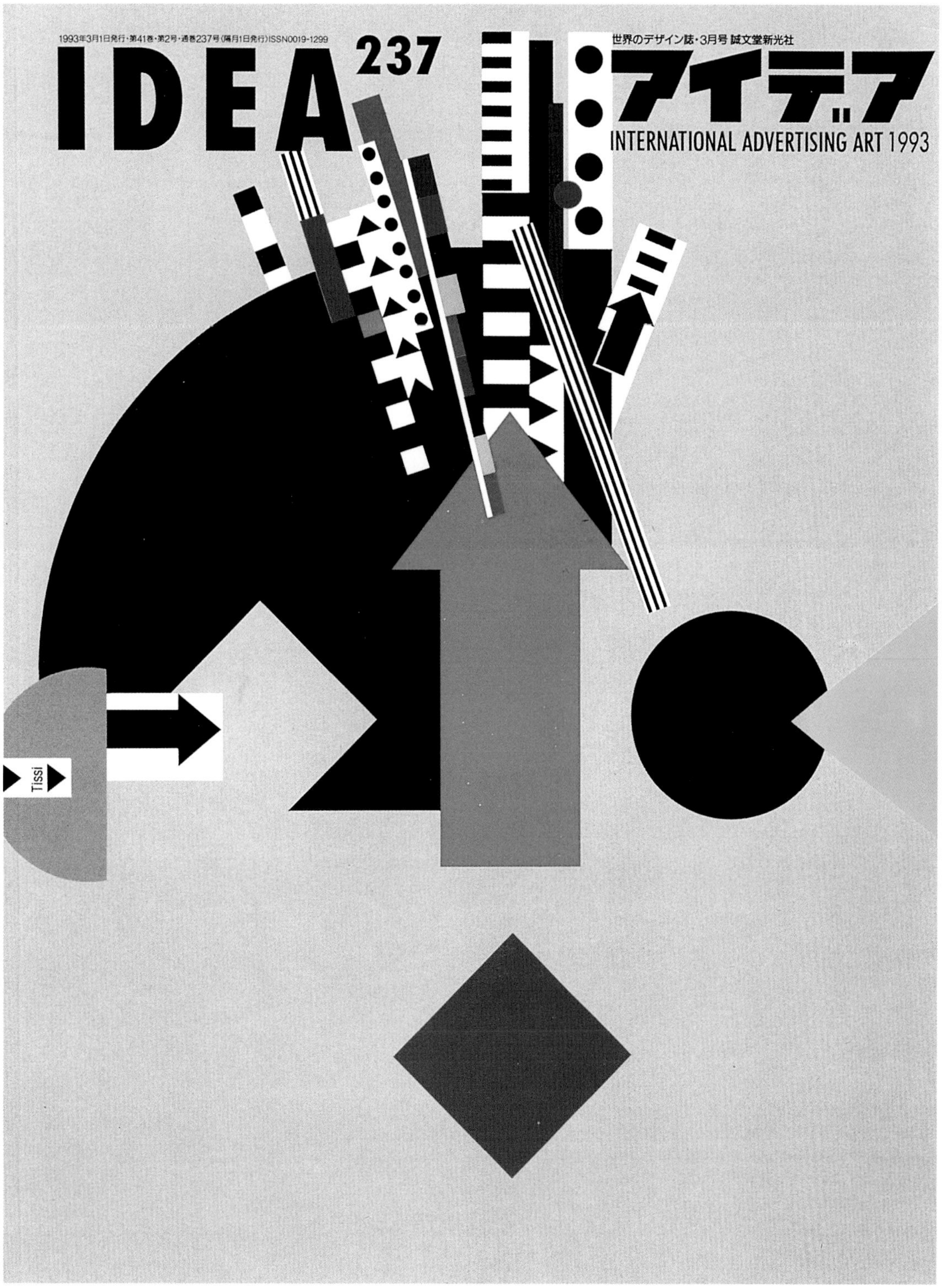

First Choice
Cover design for 'IDEA' magazine

'It was difficult for me to decide which piece to choose as number one: The poster 'World City Expo Tokyo '96' or the cover for 'IDEA' magazine. The reason why I chose this cover as my favourite is because it conveys an impression of the kind of design style I have been using for my work during the past years. I would hope it represents a typical example. I was very pleased that I was asked by a Japanese publisher to design a cover for their renowned design magazine - all the more because in the same issue a portrait of our studio Odermatt & Tissi was presented under the headline 'World Masters''

Poster for World City Expo Tokyo 96

Poster for International Festival of Music Lucerne 1994

Poster for the Exhibition of the Prized Swiss Posters 1993

Poster for Serenaden 1993 for Cultural Affairs Department

Cover design for 'Domus' magazine

Cover design for UCLA Extension

ome rain
-to-sound
leechesandjo
feet above the earth
liquid trees
boy in my
e Submassive
aller
belief ha

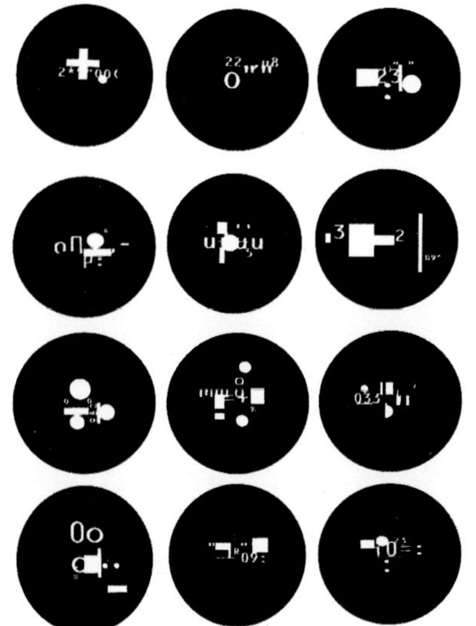

First Choice
Double page spread
from 'mmm...Skyscraper
I love you'

don't put your hand
where you wouldn't put
your face

she said

rat
with
face
onion
drag
clean
I'm a new
with urge
phone
zone
of stainless steel
got
charity
sex
rhythm
skin
meat
diggers

kissboots
recycled blondes
the
little bone
oozing
a beggar's dog
the wind

Personal project entitled 'False Sciences Series'

A page from Flux entitled 'MTV Awards Brochure'

Personal project entitled 'Agitators List'

Double page spread from Flux entitled 'MTV Awards Brochure'

Corporate Identity for Echo Records

Poster/press ad for Adidas

At Disney Consumer Products (Europe & Middle East)

...there's more **magic** than ever!

28

merchandise

"Licensing **SUCCESS** is evident

on the faces of delighted consumers..."

Disney products are the most fun and innovative in the market place. And the key to merchandise licensing is teamwork. It involves the dedicated efforts of Disney marketers and artists working with committed licensees, retailers, and promotional partners. Their success can be seen in stores and homes throughout Europe and the Middle East - and on the faces of delighted consumers of every age.

Our evergreen properties, the standard characters, are the lovable gang of Mickey, Minnie, Donald, Daisy, Goofy, Pluto, and all the rest. An unending stream of new creative concepts - brands, themes, and trends - keeps the standard characters fun, fresh, and fashionable.

The spectacular success of our recent animated films, "Beauty and the Beast," "Aladdin," "The Lion King" and others, has opened a new golden era for licensees. By turning the adventure, humor, and romance of the film themes into products, we turn film viewers into consumers.

Superb merchandise opportunities extend the life cycle of each property through home video, TV, and park events and theatrical re-releases.

Disney licensing offers fun and innovative products in:

apparel
toys
gifts
food
home furnishings
personal care
stationery
consumer electronics

First Choice
Brochure for Disney Consumer Products

'I am very proud of these chosen jobs and find it hard to choose a 'first'. I feel all the more proud that, during these recent overcautious, recessionary years, we have tried hard to produce innovative work which increased business for our clients. This brochure represents a learning curve between us and a new client. It was for the licensing department of Disney in Europe and the Middle East, and was aimed at potential 'partners', explaining what Disney brings to the partnership. The client was more used to being the 'expert' than being the 'client'. They wanted to show an avalanche of Disney products, it was part of our job to demonstrate that 'less is more'. The biggest thrill was when our client phoned to say 'NOW, I understand what you were trying to achieve with white space!''

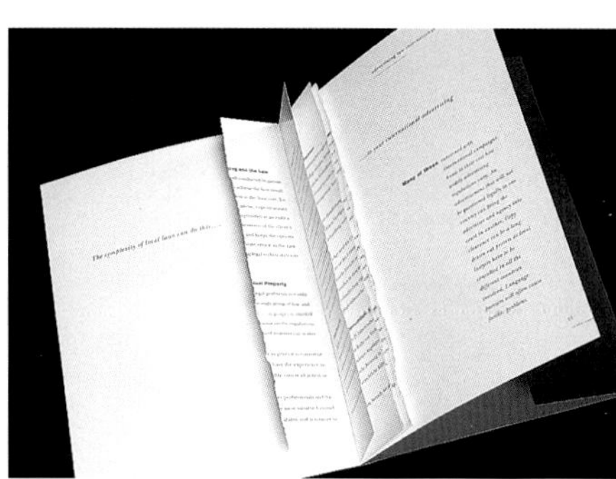

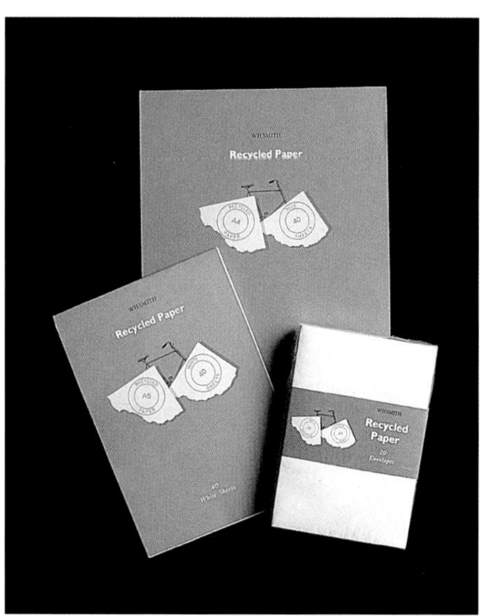

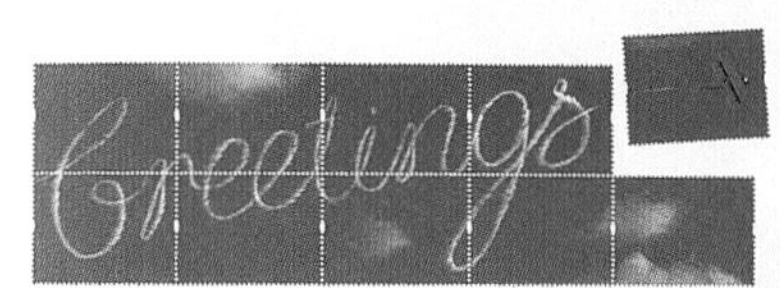

The Story of Greetings Stamps

Calendar design for photographer Robert Dowling entitled 'A Pigs Ear'

Design for a laser engraved Thank You card for ISTD Paper

Brochure design for International Consortium of Lawyers entitled 'Advertising Law'

Poster for London Transport's 60th Anniversary

Range of stationery packaging for WHSmith

Book design for Royal Mail entitled 'The Story of Greetings Stamps'

Les Diaboliques
Maggie Nicols Irene Schweizer Joëlle Léandre
Freitag 4. November 94 20.30 Uhr, Mohren
Jazz in Willisau

Eindruck
Ausdruck
Siebdruck
Bösch Stans Luzern

Jazz in Willisau
Freitag, 26. November 93
20.30 Uhr, Mohren
RAY ANDERSON ALLIGATORY BAND
feat. Lew Soloff, Jerome Harris, Tommy Campell
Gregory Jones
Frank Colon

WILLEM
BREUKER
KOLLEKTIEF

13.–23. Oktober 1994
olma
St.Gallen
Schweizer Messe
für Land- und Milchwirtschaft

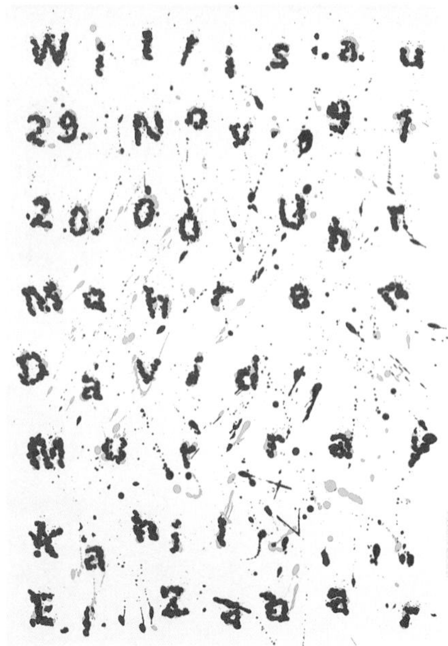

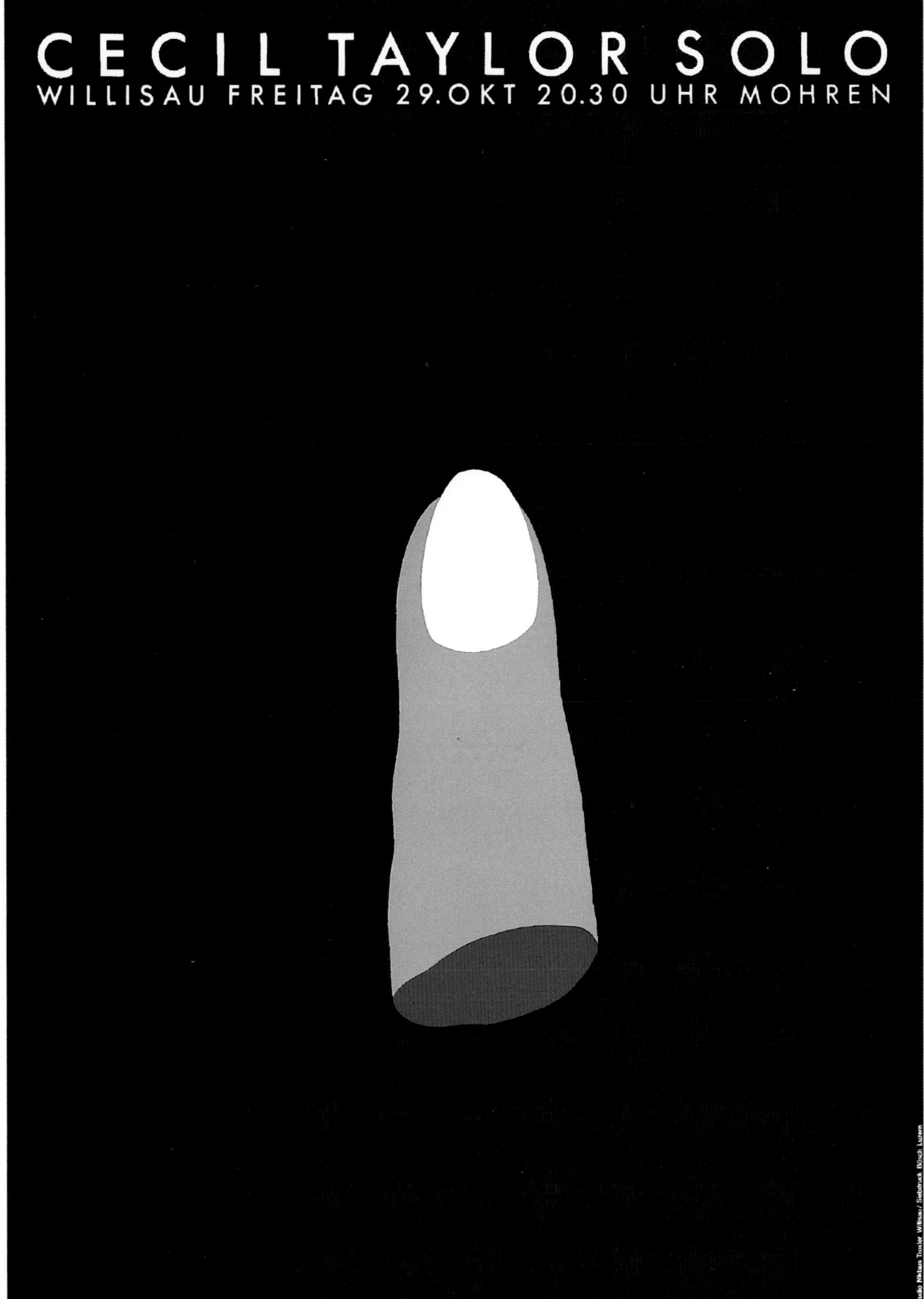

First Choice
Poster for Free Jazz piano player Cecil Taylor

'A finger, pointing like a signal to the writing, as a symbol for the kamikaze-like piano solo performance that does not admit any compromise'

Poster for Jazz in Willisau, a concert by Les Diaboliques

Poster for Bosch Siebdruck Stans Luzerne, a silkscreen printer

Poster for Jazz in Willisau, a concert by a new group called Alligatory Band

Poster for Jazz in Willisau, a concert by Willem Breuker Kollektief

Poster for OLMA St. Gallen

Poster for Jazz in Willisau, a concert by David Murray and Kahil El'Zabar

WOODS
BAGOT
·125·
YEARS

First Choice
Label for Woods Bagot Architects 125th Anniversary Celebration Gift Package

'The bottle (which contains a limited edition Aged Muscat) has a sculptural, monumental perception. The company logotype was deep-etched into the glass bottle. The outer presentation unit was especially made for this concept in stippled matt grey coated aluminium. The materials used (and the simple yet elegant forms) convey to recipients of the package, a sound, prestigious structural quality in keeping with and portraying the philosophy and status of the architectural company. A very pleasing solution...My First Choice!'

Label design for Nautilus Cabernet Sauvignon, Merlot and Cabernet Franc 1992 Vintage from Marlborough Region, New Zealand

Label design for Bluegrass Cabernet Sauvignon 1993 Vintage from Saddler's Creek, Hunter Valley

Label design for Octavius I 1988 Vintage Coonawarra Cabernet Sauvignon for Yalumba

Label design for Avon Graphics, specialist foil printers entitled 'The Christmas Spirit 1994'

Label design for Voss Chardonnay from Voss Vineyards, USA

Label design for Saddler's Creek Sauternes and Muscat, Hunter Valley

LES ENFANTS TERRIBLES
THE 1993 SAN FRANCISCO
MUSEUM OF MODERN ART
DESIGN LECTURE SERIES
PRESENTED BY THE
AMERICAN INSTITUTE
OF GRAPHIC ARTS
SAN FRANCISCO CHAPTER

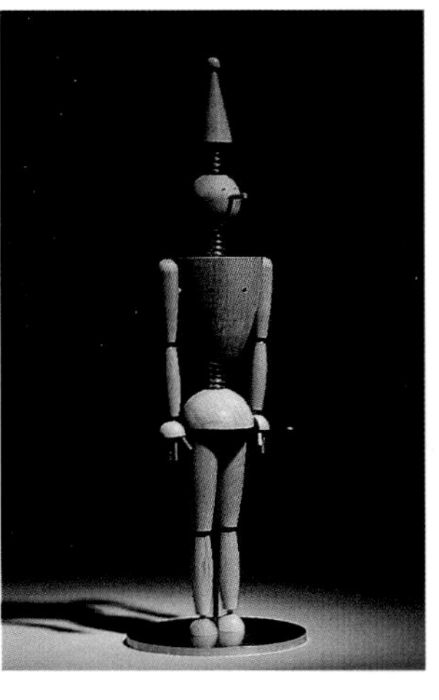

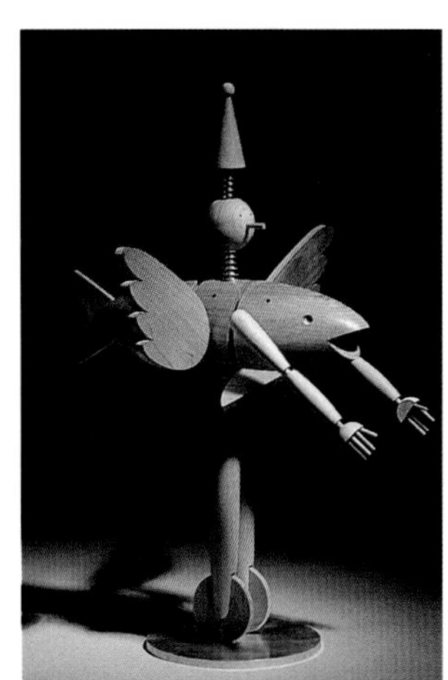

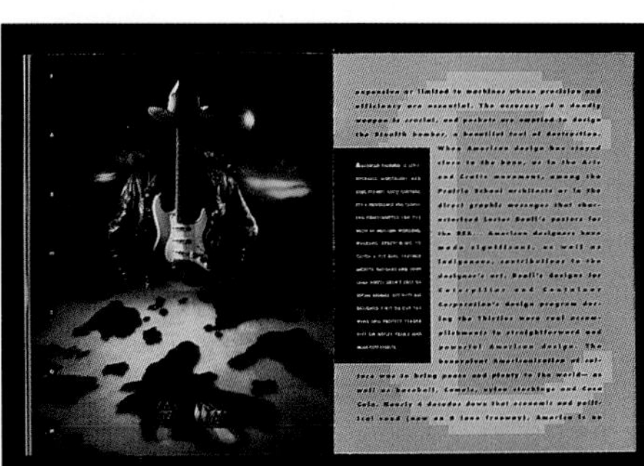

First Choice
AIGA Lecture Series
Poster entitled 'Les Enfants Terribles'

'When given the opportunity to chair the annual lecture series for the San Francisco Museum of Modern Art last year, it gave me a chance to invite three speakers who I feel are unique at this time and place in history. All working in Paris, Jean-Paul Goude, Pierre Bernard and Phillipe Starck, represent a movement and attitude, though not official, that has come to the forefront of design today. This poster represents the raw passion of these designers' work. Work that is radical, personal and inspiring. I chose the most obvious cliché of passion, 'the winged heart' and attempted to make a jarring and unconventional version of it. Much the same way as the three designers, who translate their own work-making the obvious exceptional'

Toy design for the client, George Belarian, to teach children the concept of surrealism

Promotional piece for Champion Paper entitled 'Subjective Reasoning' series

Furnishing design for the Robert Talbott Retail Store, NYC

Design for the interior of the Esprit Shoe Showroom, New York

The re-design of a 3000 square foot showroom for the contract furniture manufacturer, Keilhauer, Chicago

Poster for the Exhibitor Design Conference '93

Humour in Design AGI Conference Cambridge England
Kiss Me

SOME
OF MY
BEST
FRIENDS
R

V CTORY

TM

LEFT
RIGHT
LEFT
RIGHT
LEFT
RIGHT
BOOM!

First Choice Annual Report for Mizrahi Bank

'Following the corporate identity job done for one of the largest banks in the country, we were asked to design its annual report. It was an opportunity to present the 'Sunrise' logo concept. 'Mizrahi' in hebrew means Oriental. Its other local connotations suggest a sectorial institution - a marketing limitation. The Sunrise from the east (orient - oriental) became the concept - with all its life-giving qualities. All photographs in the 230 page report were of sunrises around the world'

Poster for Pentagram New York entitled 'You'

Poster for AGI congress on Humour in Design entitled 'Kiss me! Heart as lips'

Poster for ICU publications entitled 'Some of my best friends ARE'

Poster for ICU publications entitled 'This side up!'

Publications entitled 'Victory=blood=coffin'

Poster for an anti military, anti extremes statement entitled 'Left-Right-Boom!'

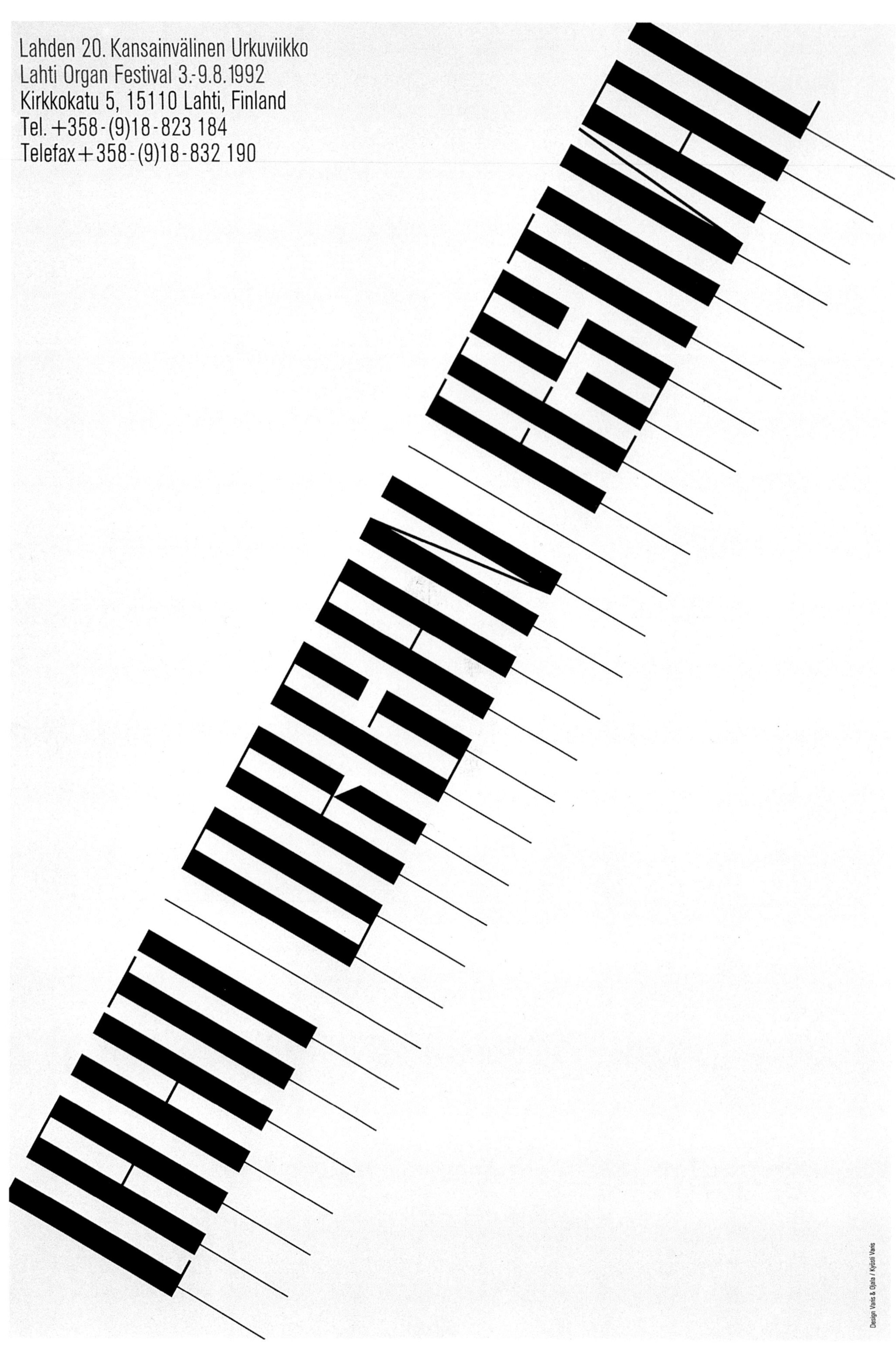
Lahden 20. Kansainvälinen Urkuviikko
Lahti Organ Festival 3.-9.8.1992
Kirkkokatu 5, 15110 Lahti, Finland
Tel. +358-(9)18-823 184
Telefax + 358-(9)18-832 190
Design Varis & Ojala / Kyösti Varis

First Choice
Poster for the Lahti Organ Festival

'In this poster, I have succeeded in integrating both the verbal and the visual messages'

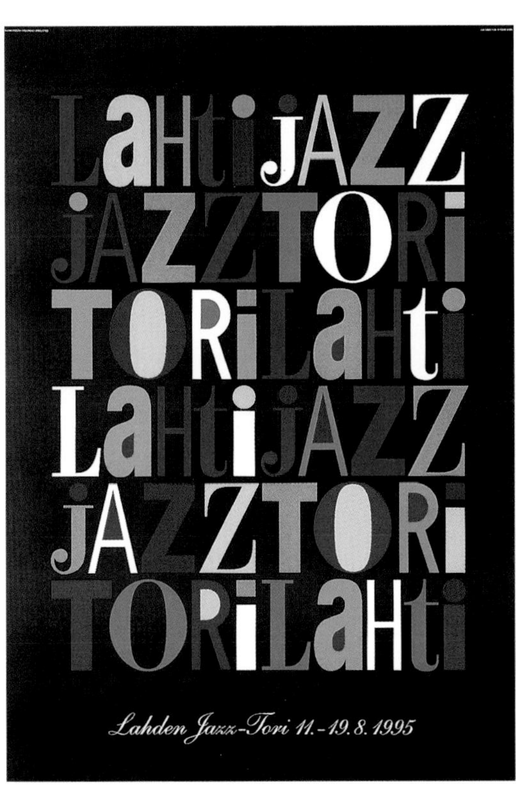

Poster for LIBRIS, 'The printers for good designers'

Annual Report Cover for the State Alcohol Monopoly

Poster for Lahti Jazz Market

Symbol for a Federation of Evangelical-Lutheran Parishes

Symbol for Soroptimist International

Symbol for the Juhani Aho salmon fishing club

Lilla Teatern
YRJÖNKATU 30
PUHELIN 643 939
GOZZI–BESSON
BENNO BESSON · OHJAUS–JEAN-MARC STEHLÉ · LAVASTUS–JUHA SILTANEN · SUOMENNOS
HIRVIKUNINGAS
RITVA VALKAMA · ELINA SALO · TOM WENTZEL · JONNA JÄRNEFELT · SIXTEN LUNDBERG · HELGE HERALA · JOUKO KLEMETTILÄ · HELENA KALLIO · MARCUS GROTH · NIKLAS GROUNDSTROEM · ASKO SARKOLA

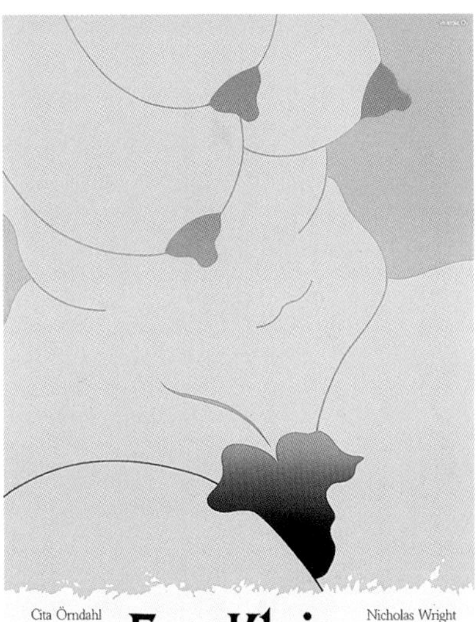

First Choice
Poster for 'The King Stag, Hirvi Kuningas', a theatre play

'This is a story where the hunter and the target are mixed. One is seeking love, the second power and the third adventure. I am very thankful that Asko Sarkola asked me to create the posters and the other material for this marvellous play. The technique is acrylic colours on canvas and it is painted nearly actual size 80 x 120cm'

Poster for the GRAFIA exhibition entitled 'Functional Surrealism'

Poster for The Best Posters of the Year Association entitled 'The Best Finnish Posters'

Poster for a theatre play entitled 'Fru Klein'

Poster for the Areal Art Exhibition

Poster for a concert for Amnesty International featuring the Oulunkylä Big Band

Poster for a public Sauna entitled 'Save Saint Peter's Sauna! Visit There!'

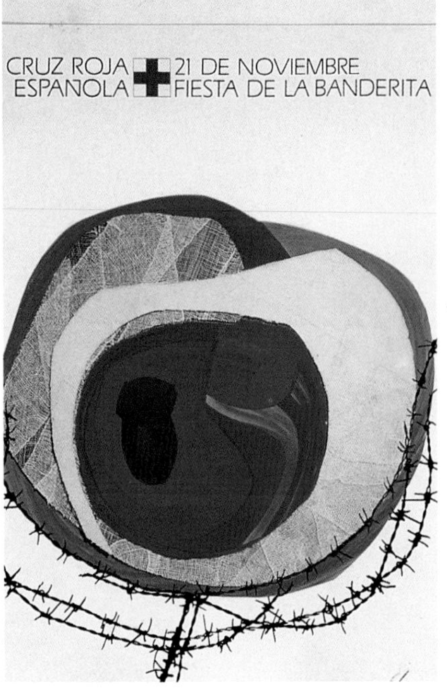

« VELLVÉ »

EL PRIMER «PALO SECO» IBÉRICO

Noviembre de 1971

Tomás Vellve Mengual

El diseño del tipo «Vellvé» del grafista Tomás Vellvé, fabricado por Fundición Tipográfica Neufville, no solamente plantea y resuelve una cuestión puramente utilitaria sino que es como si quisiera replantear el goce estético de la tipografía, el mismo que los romanos descubrieron en la escritura.

La psicología y motivación del nuevo tipo «Vellvé» intensifica y hace más entrañable «la incomparable «meditación a solas» frente a la página impresa, que constituye la lectura» como ha expresado el novelista cubano Alejo Carpentier. Ratifica el planteamiento de como el diseño gráfico, a través de la comunicación impresa, la cual permite el ejercicio de la libertad y la reflexión del receptor, puede también contribuir, hoy, a un mejoramiento social y entrañablemente humano.

Estas reflexiones las ha motivado una inédita y actual integración de nuestro país a la tipografía internacional. La aparición del nuevo tipo «Vellvé» que, a este tercer renacimiento de la familia funcionalista de tipo palo seco que vivimos hoy, aporta la novedad de la emoción y el matiz ibéricos.

Pere Creus

Hamburgo

Hamburgo

Hamburgo

Hamburgo

Hamburgo

Hamburgo

G

El tipo ha nacido pues de una feliz combinación de intuición artística y de moderna técnica de «marketing».

En Noviembre de 1971 el «Vellvé» consiguió un primer gran éxito. Aun con sólo un cuerpo totalmente grabado (el cuerpo 24) y la escala del Hamburgo, es seleccionado por ADI/FAD, y gana el premio LAUS concedido anualmente a la mejor realización gráfica.

Fundición Tipográfica NEUFVILLE, S. A.

First Choice
Poster announcing the 1992 Olympic Games in Barcelona

'This is my first choice because it has received several mentions in the design industry. On a personal level, I felt very satisfied with it and rejoiced when I completed it'

Poster announcing the Red Cross's Little Flag Day in Barcelona

Decorative Christmas poster

Advertisement for an exhibition for Fundación Tipográfica Neufville, S.A

Cover design for the client, Industrias Bures

Advertisement for an exhibition for Fundación Tipográfica Neufville, S.A

Poster for 'Brut for Men' for Faberge

Anyone
Anywhere

GALERIAS

Franciacorta Bianco
Marchesi Fassati di Balzola
Castello di Passirano
Franciacorta Rosso

Cosmit
April 11-17 '94
Salone
Furnishing Accessories
Euroluce
Milano

Frank Lloyd Wright, the great
American anarchist, once wrote:

In the new computer age the proliferation of typefaces and type manipulations represents a new level of visual pollution threatening our culture. Out of thousands of typefaces, all we need are a few basic ones, and trash the rest. So come and see

A Few Basic Typefaces

The Masters Series: Massimo Vignelli
February 22 to March 8, 1991

Reception: Thursday, February 21, 6 to 8 pm
Lecture: Tuesday, February 26, 7 to 9 pm,
School of Visual Arts Amphitheater.

The third in a series of exhibitions honoring the great visual communicators of our time.

Visual Arts Museum, 209 East 23rd Street, NYC, 10010
Museum Hours: Monday to Thursday, 9 am to 8 pm,
Friday, 9 am to 5 pm. Closed Weekends.

The Masters Series is supported in part by a grant from the Architecture, Planning and Design program of the New York State Council on the Arts. ©1991 by the Visual Arts Press, LTD.

First Choice
Poster for his personal exhibition

'One of my favorite works of the last few years is a poster I did for an exhibition of my work, based on the use of only four typefaces (Bodoni, Garamond, Century, Helvetica).
The poster was printed on both sides and what you see here is actually the two superimposed that form a full poster.
The word for poster in Italian is 'manifesto', which has become the synonym of declaration.
Playing with that semantic ambiguity I took the opportunity of designing a poster that would carry the concept of the exhibition as well as become a provocative statement on the state of typography today.
I will never tire of raising my voice against meaningless explorations, when the real tasks of the graphic designer, to fight visual pollution and visual degradation of the environment, are neglected'

A series of architectural books designed for an architectural firm

Corporate Identity for Galerias, a department store chain, Spain

Corporate Identity for the American Centre, Paris

Labels and packaging cartons for Fassati Wines, Italy

Design of mailing pieces for COSMIT, an organisation that handles trade fairs

Graphic Program for the Solomon R. Guggenheim Museum, New York

Les Maîtres
de la carrosserie italienne
DesignAutomobile

ITALIA
design / tecnologia
XVI
Compasso d'Oro
1991
30 settembre 20 ottobre
ADI

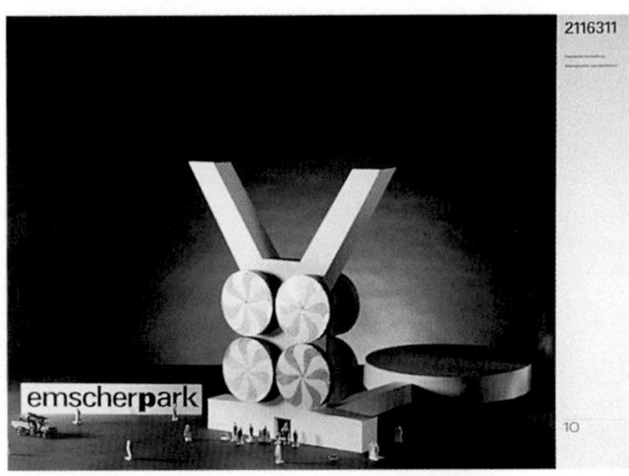
2116311
emscherpark
10

CASTER
ZELKOVA
AVENUE
We Love Keyaki

First Choice
Poster of the Seventh Violin-making Triennial, Italy

'It is my first choice because it represents a cultural event, it is not commercially characterised; it is free from business influences. The number represented in this poster (seven), is important because it refers to the Seventh Violin-making Triennal, but also it is composed of two elements belonging to two different kinds of art: music and graphic. These elements are the violin scroll and the violin neck, which are compared to two elements of the typeface. The synthesis is fundamental in this work: the essentiality of the shape, the modernity, and with this the functionality of the support; on the other hand the classicism, harmony and the musicality of the shape. One single symbol can create a synthesis, which is the result of a fusion of two different kinds of arts; music and design'

Cover of the catalogue for an Istituto Commercio Estero exhibition at the Georges Pompidou Centre, Paris

Poster and catalogue for the exhibition 'Design/Technologia' Madrid, Spain

Silkscreen design for an award for the Annual Reporter Oscar, a competition held among the biggest Italian companies

Three dimensional symbol for the Internationale Bauausstellung Emscher Park competition

Logotype for the Hi Tech Edition Car for Guglielmo Spotorno, Toyota Concessionaire,Milan

Symbol and logotype for the Caster Zelkova Avenue Event

BAŁTYCKI
TEATR
DRAMATYCZNY
IM. J. SŁOWACKIEGO
W KOSZALINIE
ALBERT CAMUS
CALIGULA

First Choice
Theatre poster designed for the play 'Caligula' for Baltycki Teatr Dramatyczny Im J.Stowackiego W Koszalinie

'Honestly I cannot say much about why I consider those selected works the best ones. I really don't know why I have chosen 'Caligula' as number one. Equally well I could have picked 'I feel like screaming' or 'White Flower' or the 'King'. Surely, the decisive factor in this case was my intuition, but do you expect me to say anything more specific on that? Definitely my choice was connected with my taste, but I don't see any point in writing about it, as one who sees my selection will know more about my taste than he could sense upon my commentary. The choice by itself is a kind of demonstration of my preferences clear enough for those who do not look at things but also see them. For those, I work'

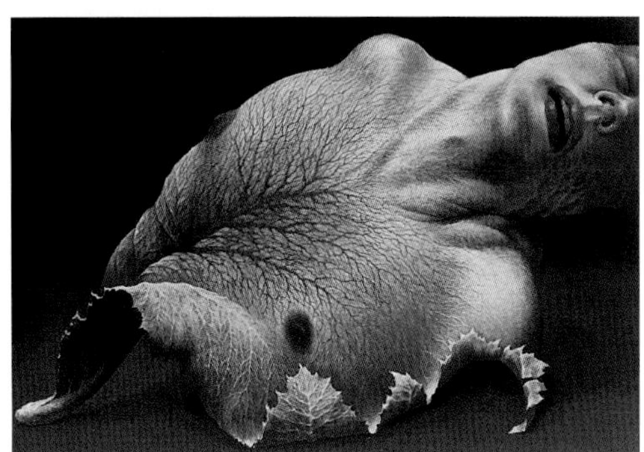

Poster for the film by Andrzej Wajda on the French revolution produced by Visual Studio entitled 'Danton'

Personal work entitled 'King'

Personal work entitled 'White Flower'

Poster for the film 'I feel like screaming' for the Karol Irzykowski Film Studio

Poster for the film 'Fiddler on the Roof' for the Visual Studio

Poster for the film 'Farewell to Autumn' for the Karol Irzykowski Film Studio

Tango
TM
Sparkling Orange
Drink

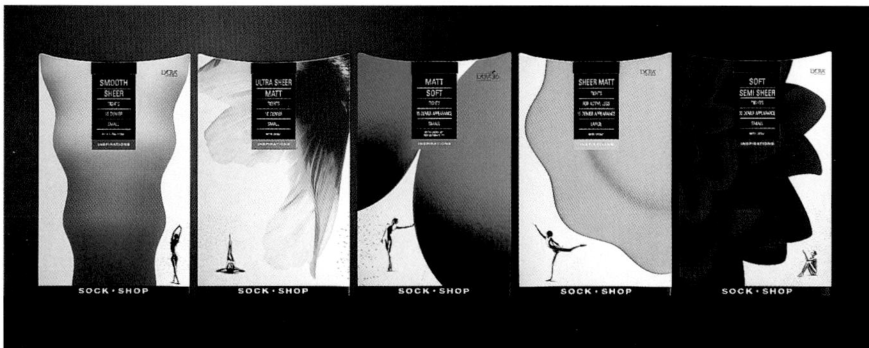

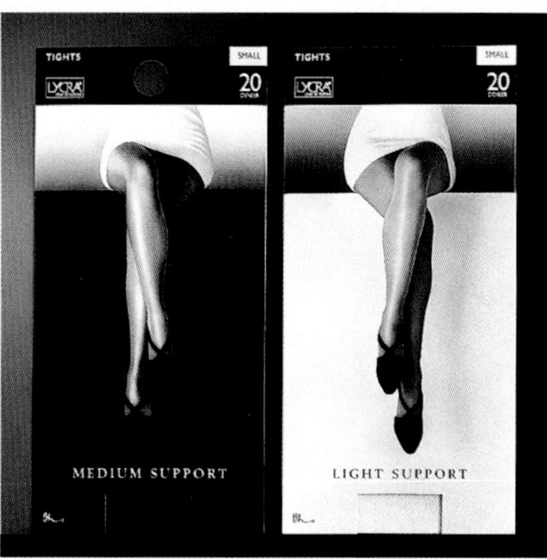

First Choice
Identity for Britivic Soft Drinks Ltd brand, Tango

'Tango is the UK's answer to the proliferation of American soft drinks, positioned more streetwise, a big brand with 'attitude'.
I have selected it as my first choice for a number of reasons.
First, it was a radical change for a well-known name. Second, it constantly reassures me of what can be achieved in spite of the enormous commercial pressures of the packaging business and the constraints of high speed can printing, when dealing with a trusting, determined client.
Third, whilst not overtly 'beautiful' it does demonstrate my belief that design should be individual and distinctive above all else. And finally, it still stands out even though almost all of its competitors have been redesigned since its introduction'

Packaging for Black Sheep Ale for the Black Sheep Brewery

Packaging for Gale's Honey for Nestlé

Packaging for Billington's Sugar

Packaging design for the Facia Group, Sock Shop

Packaging for Hosta Schokolade, Mr. Tom

Packaging design for Bhs hosiery range

AGI
Oslo 1992
40e congrès
anniversaire
de l'AGI

5e festival
d'affiches
de Chaumont
28 mai - 19 juin 94
sur le thème :
affiches d'expositions
5e rencontres
internationales
des arts graphiques
de Chaumont.
Région
Champagne / Ardenne,
ORCCA

5e festival
d'affiches
de Chaumont

Design à la maison du livre, de l'image et du son
Exposition du 4 octobre au 30 novembre 1991
jean widmer
247, Cours Emile Zola 69100 Villeurbanne
téléphone 78 68 04 04, métro Flachet,
du mardi au vendredi de 14h à 19h, le samedi de 14h à 18h

FerrØsan

observatoire international des prisons

Jean Widmer sérigraphie Syria

First Choice
Poster for the Observatoire International des Prisons

'Because it deals without concession with a humanitarian theme that pledges to respect other people. This poster made me think about an unusual creation, a considerate image at the service of a humanitarian ideology completely free of any constraint calling to mind the power of the signs of a troubled and closed atmosphere, a confined everyday, the permanent and vigilant keeping watch, the downgrading of intimacy, of unceasing successions and beyond a life one has to continue to believe in'

Postcard for the 40th Anniversary of AGI in Oslow

Poster for the Fifth Poster Festival of Chaumont

Watch produced for the Fifth Poster Festival of Chaumont

Poster for the monographic exhibition at the 'House of the Image and Sound' at Villeurbanne

Logotype for Ferrosan

Logotype for Grand Ecran (Wide Screen)

NUMERO 737 — domus — APRILE 1992
MONTHLY REVIEW OF ARCHITECTURE INTERIORS DESIGN ART

Editoriale: Progetto e durata □ John Hejduk, due monumenti a Praga □ Michael Hopkins, edificio per uffici a Londra □ Enric Miralles, cimitero a Barcellona □ Mario Botta, studio a Lugano □ Tre interni: a Londra, New York e Parigi □ Mobili: l'arredo svizzero 1925-1950 □ Saggio sul concetto di qualità □ Frank Lloyd Wright: la tecnica del *textile block* e itinerario in California.

First Choice
Cover for 'Domus' for an article on the Vatican, April, 1992

'I have often solved visual problems by combining two images and using two different techniques as I do in this one. The Cathedral (St Peter's) is an engraving from the 18th century, the Cardinal's robes are painted. The original exists on board as you see it in one piece, no computer was used to achieve this combination. I was happy with the way the red paint started 'bleeding' by wetting the illustration board at the bottom'

Designs for a promotional piece for the Westvaco Paper Company

Cover for the magazine, 'Longevity'

Poster for IBM for an exhibition of their promotional graphics

Poster for the lecture, 'The Impact of Excellence'

PAGANINI
LEHÁR
REŽIE
Oto Ševčík
DIRIGENT
Miloš Formáček
KARLÍN
HUDEBNÍ DIVADLO PRAHA

First Choice
Poster promoting the play 'Paganini' for HD Karlin

'This is one of the posters for a big Prague theatre, which is in the hands of very nice people whose tastes in posters radically differed (and perhaps still do) from mine. It was rather hard to convince them that I wanted the best for them'

Poster promoting the play 'Catherina The Great'

Poster promoting an exhibition entitled 'UPM' for the Museum of Prague

Poster promoting the play 'Land of the Smile'

Poster promoting the play 'Mam'zelle Nitouche' for HD Karlin

Posters promoting a film festival of technical films entitled 'Techfilm'

A book of this size and scope is only possible with the effort of a large number of people. Amongst those who deserve particular recognition for their contributions are: Heather Wellard for co-ordination and copy-editing; Leigh Cato and Bridgette Newbury for editing and editorial assistance; and Sue Stansfield and Chris Trutwein for artwork and assistance with design. And of course, a special thanks to all the designers who contributed such a varied and impressive range of work and made the very difficult 'first choice' that has gone into making this book as interesting as it is

m e n t

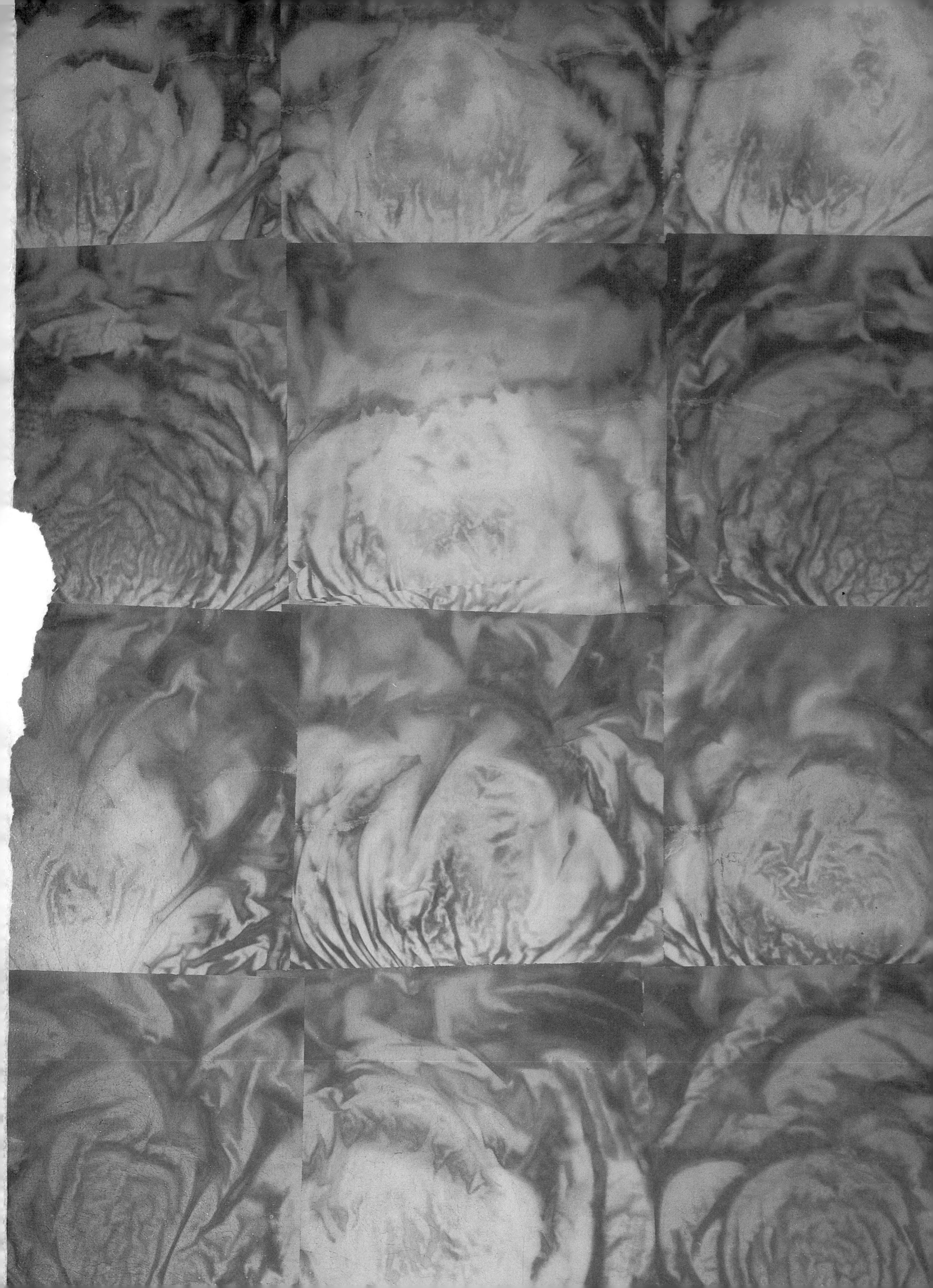

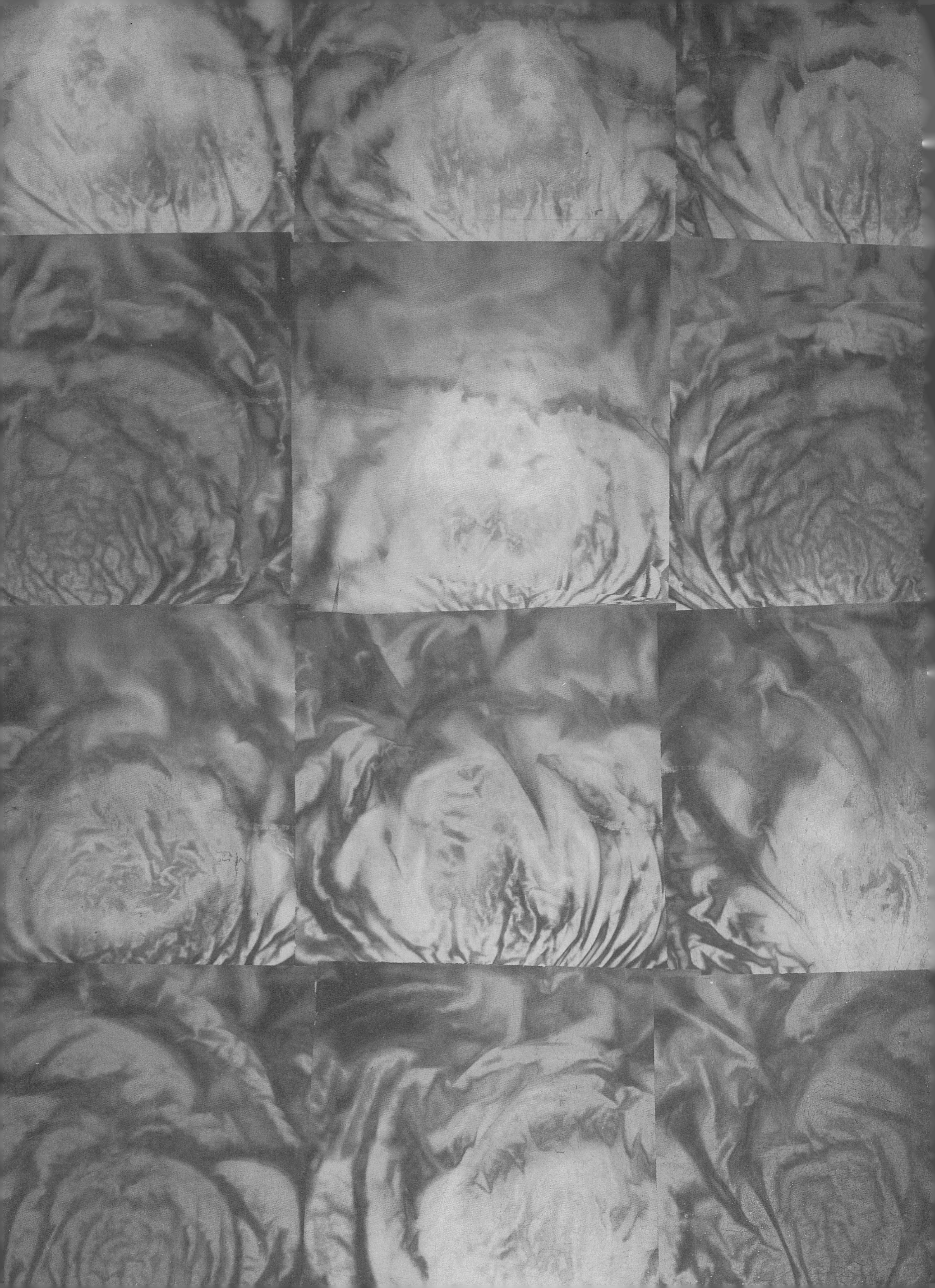